# Gandhian Philosophy

## Its Relevance today

# Gandhian Philosophy

## Its Relevance Today

by

Gummadi Veerraju

Decent Books

New Delhi

*Published and printed by*
**Decent Books**
D-36/A-1, Mohan Garden
Nagafgarh Road
New Delhi - 110 059

*Distributed by*
**D.K. Printworld (P) Ltd.**
*Regd. office : 'Srikunj'*, F-52, Bali Nagar
Ramesh Nagar Metro Station
New Delhi - 110 015
*Phones* : (011) 2545-3975, 2546-6019
*Fax* : (011) 2546-5926
*E-mail*: dkprintworld@vsnl.net
*Web*: www.dkprintworld.com

**ISBN 10: 81-86921-04-4**

First published in India in 1999
Second impression in 2009

# Preface

MAHATMA Gandhi is considered to be one of the greatest sons of the Indian soil. Although much has been written of Gandhi in the recent times and so much literature has come on his ideas and ideals, yet much more remains uncovered because of the increasing relevance and significance of his philosophy in the modern times.

As a man of action, he practised what is moral, truthful and non-violent after a thorough examination with great insight. He was multi-dimensional in his approach and left an indelible mark in the religio-moral, socio-economic and political spheres. So in the modern times, his philosophic ideas and ideals are progressively becoming significant and more relevant than before. The entire gamut of his philosophical thought is mainly based on two moral values of eternal relevance, namely, truth and non-violence.

In this study I dealt with an attempt is made in this study to understand the concepts namely, social equality, universal love, non-possession, human service, renunciation, purity of means and ends, removal of untouchability, casteless and classless society, social evils, value oriented education, economic equality, industrialisation, decentralised democracy, panchayat raj, satyagraha, environmental challenges, terrorism and global peace. These concepts were dealt earlier by Mahatma Gandhi and the solutions he offered without losing sight of truth and non-violence are of great relevance and significance to the modern times.

An attempt is made in this study to understand to incorporate issues of recent times that have occurred in India as well as in some parts of the world so as to examine and analyse them in the light of Gandhian philosophy to find out their co-relation and relevance to make the study up to date.

Gandhi covered all the aspects of the human life and he

considered man an integral whole. He offered his solutions with great insight. He was a rare personality and at the same time he was unique in many respects.

As Albert Einstein aptly puts:

> Generations to come will scarcely believe that such one as this has ever in flesh and blood walked upon this earth.

The modern society has become more acquisitive, exploitative and violent due to the imperfection in the human institution. There is no other alternative except to adapt the techniques that Gandhi followed to resolve the different levels of conflict, and to rid the evils that have beset the modern society.

My grateful thanks are due to my Research Director Dr. T. Christanandam, Associate Professor Department of Philosophy, Andhra University, for his able guidance and also for offering his critical and valuable suggestions at.

My grateful thanks are to Dr. M. Gopala Krishna Reddy, former Vice-Chancellor, and Dr. R. Radhakrishna, the present Vice-Chancellor of Andhra University for all their good wishes and encouragement.

Prof. G. Subrahmanyam, former Registrar, and Prof. J.M. Naidu, the present Registrar of Andhra University have been a constant source of inspiration and help for me. My sincere thanks to them.

I am thankful to Prof. V. Balamohan Das, Principal of Colleges of Arts and Commerce for the encouragement he gave for the completion of my thesis.

My thanks are due to Sri Ch. Bapu Haranath, Sri N. Babayya and Dr. Sudarsana Rao, Asst. Principles, Colleges of Arts and Commerce, Andhra University for their concern and the cooperation they have extended for the completion of this study.

My grateful thanks are to Prof. P. George Victor, UGC-SAP co-ordinator and Dr. Y.U. Satyanarayana, Head of the Department of Philosophy, for their kind cooperation and valuable suggestions for the completion of this book.

I am also immensely thankful to my teacher Prof. V. Gopala

Krishnaiah, Chairman, Board of Studies, Department of Philosophy, for his kind encouragement and help.

My grateful thanks are to my teacher Prof. G.V. Raju (Retired) Department of Philosophy for his able guidance and valuable suggestions at various stages of drafting of this study.

My thanks are due to Prof. G. Sundara Ramaiah, Prof. O. Deenammal, Prof. S. Satyanarayana, Prof. M.V. Krishnayya, Dr. Y.V. Satyanarayana, Dr. V.V.S. Saiababa, Dr. S.D.A. Joga Rao and Sri B. Ravi Babu for their constant encouragement and concern.

My grateful thanks are due to Prof. B. Mastanaiah, Department of History and Archaeology and Sri L.S. Ravindra Babu, Lecturer in English, Government Degree College, Palakol for their valuable suggestions and also for going through the drafts of the work. (which enabled me to complete my research successfully.)

I am thankful to Dr. K. Solomon Raju, Prof. P. Apada Rao, Dr. A. Narasimha Rao, Dr. G. Yohan Babu, Dr. (Smt.) D. Amrutamma, Mr. Abdual Rahman, Y. Ravi Kumar, Dr. T. Venkateswarlu, for all their good wishes and encouragement.

I am much grateful to my wife, Smt. G. Nagamani for her cooperation and encouragement.

*Visakhapatanam* **G. Veerraju**

# Contents

# Introduction

MAHATMA Gandhi is the father of the nation and the maker of the modern independent republic. He is held in high esteem and venerated as the great soul. His popular sayings that 'My life is my message' and 'My life is a series of experiments with truth' have literally come to be true. These statements establish his scientific temper and his adherence to the moral values.

My main aim is to study the philosophy of Mahatma Gandhi, especially in the modern context and examine its relevance to the modern times. Gandhi was not an academician and he did not make any systematic presentation of his philosophy. In order to present his philosophy in an organised and logically cogent manner, his ideas have to be culled from his various speeches and writings. Gandhi laid more stress on the basic values of the human life especially on truth and non-violence. As a defender of the human rights, he made people more conscious of their duties, to set a moral order in the society and also to make the people learn that the true source of right is duty only.

Gandhi did not like people to remain as mere silent spectators in a helpless manner. He aroused their indomitable moral will and inherent potentialities to fight against the supposed wrong or injustice in a non-violent manner. He envisaged a casteless, classless and egalitarian society against the existing acquisitive and exploitative society.

Gandhi was not a system builder, but with great understanding and insight, he could bring about the scheme of his concepts in an appropriate and relevant manner so as to suit the modern requirements. His concepts underwent evolutionary and revolutionary changes. There is need for the social scientists to combine their scientific methods and theories with the Gandhian values to achieve better results.

The modern technology poses great threat and fear than hope and happiness. The significance of man is lost and his life has lost its meaning and purpose except to reduce it to a mere mechanical drudgery. The heavy industrialisation is vulnerable to several evils like gambling and results in problems such as unemployment. His real happiness does not lie in his enjoyment of sensual pleasures and multiplication of desires but in leading a simple and ennobled life with moral consciousness and high thinking.

Gandhi formulated a pattern and a structure basing on his series of experiments with truth in the religio-moral, socio-economic and political spheres by keeping the individuality and dignity of the individual in view without losing sight of truth and non-violence.

Gandhi rejected the earlier formulated political theory that 'end justifies the means' as it tends to be opportunistic and expedient and the unscrupulous and immoral methods have been followed. He introduced a new moral code by making means as significant as end and also by establishing their convertibility to avoid the immoral means and violence to justify the end.

Gandhi stood for the economic equality. His theory of trusteeship bears the testament of his commitment to usher in an egalitarian society by reducing the economic disparities. He made a break-through in the social structure by working for the removal of the social evils such as untouchability and the creation of equal opportunities for the unprivileged for their social upliftment.

As regards his notion of village autonomy, and village development, he worked out for the village self-sufficiency. He wanted to reduce the disparities between the urban and the rural to avoid the people's craze to settle in the cities.

Gandhi subscribed to the view that power corrupts and absolute power corrupts absolutely. On the other hand, the centralised power structure has to adopt the method of violence to defend its power and implement its policies forcibly. In the modern times politics has become a great preoccupation of the people. There has been a ruthless and unhealthy competition for power in every walk of life. So Gandhi brought religion and politics together to purify politics. He stood for the decentralised democracy and *panchayat raj* system where in man is considered supreme and his role is significant.

Gandhi was opposed to the heavy industrialisation, deforestation and depletion of natural resources, pollution and ecological imbalance. These modern trends have badly effected the health of mankind. He advocated small-scale industries and technology which is intermediary with a human face that stands for the greatest good of all. He stood against terrorism. He stated that people have to rely on non-violent resistance to achieve their just cause.

The Gandhian concept of *satyagraha* is a method of conflict resolution based on non-violent resistance directed against injustice, corruption and unjust laws of the society and state. This is reckoned with great significance because of its relevance in the modern times. He stated that the lasting and enduring world peace could be established only through non-violence. However, there may be some military illusions that peace could be brought about by relying on the theories such as the doctrine of deterrence but it cannot establish world peace but promotes mutual insecurity and terror. He held that non-violence is the only answer and alternative in the modern times to establish the world peace.

Mahatma Gandhi made a multi-dimensional study reflecting on moral, religious, socio-economic and political spheres of the human life. Gandhi was influenced by a number of great religious personalities right from nurse Rambha to that of the eminent writers and thinkers like Leo Tolstoy and John Ruskin. His open mind helped him to accept any good idea from any source and adopt it in his life.

The first chapter deals with the sources and influences that have shaped his thought right from his parents to that of the great religious personalities and eminent thinkers of the East and the West. The influence of the *Bhagavad Gita*, the Sermon on the Mount, the Civil Disobedience of Henry Thoreau, the social equality of John Ruskin, the influence of Leo Tolstoy have also been dealt in this chapter.

The second chapter presents the moral and religious aspects. The religious philosophy of Gandhi was chracterised mainly by truth and non-violence. The aspects such as his interpretation of religion, the relationship of religion and morality, the cardinal virtues, viz., non-violence, truthfulness, non-stealing, non-possession and celibacy, the concept of universal religion, the purity of means and ends, the significance of truth in religion, the role of religion in purifying politics, have been dealt.

In the third chapter 'Social Problems and Gandhian Solutions', the social aspects such as caste, the evil of untouchability, his concept of egalitarian society, his progressive and evolutionary views on inter-dining and inter-caste marriages, the status of women and their problems, their role in the society, the evil aspects of alcoholism, the significance of prohibition, value oriented education, the significance and relevance of basic education, have been dealt.

The fourth chapter presents the economic views of Gandhi and his concept of economic reorganisation, the theory of trusteeship, economic equality, the evils of industrialisation, the revival of the small-scale and rural industries for rural development and co-operative forming of the villages.

The fifth chapter is on the Gandhian approach to the contemporary political issues. The aspects such as welfare state, democracy, the significance of minority in the democracy, his notion of political power, non-violence and democracy, decentralisation, *panchayat raj* and its significance, the three-tier system of decentralised administration, duties and rights, significance of freedom, *satyagraha* and its application, non-cooperation and civil disobedience have been dealt in this chapter.

In the sixth chapter 'Global issue's and Gandhian Solutions', the contemporary issues such as environment its sustainability and challenges, the evil effects of modern civilisation, the problem of terrorism and violence, non-violence and world peace, the military illusions, the doctrines of deterrence has been discussed.

The last chapter presents the summary and conclusion. A careful examination of all the aspects of the Gandhian Philosophy covered in this study in the context of modern developments, establish relevance to the modern times as the entire gamut of his philosophy is laid firmly on two eternal values — Truth and Non-violence.

# 1

# Sources of Gandhian Philosophy

MAHATMA Gandhi made a multi-dimensional study reflecting on moral religious, socio-economic and political aspects of the human life. He devoted his entire life in the service of the humanity. He has an open mind and willingness to adopt any good idea from any source.

## Indian Influences

Gandhi was influenced by a number of religious personalities and intellectuals right from his nurse Rambha to that of the eminent writer and thinker Leo Tolstoy. At the outset, his parents exerted profound influence on him. His mother Putlibai, a lady of most devout temperament, influenced his religious thought. Gandhi says,

> The outstanding impression, my mother has left on my memory is that of saintliness. She was deeply religious. She would not think of taking her meals without her daily prayers.[1]

His mother Putlibai had strong commonsense. She was well-informed of matters of the state and the ladies of the court had high opinion of her intelligence.[2] He learnt the popular Indian maxim 'There is nothing higher than Truth.' He also learnt from his mother *ahimsa paramodharmah*[3] that the practice of harmlessness or non-

---

1. M.K. Gandhi, *The Story of My Experiments with Truth*, p. 2.
2. *Ibid.*, p. 3.
3. D.M. Dutta, *The Philosophy of Mahatma Gandhi*, p. 9.

violence was the highest virtue or *ahimsa* is universally acknowledged and rigidly practised especially by the Jainas and Vaishnavas and Gandhi grew in that atmosphere.

Gandhi learnt a lot from his father Kaba Gandhi. Although his father had a little bit of religious training, he had imbibed religious culture by his frequent visits to temples and listening to religious discourses. He pointed out:

> His rich experience of practical affairs stood him in good stead in the solutions of the most intricate questions and in managing hundreds of men.[4]

Gandhi recalled the affection he had obtained from his nurse Rambha. In his childhood he used to have the fear of ghosts and the spirits. Rambha suggested to him to repeat the name of Rama as a sovereign remedy of his fear. He considered the name of Rama as infallible remedy for him which as a seed of faith in God nurtured him and it is due to Rambha.[5]

Gandhi has developed a passion for truth. He writes in his autobiography that the passion for truth was innate in him.[6] Gandhi quoted an incident which occurred at the examination hall when he was studying first year at the high school. Although the teacher tried to prompt him, he would not be prompted and could never learn the art of copying. Gandhi referred to the other two incidents which have the basis in truth and devotion to service. They had always clung to his memory and shaped his thought. His first impression was the book on *Shravana Pitrubhakti Nataka* (a play relating to Shravana's devotion to serve his parents). He read the book evincing keen interest in it. He also saw a picture of Shravana carrying blind parents by means of slings fitted to his shoulders on a pilgrimage. The book and the picture of Shravana led to an indelible influence on his young mind. He said to himself that here was an example for him to copy. The agonised lament of the parents over the death of Shravana was fresh in his memory. This

---

4. M.K. Gandhi, *The Story of My Experiments with Truth*, p. 2.
5. *Ibid.*, p. 23.
6. *Ibid.*, p. 7.

impression had made Gandhi to render service to the humanity.[7]

Another important effect on Gandhi's life was the play of Harischandra performed by certain dramatic company which captured his heart. He could never be tired of seeing the drama. He asked himself day and night the question "Why should not all be truthful like Harischandra?" to follow truth and to go through all the hardships Harischandra went through. The ideal of Harischandra inspired Gandhi. He literally believed the story of Harischandra. For him both Harischandra and Shravana are living realities.[8]

Jainism exerted profound influence on Gandhi which has been great living force in Gujarat. The Jaina system of thought has influenced him the utmost. Pyarelal says,

> They were, Ahimsa on the religious side, anekantavad or Syadvad on the philosophical side, and the institutions of vows on the ethical side. He was greatly attracted, too, by the Jaina theory of knowledge. On the religious side, the Jaina doctrine is pluralistic. In its philosophical aspect it is characterised by a dialectical way of thinking. According to Jaina Shastras, Ahimsa is not a negative virtue — a mere mechanical abstention from violence — but a positive quality based on universal love resulting from the recognition of oneness of life and, therefore, kinship of all living beings. One who has realised this ideal cannot be indifferent to the suffering of others. Further, the Jaina religion, it is claimed, has been the first, perhaps the only religion in the world to include in its conception of universal love, not only human beings, but the entire sub-human creation, including plant life.[9]

The Jaina thinkers on the philosophical side have propounded the principle of *anekantavada* or 'manyness' of Truth or Reality. This view holds that reality has a very complex structure. The proposition

---

7. *The Story of My Experiments with Truth*, p. 4.
8. *Ibid.*
9. Pyarelal, *Mahatma Gandhi, The Early Phase*, Vol. I, p. 276.

is true only from a particular standpoint. But what is true from one's standpoint may not be true from another, and thus truth is relative. It occupies one's standpoint but does not deny other standpoint. The possibility of many standpoints with contradictory propositions relating to the same subject which is true from its relative standpoint is known as *syadvada* or the doctrine of 'may be'. Reality must be examined from all the angles taking various aspects, with an integrated view of the whole to comprehend the reality.[10]

Reality has been defined by the Jaina thinkers as a "permanence in the midst of change, identity in the midst of diversity, and unity in the midst of multiplicity".[11] As reality is multi-formed and ever-changing, it follows from its corollary that no statement could hold good at all times, always and in all places. So no man can claim exclusively truth of his own.[12]

Gandhi was fundamentally influenced by the Jaina institutions of vows. The Jaina *shastras* lay down that one should regulate his conduct in his daily life by not allowing evil channels of *karma*. That means one should restrict the field of his activity. For this purpose, certain rules or vows have been recommended. They are Truth, Celibacy, Non-violence, Non-stealing, and Non-possession. The Jaina thinkers hold that the absolute renunciation of certain categories of activity through the observance of vows, tend to separate the association of soul with matter which is the cause of its bondage.[13] Gandhi referred to the song of Nishkulanand "Renunciation of objects, without the renunciation of desires, is short-lived, however hard you may try."[14]

The observance of vows for Gandhi was primarily and essentially a means of cultivating self-discipline and overcoming himself in the

---

10. *Mahatma Gandhi, The Early Phase*, p. 276.
11. *Ibid.*, p. 277.
12. *Ibid.*
13. *Ibid.*, p. 278.
14. M.K. Gandhi, *The Story of My Experiments with Truth*, p. 6.

event of temptation and doubt. He holds that a man whose mind is undisturbed by sense storms and completely emptied of self, develops an unerring institution.[15]

Violence or infliction of suffering to others is the great sin in Jainism. Other sins include untruthfulness, dishonesty, unchastity, covetousness, anger, conceit, deceit, avarice, which lead to bondage in this world, and their opposites, patience, humility, simplicity and contentment, further the spiritual growth.[16]

The chief feature embodied in Jainism is non-violence (*ahimsa*) which implies reverence for everything that has life and abstinence for violence.[17] Mahavira contended that man's emancipation does not depend on the mercy of any super-being. Man is held to be the architect of his own destiny. He has to strive for his salvation.[18]

Gandhi read a number of times Arnold's *Light of Asia* dedicated to the life of Lord Buddha. "Look at Gautama's compassion," Gandhi says, "it is not confined to mankind, it was extended to all human beings."[19]

Professor Arnold Toynbee, an outstanding historian, referred to the Buddha's way as the "contemplative way of the creative withdrawal into the spirit, without which man may not live".[20]

*Dhammapada* is the most popular and influential book of Buddhist literature. *Dhamma* is described as a discipline, law and religion and *pada* is path which means a way. *Dhammapada* is thus the path of virtue and the foundation of religion.[21]

Buddha saw the whole universe as a system of law composed of struggling features continually passing away from one form of existence and taking shape in another form [22] Buddha assessed

15. Pyarelal, *Mahatma Gandhi, The Early Phase*, Vol. I, p. 278.
16. S. Radhakrishnan, *Indian Philosophy*, Vol. I, p. 326.
17. *Ibid.*, p. 327.
18. George Kotturan, *Ahimsa: Gautama to Gandhi*, p 11.
19. M.K. Gandhi, *The Story of My Experiments with Truth*, p. 120.
20. Pyarelal, *Mahatma Gandhi, The Early Phase*, Vol. I, p. 65.
21. S. Radhakrishnan, *Dhammapada*, p. 1.
22. *Ibid.*, p. 8.

religion on the rational basis. He stated that one should not accept what he receives by the report, and by tradition. Lord Buddha says,

> Birth is sorrow. Decay is sorrow. Sickness is sorrow. Death is sorrow. . . . To be conjoined to things which we dislike, to be separated from things which we like — that also is sorrow. Not to get what one wants — that too is sorrow. Birth and death, suffering and love are universal facts. They are the signs of a lack of harmony, of a state of discord. Conflict is at the root of man's misery, of his spiritual disease. It is a pervasive feature of all empirical existence, which is impermanent and transitory and escape from it can, and must, be found. Everything has a cause and produces effect. This simple principle governs the whole universe, gods and men, heaven and earth.[23]

Buddha held while detecting and eliminating the cause of suffering, suffering itself could disappear. Due to ignorance, man experiences rupture in life which is the violation of its organic integrity. Ignorance is destroyed by intuition and desire by ethical striving.[24]

The Eight-fold Path of Lord Buddha represents the ladder of perfection. The first step relates to the right views, and the knowledge of the four truths. Buddha says,

> Conquest of self indeed better than the conquest of other persons; of one who has disciplined himself, who always practices self-control.[25]

Lord Buddha says that a man should set his heart towards good, and restrain his thoughts from evil. If a man is lacking in doing what is good, his mind rejoices in evil. If a man commits sin, let him not do it again. Let his heart be not set on evil. If a man does what is good, let him do it again and again and let him set his heart on it.[26] Lord Buddha says,

---

23. *Dhammapada*, p. 16.
24. *Ibid.*, pp. 16-17.
25. *Ibid.*, p. 94.
26. *Ibid.*, p. 98.

> Victory breeds hatred the conquered dwells in sorrow. He who has given up (thoughts of both) victory and defeat, he is calm and lives happily.[27]

Lord Buddha held that there is no fire like passion, no evil like hatred. There is no sorrow like this physical existence, and there is no happiness higher than tranquillity. Greediness is held to be the worst of all diseases. Contentment is the greatest wealth and the trust is best of all relationships.[28] Lord Buddha says,

> Let a man overcome anger by non-anger (gentleness), let him overcome evil by good, let him overcome the misery by liberality, let him overcome the liar by truth.[29]

Buddha pointed out that he who carries out his purpose by violence is not righteous. He who guides others by non-violent means is said to be a guardian of the law, wise and righteous. A man who is tranquil, free from hatred, and fear is said to be learned. A man in whom truth, virtue, non-violence, restraint, and control dwell and who is free from impurity, is wise, and he is called an elder.[30]

Among the books that influenced Gandhi's thoughts and ideas, *Gita* can be ranked first. It has become an infallible guide of conduct and the dictionary of daily reference.[31]

Late Sir Edwin Arnold poetically called the *Bhagavad Gita* as the *Song Celestial*. Mahadeva Desai says,

> The Gita performs the unique function of making what was an esoteric doctrine a living reality for the unlettered, the lowly and the lost, and present the highest form of practical religion to enable each and all to realise his or her purpose in life.[32]

---

27. *Dhammapada*, p. 126.
28. *Ibid.*, pp. 126-7.
29. *Ibid.*, p. 131.
30. *Ibid.*, pp. 140-1.
31. M.K. Gandhi, *The Story of My Experiments with Truth*, p. 198.
32. Mahadev Desai, *The Gita According to Gandhi*, p. 19.

The theme of the *Gita* is to indicate the end of man's existence on earth and the means for the attainment of it.[33]

The *Gita* is an unerring psychological insight into the human life. *Gita* indicates the ladder of broom in which the first step is brooding over the sense-objects. The second is attachment to them; the third is hankering after them; the fourth is resentment over the unfulfilled hankerings; the fifth is heedlessness with all resentment beings; the sixth is self-lessness and forgetfulness; the seventh is restriction of all desires which takes one finally down to the abyss.[34]

Gandhi was acquainted with the *Gita* in 1888 with the translation by Sir Edwin Arnold known as the *Song Celestial*. The *Gita* has become for him a spiritual reference book.[35]

The *Gita* deals with the subject of self-realisation. Gandhi says,

> The object of the *Gita* appears to me to be that of showing the most excellent way to attain self-realisation.[36]

Renunciation is the central theme of the *Gita*. Renunciation of fruits of action is matchless remedy. All religions proclaimed that it is possible to man to attain freedom by treating the body as the temple of God. How could one be free from action, i.e., from the taint of sin? The *Gita* answered the question in these important words:

> By desireless action; by renouncing fruits of action: by dedicating all activities to God, i.e., by surrendering oneself to Him body and soul.[37]

Renunciation means the absence of hankering after fruit which is the acid test of faith. A man who is after the result becomes impatient giving vent to anger and, if he does not get the result, resorts to unfair and foul means to attain his end.

Gandhi felt that the central teaching of the *Gita* is bounded by truth and non-violence. It is stated that when there is no desire for

---

33. *The Gita According to Gandhi*, p. 52.
34. *Ibid.*, p. 60.
35. *Ibid.*, p.126.
36. *Ibid.*, p. 129.
37. *Ibid.*

truth, there is no temptation for untruth or violence. If any instance of untruth or violence is found, the desire to achieve the cherished goal could be found. While enforcing the teaching of the *Gita* in his own life, Gandhi felt that perfect renunciation without the perfect observance of non-violence in every shape and form is impossible. While the desire for fruit is only universal prohibition, desirelessness is obligatory.[38]

Towards the end of his second year stay in England, he came in contact with the Theosophists. They talked to him about the *Gita* and invited him to read Sir Edwin Arnold's *Gita* translation — the *Song Celestial*. The verses, especially 62 and 63 of the second chapter, have made a deep and lasting impression on him. They are as follows:

> If one ponders on objects of the sense, there springs
> Attraction; from attraction grows desire,
> Desire flames to fierce passion, passion breeds Recklessness;
> then the memory — all betrayed.
> Let's noble purpose go, and saps the mind,
> Till purpose, mind, and man are all undone.[39]

The book struck him as one of priceless worth. He regarded the book *par excellence* for the knowledge of the truth. It has offered to him invaluable help in his moments of gloom. The *Gita* became for Gandhi an infallible guide of conduct and a dictionary of daily reference. Just as one refers to the English dictionary for the meanings of the English words, Gandhi referred to this dictionary (*Gita*) of conduct for a ready solution for all his troubles and travails. The words like *aparigraha* (non-possession) and *samabhava* (equability) gripped him to the utmost. The study of English law helped him to understand more clearly the implication of the word 'trusteeship' in the light of the *Gita*. He understood the teaching of the *Gita* about non-possession to mean that who desires salvation should act like Trustee. He should not regard an iota of their great possessions as their own. It became clear to Gandhi that non-

---

38. *The Gita According to Gandhi*, pp. 132-4.

39. M.K. Gandhi, *The Story of My Experiments with Truth*, p. 48.

possession and equability presupposed the change of heart and the change of attitude.[40]

Gandhi held that fasting could help to curb passion, if undertaken with a view of self-restraint, and fasting is futile unless it is followed by an incessant longing for self-restraint. Gandhi in this connection referred to the famous verse of the second chapter from the *Bhagavad Gita*:

> For a man who is fasting his sense outwardly, the same objects disappear, leaving the yearning behind; but when he has seen the Highest, even the yearning disappears.[41]

Gandhi was influenced by Raichand who was introduced to him by Dr. Mehata. He was a partner of a firm of jewellers. His first meeting with Raichand convinced him that he was a man of great character and learning. He was also known as 'Shatavadhani'. He had wide knowledge of the scriptures and spotless character and has a burning passion for self-realisation. Gandhi found that he only lived to the last for self-realisation. The following lines of Muktanand were always on the lips of Raichand:

> I shall think myself blessed only when I see Him in every one of my daily acts;
> Verily He is the thread, which supports Muktanand's life.[42]

Although Raichandbhai's commercial transactions covered hundreds of thousands, and even though he was a connoisseur of pearls and diamonds, all these things were not the centre round which his life revolved. The centre was the passion to see God face to face. Apart from the things of his business, the other things invariably found were some religious books and his diary on his table. The moment he finished his business, he used to open the religious book or diary. Immediately after finishing his talk about weighty business transaction, he would begin to write about things that were hidden of the spirit. Evidently he was not a businessman but a real seeker of Truth. Gandhi found Raichandbhai thus absorbed in godly

40. *The Story of My Experiments with Truth*, p. 198
41. *Ibid.*, p. 250.
42. *Ibid.*, p. 64.

pursuits in the midst of business quite often without losing his state of equipoise.[43]

When Gandhi did not pay any serious interest in the religious discussions, still he found the talk of Raichandbhai to be of absorbing interest. Gandhi tried to meet the heads of various faiths but no one else had ever made the impression that Raichandbhai could make on him.[44] Gandhi says,

> His words went straight home to me. His intellect compelled as great a regard from me as his moral earnestness, and deep down in me was the conviction that he would never willingly lead me astray and would always confide to me his innermost thoughts. In my moments of spiritual crisis, therefore, he was my refuge.[45]

This found expression when he was at the age of eighteen in this poetical form:

> O, for the hour of that unique bliss,
> When all the knots untied — within, without,
> And all the subtlest bonds removed, I shall.
> Walk on the blessed path that sages trod of yore
> Transcending mind and all its fleeting moods,
> And fixed in deep detachment evermore,
> Regarding body only as the means,
> For self-discipline,
> And nothing else for any cause whatever,
> No more deluded I shall be
> By the sense-magic, or this earthly frame of mine.[46]

Raichandbhai enabled Gandhi finally to find the answer to the question he had been struggling with since his childhood:

---

43. *The Story of My Experiments with Truth*, p. 64.
44. *Ibid.*
45. *Ibid.*, p. 65.
46. Pyarelal, *Mahatma Gandhi, The Early Phase*, Vol. I, p. 274.

> Which was the one true religion that he could adopt and reject the others as false.[47]

Religion is not an 'ism' and it is not merely intellectual knowledge or belief in any set of doctrines, but an innate attribute of the soul. It enables to define the human duties in life and establish correct relationship with the fellow-beings. But before this, there is need to have the knowledge of the self of its true nature. Thus, religion is the means, in the first place of the self-realisation or realisation of the true nature of self.[48]

Gandhi went through the secrets of the sacred books — the *Ramayana* of Tulsidas, the *Mahabharata* of Vyasa and the *Manu-smriti*. Gandhi used the term religion in its broader sense which meant self-realisation or the knowledge of the self. The belief that renunciation as the highest form of religion appealed to him greatly.[49] Gandhi says,

> One thing was deep rooted in me that is the conviction that morality is the basis of things, and that truth is the substance of all morality. Truth became my sole objective. It began to grow in magnitude everyday, and my definition of it also has been ever widening.[50]

The reading of the *Ramayana* left a deep impression on Gandhi. When Ladha Maharaj began his reading of *Ramayana*, Gandhi was deeply enraptured. That laid the foundation of his deep devotion to the Ramayana. He regarded the *Ramayana* of Tulsidas as the greatest book in all devotional literature.[51] Tulsidas advised to *sant* (the good) to shun the *asant* (evil doer).[52]

The influence that *Mahabharata* exerted on the life of Gandhi

---

47. *Mahatma Gandhi and Shrimad Rajchandra* (in Gujarati) published by Bhogilal Naginadas, Unjha Pharmacy Ltd., Unjha (Gujarat), (Samvat 2005), p.18.
48. *Ibid.*, p. 21.
49. M.K. Gandhi, *The Story of My Experiments with Truth*, p. 198.
50. *Ibid.*, p. 25.
51. *Ibid.*, p. 23
52. *Young India*, 4.8.1920, p. 4.

cannot be minimised. Gandhi says,

> I have maintained in the teeth of orthodox Hindu opposition that *Mahabharata* is a book written to establish the futility of war and violence.[53]

Gandhi was introduced to Edward Maitland with whom he opened correspondence. "I greatly liked Maitland's book" he says, "they seem to support Hinduism."[54] Maitland's writings helped Gandhi to give a reasoned presentation of some of the basic tenets of Hinduism like the doctrines of rebirth, transmigration, the essential identity of God, the individual soul, and the salvation from the possibility of fall by realising the Supreme. He applied Maitland's method of allegorical interpretation of the Gospel of Indian ethics — the *Ramayana* and the *Mahabharata* and the *Gita*. He insisted that these should not be regarded as historical works or philosophical poems presented in a historical setting. He was very much impressed with Maitland's insistence on 'reasoned faith'. Later on he declared that while faith transcends reason, it must not contradict reason.[55]

The fact that Gandhi had learnt to be tolerant of all other religions did not mean that he did not have living faith on God. He came across *Manusmriti*[56] which was among his father's collections. The story of the creation and similar other concepts written in it, did not impress him much but on the contrary led him to be inclined towards atheism.[57]

*Manusmriti* did not teach him non-violence, but seemed to support it. He felt that it was quite moral and justified to kill serpents, birds and similar other insects. He remembered to have killed at that age bugs and such other insects as he regarded it as his duty.[58]

---

53. N.B. Sen (ed.), *Wit and Wisdom of Mahatma Gandhi*, p.146.
54. M.K. Gandhi, *The Story of My Experiments with Truth*, p. 102.
55. Pyarelal, *Mahatma Gandhi, The Early Phase*, Vol. I, p. 324.
56. Laws of Manu, *A Hindu Law Giver*.
57. M.K. Gandhi, *The Story of My Experiments with Truth*, p. 24.
58. *Ibid.*, p.25.

A Gujarati didactic stanza gripped his mind and heart. Its precept — return good for evil became his guiding principle. Those wonderful lines are as follows:

> For a bowl of water give a goodly meal
> For a kindly greeting bow thou down with zeal
> For a simple penny pay thou back with gold
> If thy life be rescued, life do not withhold.
> Thus the words and actions of the wise regard;
> Every little service tenfold they reward.
> But the truly noble know all men as one,
> And return with glandness good for evil done.[59]

Gopala Krishna Gokhale exerted profound influence on Gandhi. He was an economist, a parliamentarian and a statesman. His budget speeches had been studied as classics on the subject, and his advice, morally valued. Lord Curzon heard and respected him as a worthy foreman. He was founder of 'Servants of Indian Society' which had as its object the training of youngmen for political work spurning worldly prospects to dedicate themselves only to the service of the Motherland. It was Gokhale who gave India the *mantra* 'Politics must be spiritualised'. The personal relationship that Gandhi established led him to adopt Gokhale as his political *guru*. Gokhale spiritualised politics bringing religion and politics together. Gandhi learnt about the purity of means from Gokhale. Gandhi says,

> Gokhale taught me, that the dream of every Indian who claims to love his country should be not to glorify in language but to spiritualise the political life of the country and the political institutions of the country. He inspired my life and is still inspiring and in that I wish to purify myself and spiritualise myself. I have dedicated myself to that ideal.[60]

---

59. *The Story of My Experiments with Truth*, p. 25.
60. M.K. Gandhi, *In Search of the Supreme*, Vol. II, p. 3.

Gandhi was greatly influenced by the life and teachings of Swami Vivekananda. Vivekananda's conception of *daridra narayan* — the God of the poor had been adopted, elaborated and practised by Gandhi himself. It was after the death of Sri Ramakrishna, Vivekananda with his disciples took the vow of a life-long renunciation and dedication to disinterested service of humanity. He wandered all over the country from the Himalayas to Cape Comorin. His travels revealed to him that India, with her bewildering diversity of races and cultures, has the spirit of fundamental unity. The impoverished state of the masses and their misery overwhelmed him.[61] Vivekananda's Master remark that "religion is not for empty bellies" impressed him much. Vivekananda says,

> I have now travelled all over India But alas: It was agony to me to see with my own eyes the terrible poverty and misery of the masses. It is now my firm conviction that it is futile to preach religion among them without first trying to remove their poverty and their sufferings.[62]

Vivekananda addressed the delegates in the Parliament of World Religions in Chicago on 11 September 1893. He stated that the Indians believe in the universal tolerance and accept all religions as true. He stood against fanaticism and persecution. In his address on the closing day, he pleaded for a comity of religion by the synthesis but not by the destruction of other religions. He held that each religion must assimilate the spirit of the other religion, preserving its individuality, and growing in accordance with the law of its growth.[63]

Vivekananda upheld the ideals of self-help, unity, uplift of the masses, elevation of the status of the women and the dissemination of the ancient long forgotten truths of the Upanishads in his message, so that the Indian masses might realise their inherent strength and overcome their ignorance and poverty. For this purpose, he held that religion must come out of the narrow, traditional grove

---

61. Pyarelal, *Mahatma Gandhi, The Early Phase*, Vol. I, p. 90.
62. *Ibid.*
63. *Ibid.*, p. 91

and cease to think in terms of individual salvation, and combine the ideal of renunciation with the ideal of the service to regenerate the nation.[64] Vivekananda says,

> After so much tapasya, I have come to realise that the highest truth is this: He is present in all beings. They are all His multiple forms. There is no other God to seek. He alone serves God who serves all other beings.[65]

Swami Vivekananda humanised the concept of God and stated that 'service to the poor is service to God' which made Gandhi to say:

> I had made the religion of service my own, as I felt that God could be realised only through service. And service for me was the service of India.[66]

Gandhi made a flying visit to Burma (now Myanmar), and saw the Golden Pagoda there. He found the innumerable little candles burning in the temple to his dislike. He found the rats running about the sanctum, reminding him of Swami Dayananda's experience at Morvi.[67] This speaks of his rational assessment of the religious faith.

Swami Dayananda was a devout worshipper of Shiva. At the age of fourteen, Dayananda experienced the religious crisis. He participated in a vigil and when commanded by his father, he fasted in a Shiva temple on a *Shivaratri* night. When the other devotees had fallen fast asleep, the young lad tried to conscientiously keep his eyelids open by dashing water against them. He was shocked to find rats frolicking all over the image of the deity. He felt within himself that it could not be true God, as it could not even keep the rats away. The explanation given by his father to resolve the doubts could not satisfy him.[68]

---

64. *The Early Phase*, pp. 92-3.
65. Vivekananada, *Prophets of the New India*, p. 572.
66. M.K. Gandhi, *The Story of My Experiments with Truth*, p. 118.
67. *Ibid.*, p. 174.
68. Pyarelal, *Mahatma Gandhi, The Early Phase*, Vol. I, p. 73.

Dadabhai Naoroji exerted profound influence on Gandhi. Naoroji was the founder of Indian National Movement. He was a journalist, an economist, and a passionate advocate of women's education. He was the first and foremost among the Congress patriots. As an ardent social reformer and supporter of the temperance movement, Naoroji led an uncompromising crusade against the immoral opium trade. He tirelessly laboured to create an organised public life in India before the formation of the Congress. He was elected as the President of the Indian National Congress thrice and lived to be universally revered by his countrymen as the **Grand Old Man of India**.[69]

Gandhi admitted that he had learnt the first lesson of *ahimsa* from Dadabhai Naoroji. Romain Rolland says,

> It was Dadabhai who is trying to moderate Gandhi's youthful ordour, gave him in 1892 his first lesson in Ahimsa by teaching him to apply heroic passivity — if two such words may be linked to public life by fighting evil, not by evil but by love.[70]

There is no doubt that Gandhi was very much influenced by Dadabhai Naoroji as the following saying about him confirms the reverence he had for Naoroji.

> I am . . . inexperienced and young . . . guide me . . . . Indians look upon you as children to the father.[71]

Gandhi met Lokamanya Tilak for the first time and it revealed to him the secret of the latter's unique personality. Tilak was the celebrated author of the *Gita Rahasya* and a daring man of action. He was a skilled organiser and born leader of men, deeply respected by his admirers and antagonists alike, for his personal purity, renunciation and self-sacrifice. He was called a man of the people for it was he who brought the Indian masses to the arena of the political field. He had the courage to give voice to his convictions

---

69. *Mahatma Gandhi, The Early Phase*, p. 128.
70. Romain Rolland, *Mahatma Gandhi*, p.16.
71. Pyarelal, *Mahatma Gandhi, The Early Phase*, Vol. I, p. 133.

unhesitatingly despite all the bureaucratic thunder and he was ready to suffer for it. He gave to India the first *mantra* of freedom "Swaraj is my birth-right and I shall have it" and Gandhi added later the other half, viz., "the means thereto are truth and non-violence."[72]

Tilak held that, while persuasion must be the weapon of choice and social reform, compulsion also might be necessary in politics. Ignorance of the people stands as an obstacle that comes on the way of social reformer. Patient reasoning helps to overcome this obstacle. And people could change their way of life by heeding to the voice of the social reformer and this was in their interest. Tilak held that the obstacle that stood on the path of freedom was their self-interest of those wielding power and they never yield to the verbal persuation alone.[73] Before Gandhi preached the Gospel of non-cooperation, it was Tilak who set before the nation, the entire programme of non-cooperation.[74]

The other great person who shaped Gandhi was Sir Pherozeshah. He was a luminary of the legal profession, before he joined the Congress. After his return from South Africa, Gandhi considered that Bombay was the first city to educate the public, relating to problems of the Indian immigrants settled in South Africa. Gandhi tried to ventilate their grievances through pamphlets. Gandhi says,

> Sir Pherozeshah had seemed to me like the Himalaya, the Lokamanya like the ocean. But Gokhale was as the Ganges. One could have a refreshing bath in the holy river. The Himalaya was unscaleable, and one could not easily launch forth on the sea, but the Ganges invited one to its bosom.[75]

---

72. *Mahatma Gandhi, The Early Phase*, p. 140.
73. *Ibid.*, p. 142.
74. D.K. Dutta, *Social, Moral and Religious Philosophy of Mahatma Gandhi*, p. 31.
75. M.K. Gandhi, *The Story of My Experiments with Truth*, p.129.

## Western Influences

Although Gandhi was an Indian, he was deeply influenced by the Western thinkers, writers, and prophets who are both ancient and modern. Gandhi owed indebtedness to the West. He did not think that everything Western had to be rejected. He learnt about *ahimsa* from the Western tradition also. Gandhi says,

> I have nothing to be ashamed of if my views on 'ahimsa' (non-violence) are the result of my Western education. I have never tabooed all Western ideas nor am I prepared to anathematise everything that comes from the West are inherently evil. I have learnt much from the West and I should not be surprised to find that I had learnt something about ahimsa too from the West.[76]

The Ancient Greek Philosopher Socrates, as seeker of truth, influenced Gandhi greatly. Commenting on Socrates and his stand for truth, Gandhi pointed out:

> Socrates would not refrain from preaching what he knew to be truth to the Athenien youth and bravely suffered the punishment of death. He was in his case a Satyagrahi.[77]

Gandhi regarded Socrates as a great *satyagrahi*. He had great admiration for Socrates and found in him a soul force which is capable of fighting against injustice, Socrates was courageous enough to prefer a cup of hemlock to give up his pursuit of truth and resisted superstitious beliefs of his people through non-violent means.

*New Testament*, especially *The Sermon* on the Mount, went straight into his heart. Gandhi compared The Sermon on the Mount with the *Gita* and referred to Jesus saying written in the *New Testament* — Matthew 5th Chapter — 39th, 40th verses:

> But I say unto you.' That ye resist not evil but whosoever shall smite thee on Thy right, cheek, turn to him the other

76. M.K. Gandhi, *Hindu Dharma*, p. 199.
77. M.K. Gandhi, *On the Back Flap of The Science of Satyagraha*.

> also. And if any man will sue thee at the law, and take away thy coat, let him have thy cloak also.[78]

These verses delighted him beyond measure. He was reminded of Shamal Bhatt's "For a bowl, of water, give a goodly meal".[79] His young mind tried to unify the teachings of the *Gita*, *The Light of Asia*, and *The Sermon on the Mount*.[80] He found the spirit of renunciation present in *Sermon on the Mount* appealed to him greatly. Gandhi says,

> I have not been able to see any difference between the Sermon on the Mount and the Bhagavad Gita. What the Sermon describes in a graphic manner, the Bhagavad Gita reduces to a scientific formula. It may not be scientific in the accepted sense of the term, but it has argued out of the law of love — the law of abandon as I could call it in a scientific manner. The Sermon on the Mount gives the same law in wonderful language. The New Testament gave me comfort and boundless joy as it came after the repulsion that parts of the old has given me. Today supposing I was deprived of the Gita and forgot all its contexts but I had a copy of the Sermon, I should derive the same joy from it as I do from the Gita.[81]

Gandhi's Christian friends taught him the essence of Christianity.[82] According to Gandhi, Jesus was one of the greatest teachers, that the humanity has ever produced. He held that Jesus does not belong solely to Christianity alone, but to the entire world and all races and people.[83] Gandhi wondered at the non-violent character of Christ and called him "The Prince of Satyagrahis". In England Gandhi renewed the study of the Bible and admitted that Jesus

---

78. M.K. Gandhi, *The Story of My Experiments with Truth*, p. 51.
79. *Ibid.*, p. 102.
80. *The Story of My Experiments with Truth*, p. 102.
81. *Young India*, 22.12.1927, p. 426.
82. Louis Fischer, *The Life of Mahatma Gandhi*, Part I, p. 59.
83. *The Modern Review*, October 1941, p. 407.

played a great role in his life. He felt the beauty of the *Sermon on the Mount* by reading it. He chose several words from the Bible and referred to the *Bible* many times in his talks.

Theosophy believes in the equality of all religions and considers them as the branches of one religion. Gandhi read Madame Blavatsky's *Key to Theosophy* which stimulated him the desire to read books on Hinduism, and disabused him of the notion fostered by the missionaries that Hinduism was ripe with superstition.[84] Gandhi was introduced to the literature of other religions also and advocated the view that although a tree has single trunk, it has many branches and leaves. Similarly is the case with the true religion which becomes many when it passes through the human medium. He felt that no religion denies the creed of truth and non-violence.

Leo Tolstoy guided Gandhi across the continents and in his writings Gandhi found solace in his struggle. Tolstoy's book *The Kingdom of God is Within You* overwhelmed him leaving an abiding impression on Gandhi. As an exponent of the doctrine of passive resistance, Tolstoy lived in accordance with it.[85] Gandhi says,

> When I was passing through a severe crisis of scepticism and doubt that I came across his book, *The Kingdom of God is Within You* and was deeply impressed by it. I was at that time a believer in violence. Its reading cured me of my scepticism and made me a firm believer in Ahimsa (non-violence). What has appealed to me most in Tolstoy's life is that he practised what he preached and reckoned no cost too great in his pursuit of truth.[86]

The writings like *War and Peace*, the world's greatest novel *Resurrection*, *Annacarenina* (The World's classics) *The Kingdom of God is Within You*, *Christianity and Patriotism* brought Tolstoy universal recognition and colossal success. He noticed the glaring discrepancy between Christ's message and man's way of life which troubled him.

---

84. M.K. Gandhi, *The Story of My Experiments with Truth*, p. 51.
85. *Speeches and Writings of Mahatma Gandhi*, p. 165.
86. *Young India*, 20.9.1928, p. 319.

Tolstoy noticed many divergences from the teachings of Christ. He pointed out that the law of non-resistance to evil by violence indicates evidently how the Church doctrine perverts the teaching of Christ.[87]

While giving conscientious summary of Tolstoy's book — *The Kingdom of God is Within You* Canon Farrar pointed out:

> Tolstoy came to the conclusion that a coarse deceit was palmed upon the world when these words were held by civilised society to be compatible with war, courts of Justice, capital punishment, divorce, oaths, national prejudices, and indeed most of the institutions of civil and social life. He now believes that the Kingdom of God would come if all men kept those five commandments: (1) Live in peace with all men; (2) Be pure; (3) Take no oaths; (4) Never resist evil; (4) Renounce national distinctions.[88]

Tolstoy stated that people cannot believe in the obedience to civil or state laws which can promote their interest, or satisfy the demands of reason or of human nature. So they have arrived at the conclusion that it is unreasonable to obey the law of justice which is doubtful. So they cannot but suffer submitting to a law which they do not recognise as reasonable and binding.[89]

Tolstoy noticed the difference of the preaching of the past and the present. He said that the men who preached two thousand years ago believed what they preached. But the preachers themselves do not believe what they said because their preaching no longer has any meaning.[90] Tolstoy says,

> The social conception of life to justify itself only as long as men voluntarily sacrificed their own interests to the interests of the community. But as soon as there were individuals who did not voluntarily do so and power was needed to restrain them, there crept into the social life —

87. Leo Tolstoy, *The Kingdom of God is Within You*, p. 1.
88. *Ibid.*, p. 47.
89. *Ibid.*, p. 145.
90. *Ibid.*, p. 161.

> conception and the structure of life founded on it the disintegrating principle of violence, that is, coercion averted by some people against others.[91]

Tolstoy held that the destruction of life is not an act of ameliorating life but an act of sucide.[92] The recognition of Truth which is the cause of all manifestation of human life depends on certain inner qualities of man without his observation but does not depend upon external phenomena.[93] Tolstoy observes:

> Man would not be free if he knew no truth at all, and he would not be free or even have any idea of freedom, if the whole truth that should guide him in life were revealed to him once for all in complete purity with no admixture of error.[94]

Tolstoy pointed out that the sole meaning of human life lies in serving the world by promoting the establishment of the Kingdom of God.[95] Tolstoy said that it is not peace which is obtained by the diplomatic negotiations, the visits of Emperors, the Kings, banquets, speeches, fortresses, artillery, dynamite, by exhausting the people by taxation or tearing the flower of the nation from toil and corrupting it. But the peace which is secured by free advocacy of the truth by each individual would be lasting which has been established.[96] Tolstoy said that people themselves are not free because they do not make themselves free.[97] Tolstoy's philosophy of life is marked by his famous saying that "one should live so as to have the best for oneself and one's family and not to try to be wiser than life and Nature.[98]

---

91. *The Kingdom of God is within You*, p. 201.
92. *Ibid.*, p. 373.
93. *Ibid.*, p. 423.
94. *Ibid.*, p. 425.
95. *Ibid.*, p. 444.
96. Leo Tolstoy, *The Christianity and Patriotism*, p. 539.
97. Louis Fischer, *The Life of Mahatma Gandhi*, Part I, p. 113.
98. B.R. Nanda, *Mahatma Gandhi — A Biography*, p. 73.

Gandhi considered Leo Tolstoy as one of his best teachers. Commenting on Tolstoy, Gandhi puts:

> There is no doubt that there is nothing new in what Tolstoy preaches. But his presentation of the old Truth is refreshingly forceful. His logic is unassailable. And, above all, he endeavours to practise what he preaches. He preaches to convince. He is sincere and earnest. He commands attention.[99]

The study of Tolstoy's, *The Gospel in Brief What to Do*? and other books made an indelible impression on Gandhi. And he "began to realise more and more the infinite possibilities of universal love".[100]

If a person lives too much for himself instead of feeding others, he not only loses possibility of giving away the surplus, but also by eating too much he is deprived of the power to help others.

Tolstoy says,

> To be good and lead a good life means to give to others more than one takes from them,[101]

From this Tolstoy derived the concept of bread labour enunciated by the Russian writer and peasent philosopher T.F. Bondareff who stated "If a man work not, neither shall he eat." For Tolstoy it was "a test of sincerity in recognising equality of all men". This helped Tolstoy to be nearer to the majority of the labour class from whom he was fenced by a war.[102] Gandhi was very much attracted towards the concept of 'bread labour'.

Next to Tolstoy it was the modern writer John Ruskin who profoundly influenced Gandhi. Mr. Polak came to see off Gandhi at the railway station on his journey from Johannesburg to Durban and left with him a book to read during his journey. It was Ruskin's *Unto This Last*. It became impossible for Gandhi to lay aside the book when once he started reading it gripped him. Gandhi

99. M.K. Gandhi, *Collected Works of Mahatma Gandhi*, Vol. X, p. 2.
100. M.K. Gandhi, *The Story of My Experiments with Truth*, p. 119.
101. Leo Tolstoy, *Essays and Letters*, p. 70.
102. Pyarelal, *Mahatma Gandhi, The Early Phase*, Vol. I, p. 667.

determined to change his way of life in accordance with the ideals presented in the book. Apart from the other books he read, the one that brought about an instantaneous and practical transformation in his life was the book — *Unto This Last*. He translated this book later into Gujarati entitling it as *sarvodaya* (the welfare of all).

Gandhi discovered some of his deepest convictions reflected in this book of Ruskin. As a result it captured and transformed his life. The teachings embodied in the book *Unto This Last* understood by Gandhi are as follows:

1. That the good of the individual is contained in the good of all.
2. That a lawyer's work has the same value as the barber's in as much as all have the same right of earning their livelihood from their work.
3. That a life of labour, i.e., the life of the tiller of the soil and the handicraftsman is the life worth living.

Gandhi said:

> The first of these I knew. The second I had dimly realised. The third had never occurred to me. 'Unto This Last' made it as clear as daylight for me that the second and the third were contained in the first. I arose with the dawn, ready to reduce these principles to practice.[103]

Ruskin was a very great artist critic, essayist, and a modern writer on ethics, sociology and political economy. Ruskin held that riches are a power like that of electricity acting through inequalities and negations of itself. What people really desired under the name of riches is essentially power over men. Men should seek consequently not greater wealth but simpler pleasure, not higher fortune but deeper felicity and harmless pride and pursuit of peace. Being conscious of the fact that what one person has, another person cannot have; the rich should abstain from luxuries until the poorest shall have enough. For Gandhi it meant only such economy is good that conduces its good of all. Ruskin merely contended that the

---

103. M.K. Gandhi, *The Story of My Experiments with Truth*, p. 221.

under-privileged must find protection in the morality of the fortunate. Ruskin was hopeful of alleviating the hardships arising out of inequality by an appeal to the human conscience.[104]

Ruskin in his *Unto This Last* shows the evidence of his growing interest in formulating the theory of political economy. He pronounced his ideas in extremely hostile manner which ran counter to the already established economic theories formulated in the Victorian era in England. *Unto This Last* is marked by promulgation of new ideas and brave redefinition in human terminology which makes this book a document of timeless relevance. Ruskin's vocabulary is confined to simple words creating an aura of humanity, affection and controlled sentiment.

Ruskin's main object was to give an accurate and stable definition of wealth. His second object was to show that the acquisition of wealth was finally possible only under certain moral conditions of society with the belief in the existence for the practical purposes, the attainability of honesty. He held that the old and destitute have to be rehabilitated for their comfort. John Ruskin says,

> A labourer serves his country with his spade, just as a man in the middle ranks of life serves it with sword, pen, or lancet. If the service be less, and, therefore, the wages during health less, then the reward when health is broken may be less, but not less honourable; and it ought to be quite as natural and straight forward a matter for a labourer to take his pension from his parish, because he has deserved well of his parish, as for a man in higher rank, to take his pension from his country, because he has deserved well of his country.[105]

Ruskin held that the modern self-styled science of political economy is based on the idea that an advantageous code of social action may be determined irrespectively of the influence of social affection.[106] There is need to include affection which one man owes to another

---

104. Louis Fischer, *The Life of Mahatma Gandhi*, Part I, pp. 83-4.
105. John Ruskin, *Unto This Last*, p. 6.
106. *Ibid.*, p. 9

in justice. "All right relations between master and operative, and all their best interests, ultimately depend on these.'[107]

Gandhi was also influenced by the American anarchist, Henry David Thoreau. He wrote the book on *Civil Disobedience*. When Gandhi was imprisoned due to *satyagraha* campaign in South Africa, he read Thoreau's book with great interest. Gandhi defined *Civil Disobedience* as "civil breach of the unmoral statutory enactments without the fear of its sanctions". Gandhi held that this expression coined by Henry Thoreau signified his own resistance against the unmoral laws of a slave state. He has left a masterly treatise on the duty of *Civil Disobedience*. Thoreau limited his breach of statutory laws to the revenue laws, i.e., payment of taxes. By the time the *Civil Disobedience* was practised by Gandhi, it covered a breach of any statutory and unmoral law. It signified the resister's outlawry in a non-violent manner.[108] Gandhi says,

> To me political power because there is not state. But the ideal is never fully realised in life. Hence the classical statement of Thoreau that Government is best which governs the least.[109]

*Civil Disobedience* is considered to be the most powerful political essay of Henry Thoreau. It is laid on the fundamental principle which is transcendental in nature. It holds that there is no law higher than Civil law — law of conscience. In the event of any conflict in the laws, it is the duty of the citizen to obey the voice of God rather than that of civil authority. Thoreau stated that the law will never make men free, but it is men who have God to make the law free. Men are the lovers of law and order and the duty is to observe the law when the government breaks it.[110]

Thus, Gandhi drew great inspiration from the Indian and Western influences and they shaped his thought to a greater extent. The aspects that exerted profound influence on Gandhi bear great significance and relevance to the modern times.

---

107. John Ruskin, *Unto This Last*, p. 13.
108. M.K. Gandhi, *Satyagraha*, pp. 3-4.
109. *Young India*, 2.7.1931, p. 162.
110. Walter Harding, *The Days of Henry Theoreau*, pp. 206-7.

# 2

# Moral and Religious Aspects of Gandhian Philosophy

## Meaning of Religion

THE word religion is used by different people in different ways. The *Oxford Dictionary* defines religion as

> human recognition of superhuman controlling power and especially of a personal God entitled to obedience, effect of such recognition on conduct and mental attitude.

Religion is also a belief in the ultimate values which are in harmony with the enduring structure of the universe. "Religion is a pervasive and almost universal phenomenon in human societies."[1] Whitehead says,

> Religion is the vision of something which stands beyond, behind, and within, the passing flux of immediate things; something which is real, and yet waiting to be realised, something which is a remote possibility and yet the greatest of present facts; something which gives meaning to all that passes and yet eludes apprehension, something whose possession is the good and yet is beyond all reach, something which is the ultimate ideal and the hopeless quest.[2]

---

1. George L. Abernethy & Thomas A. Longford, *Philosophy of Religion*, p. 1.
2. A.N. Whitehead, *Science and the Modern World*, chapter 12.

Radhakrishnan says that the religion is an insight into reality, and though inaccessible to reason, is consistent with it.[3] True religion should be distinguished from mere knowledge of dogmas or rituals.[4] Religion awakens the reality in man.[5] Religion has its basis in the discovery of the essential worth and dignity of the individual and his relation to a higher world of reality.[6]

The aim of religion is not reflection or ecstasy, but identification with the current of life, and therefore participation in its creative advance. The religious man transcends the limitations imposed on him by his material nature or social conditions, and enlarges the creative purpose. Religion is a dynamic process, a renewed effort of the creative impulse working through exceptional individuals, and seeking to uplift mankind to a new level.[7]

### Gandhi and Religion

Gandhi brought down religion from the cloistered seclusion of yogic contemplation to man's socio-economic and political plane. On the other hand, he sought to lift the political struggle to the higher level of moral and spiritual endeavour.[8] Religion is not a refuge from the world but a great source of inspiration to act in this world.[9]

Gandhi defined religion as

> a belief in the ordered and the moral Government of the universe.[10]

For Gandhi religion is not sectarianism, but it pervades everyone and binds indissolubly to truth which is a permanent element

---

3. S. Radhakrishnan, *Religion in a Changing World*, p. 102.
4. *Ibid.*, p. 104.
5. *Ibid.*, p. 106.
6. *Ibid.*, p. 42.
7. S. Radhakrishnan, *Religion and Society*, p. 78.
8. N.K. Devaraja, *Philosophy, Religion and Culture*, p. 206.
9. S. Radhakrishnan, *Religion in a Changing World*, p. 139.
10. *Harijan*, 10.2.1940, p. 445.

present in human nature.[11]

## Religion and Morality

Morality constitutes the basis of human life. The real progress of the individuals of the society depends on morality which checks the passions and impulses that retard the human progress and lead to discord and strife. Morality, on the other hand, contributes to peace, happiness and progress and creates an atmosphere to be in harmony. In the moral context the human conscience acts as a man's inner guide.

In the philosophical context religion and morality have to be dealt with separately as the two concepts are basically different. Moral values have bearing on this world and determine the way of life to be led, but the religious values have transcendental reference and determine the way of life to be led for the life beyond. Although both religion and morality co-exist conceptually, they are different.[12] In Gandhian thought such difference does not exist.

For Gandhi:

> True religion and true morality are inseparably bound up with each other. Religion is to morality what water is to the seed that is sown in the soil.[13]

Gandhi rejected unhesitatingly any religious doctrine that is in conflict with morality. He holds that "as soon as we lose moral basis, it ceases to be religious".[14] Morality is not possible without religion. On the other hand, religion contributes greatly to the growth of morality.

Gandhi took every aspect of human life only from the moral standpoint. His main object was to equalise religion with morality in order to make religion dynamically operative in human life.[15]

---

11. *Young India*, 12.5.1920, p. 2.
12. Basant Kumar Lal, *Contemporary Indian Philosophy*, p. 125.
13. N.K. Bose (ed.), *Selections from Gandhi*, p. 255.
14. *Young India*, 24.11.1921, p. 365.
15. K.M.P. Verma (ed.), *Philosophy of Religion*, p. 71.

Gandhi was prepared to reject any religious sentiment if it is not moral.

He declared:

> As soon as we lose the moral basis, we cease to be religious. There is no such thing as religion over-riding morality. Man for instance cannot be untruthful, cruel and incontinent and claim to have God in his side.[16]

Gandhi held that the great religions of the world are practically laid on the basis of conduct and morality. He said that

> True religion is identical with morality. There is no religion higher than Truth and Righteousness.[17]

Gandhi synthesised religion and morality for he thinks that morality does not preclude religion.

According to D.M. Dutta, every individual is a definite centre of the life of God, manifested under particular physical and mental conditions. Every individual has to know of himself and reform himself and gradually widen his outlook towards the Infinite Self. The vision of God becomes possible when he considers and promotes the interest of others.

As D.M. Dutta aptly puts it

> The path to the realisation of the True Self or God, therefore, lies through the love of others and the performance of duties towards others as such love demands. Morality thus becomes the essence of religion.[18]

Morality is fused with historical action, love and truth as its linked moments. The moral approach transforms the disturbed situation into serene situation and the pang of passion into the emblem of pity.

Krishna Murty wrote:

> The quest of a moral idea, the growth of the soul, heroic self-

---

16. *Young India*, 24.11.1921, p. 365.
17. M.K. Gandhi, *Ethical Religion*, p. 19.
18. D.M. Dutta, *The Philosophy, Mahatma Gandhi*, p. 75.

> sacrifice and freedom as political religion constitute the true historical moment.[19]

Man cannot reach truth without morality. Morality is held to be the fundamental pre-supposition to achieve the knowledge of the truth and self-realisation.[20] Morality is a necessary means for achieving the right goal.

According to Gandhi, the highest moral law is that in which we should unremittingly work for the good of mankind.[21] Gandhi regarded only voluntary actions as moral. He maintained that "no action which is not voluntary can be called moral".[22] Humanism believes in doing good to others as the way of highest moral life. Religion without morality would mean a mere escape from responsibility.[23]

Religion has to integrate various aspects of the human life and ethics is held to be the science of ideals. Gandhi synthesised religion and ethics. The careful examination and observation help to make the ethical concepts as guide to the human conduct.

Gandhi pointed out:

> So long as we act like machines, there can be no question of morality. If we want to call an action moral, it should have been done consciously and as a matter of duty. Any action that is dictated by fear, or by coercion of any kind, ceases to be moral. It also follows that all good deeds that are prompted by hope of happiness in the next world cease to be moral.[24]

Religion and Morality are interrelated and interconnected. Religion without morality is meaningless and morality without religion is purposeless. According to Gandhi, means and ends are inextricably

---

19. Y.G. Krishna Murti, *Gandhism will Survive*, p. 7.
20. Unto Tahtinen, *The Core of Gandhi's Philosophy*, p. 36.
21. M.K. Gandhi, *Ethical Religion*, p. 39.
22. *Ibid.*, p. 40.
23. *The Humanist*, Vol. XII, p. 98.
24. M.K. Gandhi, *Ethical Religion*, p. 43.

bound with each other. While morality offers means and a purpose to the human life, religion leads to the goal. As such, both are complementary but not contradictory to each other. So Gandhi emphasised the need for the synthesis of morality and religion.

Gandhi held that freedom of free-will is a necessary postulate of morality. But man is not completely free to choose his own way of life, determined by any conditions such as laws of nature, social conditions, traditions and human tendencies. But man has scope to assert himself and exert his will to mould the environment, morally.

Mahatma Gandhi says:

> A moral act must be our own act, it must spring from our own will. If we act mechanically, there is no moral content in our act. Such action would be moral, if we think it proper to act like a machine and do so. For doing so, we use our discrimination. We should bear in mind the distinction between acting mechanically and acting intentionally.[25]

For Gandhi religion and morality are convertible terms.

Gandhi wrote:

> For me, morals, ethics, and religion are convertible terms. A moral life without reference to religion is like a house built upon sand. And religion divorced from morality is like 'sounding brass' good only for making a noise and breaking heads.[26]

## Cardinal Virtues

Gandhi advocated some virtues of life which are essential to lead a pious and moral life. Traditional Indian philosophy emphasises the need for the observations of cardinal virtues for the reason that the world is governed by the moral law. Every kind of action produces either good or bad effect which has relevance at the same time. It is in accordance with the principle "As you sow you will reap".[27]

---

25. *The Collected Works of Mahatma Gandhi*, Vol. VI, p. 284.
26. *Harijan*, 3.10.1936, p. 268.
27. B.K. Lal, *Contemporary Indian Philosophy*, p. 134.

There is need to develop certain basic virtues which enable individuals to lead a righteous life. Indian ethics talk of five virtues viz., non-violence (*ahimsa*), truthfulness (*satya*), non-stealing (*asteya*), non-possession (*aparigraha*), and celibacy (*brahmacarya*). While admitting all these, Gandhi added some more. He interpreted all these virtues in his own fashion depending on his own experience. His idea was that these virtues must be consistent with the needs and requirements of the time.[28]

Gandhi followed the Indian formula in thought, word and deed to perfectly practice the cardinal virtues. The purity of life cannot be maintained unless the entire human life of thought, word and deed becomes pure.

## Non-Violence (Ahimsa)

Gandhi gave utmost importance to non-violence as a great virtue. The moral aspects such as tolerance and love have been manifested in this virtue. Literally speaking non-violence means non-injury and non-killing. It is an action based on the refusal to harm. Gandhi gave a new interpretation to the concept of non-violence and redefined the meaning with the new perspective. He pointed out that non-violence in the past was made to appear crude. It is doubtless that to hurt any living being is a part of non-violence which is its least expression. He stated that the principle of non-violence is hurt by evil thought, undue haste, lying, hatred, wishing ill-will to anybody. On the other hand, he made a distinction between the positive and negative meaning of non-violence:

> Ahimsa is not merely negative state of harmlessness but it is a positive state of love, doing good even to the evil doer. But it does not mean helping the evil doer to continue the wrong or tolerating it by passive acquiescence. On the contrary, love, the active state Ahimsa, requires you to resist the wrong-doer by disassociating yourself from him even though it may offend him or injure him physically.[29]

---

28. *Contemporary Indian Philosophy*, p. 134.
29. *Young India*, 25.8.1920, p. 2.

He further says:

> In its positive form Ahimsa means the largest love and the greatest charity.[30]

According to Gandhi, non-violence is the law of the human race; infinitely greater and superior to the brute force which can be wielded equally by all. He held that non-violence as a moral virtue is law of being. Gandhi noticed that man has steadily progressed towards non-violence. He referred to the history of mankind and stated that the remote ancestors were cannibal who were violent; but in the next stage he became a hunter; and became an agriculturist in the later stage discontinuing hunting in which violence was involved and adapted himself to the civilised conduct of life. All these stages are indicative of the progressing non-violence and diminishing violence in recognition of non-violence as a great moral virtue.[31]

Gandhi stated that non-violence is not merely for the *rishis* and saints but it is also meant for the common people. Those that have discovered non-violence as a great virtue established the fact that the real salvation lies in non-violence but not in violence.[32]

Non-violence as a great virtue contributes to the highest good of mankind not only in the future days to come but also to the present. "While violence appears to do good, the good derived out of it is temporary and the evil it does is permanent", says Gandhi.[33]

## Truthfulness (Satya)

Gandhi held that regard for truth or to be truthful is a virtue. His life was a series of experiments with truth. For him truth is the sovereign principle, inclusive of numerous other principles. This truth is not merely truthfulness in word but truthfulness in thought and deed. In his conception there is relative truth and also Absolute Truth which he identified with God. As long as Absolute

30. *Speeches and Writings of Mahatma Gandhi*, p. 346.
31. *Harijan*, 11.8.1940, p. 245.
32. *Young India*, 11.8.1920, p. 3.
33. *Ibid.*, 21.5.1925, p. 178.

Truth is not realised, so long must relative truth be held, which will meanwhile be Beacon, Shield and Buckler.[34]

Gandhi stated that for marching towards truth man has to give up anger, selfishness, hatred, etc., as otherwise it is not possible to attain Truth. A man swayed by passions may have good intentions, may be truthful in word, but will not be truthful in deed.

> A successful search for Truth means complete deliverance from the dual throng such as of love and hate, happiness and misery.[35]

In his opinion the only means of realisation of truth is non-violence. The result of all his experiments reveals that a perfect vision of Truth can only follow a complete realisation of non-violence.[36]

Gandhi stated that moral degeneration or deviation causes ignorance and made it explicit that six deadly enemies viz., lust, anger, greed, infatuation, pride and falsehood are to be avoided to practice truth.

### Non-Stealing (Asteya)

*Asteya* implies the observance of the rule of not taking away the property or anything belonging to anybody unless it is given by the person concerned. Apart from this, there is another meaning which is more rigorous in its application which forbids holding in possession of such thing that is not needed or required by the person concerned. Gandhi made use of this term in both these senses.[37]

Gandhi says that it is impossible for a person to steal and simultaneously claim to know Truth. Most of the people, knowingly or unknowingly, cautiously or uncautiously, are more or less guilty of theft. To receive any single thing that is not needed is wrong. He said that it is theft for any person to take any fruit that is not needed

---

34. M.K. Gandhi, *The Story of My Experiments with Truth*, Introduction, p. xv.
35. *Ibid.*, pp. 254-5.
36. *Ibid.*, p. 370.
37. B.K. Lal, *Contemporary Indian Philosophy*, p. 136.

or to take it in a larger quantity than is necessary. People are not always aware of their real needs and most of them improperly multiply their wants, and thus unconsciously are thieves of themsleves.[38] By observing non-stealing, one could bring about a progressive reduction of his wants and poverty could be alleviated to the possible extent.[39] Gandhi held that it is theft to desire mentally to acquire anything belonging to others or cast a greedy eye upon it. One who observes the principle of non-violence, refuses to bother himself about things to be acquired in the future.[40]

Jainism and Buddhism, which have exerted much influence on Gandhi, laid more stress on this virtue. Gandhi considered this a moral virtue which has its basis in love, free from exploitation and violence.

## Non-Possession (Aparigraha)

*Aparigraha* (non-possession) is a significant virtue allied to *asteya*. For Gandhi *aparigraha* is contentment, to be contented with the necessities of life without the desire for more. According to him possessing a thing which is not originally stolen but holding it without the need of it, must nevertheless be classified under the stolen property. Possessing implies provision for the future. A seeker of Truth is the follower of the law of Love who cannot hold anything against tomorrow.[41]

Due to the ignorance or negligence in observing the Divine Law which provides man with his daily bread in his day-to-day life, has given rise to inequalities and miseries. While the rich have a store of things which they do not need and which is superfluously neglected and wasted, millions are starved to death for want of sustenance.[42]

Perfect fulfilment of the ideal of non-possession requires that

38. M.K. Gandhi, *From Yeravda Mandir*, p. 20.
39. *Ibid.*
40. *Ibid.*, p. 21.
41. *Ibid.*, p. 23.
42. *Ibid.*

like birds, man should have no stock of food for tomorrow. In the absolute sense of the term non-possession, it may be impossible to observe it in life but there is need to keep the ideal constantly in view and critically examine the possessions and reduce them to the extent possible. Civilisation in the real sense of the term, consists not in the multiplication but in the deliberate and voluntary reduction of wants.[43] This alone promotes real happiness and contentment increasing the capacity for rendering service.[44]

Gandhi realised that love and exclusive possession could never go together. Perfect love demands readiness to give up everything including the body, stands as an ideal towards which man should progress though it cannot be realisable completely in the human life.

Therefore Gandhi wrote:

> Theoretically when there is perfect love, there must be perfect non-possession. The body is our last possession. So a man can only exercise perfect love and be completely dispossessed, if he is prepared to embrace death and renounce his body for the sake of human service. But that is true in theory only. In actual life, we can hardly exercise perfect love, for the body as a possession, will always remain with us. Man will ever remain imperfect, and it will always be his part to try to be perfect. So that perfection in love or non-possession will remain an unattainable ideas as long as we are alive, but towards which we must ceaselessly strive.[45]

## Celibacy (Brahmacharya)

*Brahmacharya* has been practised as a cardinal virtue. Etymologically speaking, it is a way of life dedicated to the practice of Brahma. In the general context, it is a life of purity which is regarded as essential to devote oneself exclusively for the realisation

---

43. *From Yeravda Mandir*, p. 24.
44. *Ibid.*
45. Bose, *Selections from Gandhi*, p. 17.

of God. All kinds of restraint have been associated with it.

Gandhi described the root meaning of *brahmacharya* as the conduct adapted to the search of Brahma, i.e., Truth and in its special meaning it is a control of all the senses.[46]

According to Gandhi, all the observances are deducible from Truth to subserve it. Realisation of Truth through self-gratification should, after what has been said before, appear a contradiction in terms.[47] The fulfilment of non-violence is not possible without selflessness which is a state of universal love. It is only when the limitations of family interests are transcended, could there be universal love. Gandhi says that *brahmacharya* means control in thought, word and action of all the senses at all times and in all places. A man or woman who practises complete *brahmacharya* is absolutely free from passion.[48] A person who appears to have control over his body but nurses evil thoughts in his mind makes vain effort.[49]

> Brahmacharya means control of all the organs of senses. He who attempts to control only one organ, and allows all the others free play, is bound to find his efforts futile.... He, therefore, who is resolved to control the one, must be likewise determined control the rest. I have always felt that much has been done by the narrow definition of *brahmacharya*. If we practise simultaneously self-control in all directions, this attempt will be scientific and possible of success.[50]

## Fearlessness (Abhaya)

Gandhi added another virtue, namely, *abhaya* (fearlessness) to the five cardinal virtues. As a vow, this is important especially for the workers who have been trained to face death and experience untold

46. M.K. Gandhi, *From Yeravda Mandir*, p. 14.
47. *Ibid.*, pp. 10-11.
48. *Young India*, 5.6.1924, p. 186.
49. M.K. Gandhi, *From Yeravda Mandir*, p. 12.
50. *Speeches and Writings of Mahatma Gandhi*, p. 130.

suffering in their non-violent fight against those that are armed with deadly weapons.[51]

Gandhi stated that one cannot seek truth or cherish Love without fearlessness. He quoted Pritam who says that "the path of Hari (the Lord) is the path of the brave, not of cowards". By Hari, Gandhi meant Truth and the brave is those armed with fearlessness, but not with the sword, the rifle, etc. These arms are held to be taken up by those who are possessed by fear. According to Gandhi,

> Fearlessness connotes freedom from all external fear — fear of disease, bodily injury and death, of dispossession, of losing reputation or giving offence, and so on.[52]

For Gandhi moral bravery is the highest heroism which does not consist in striking and causing injury to others but in the readiness to sacrifice, patiently and fearlessly everything including life for the sake of good of other fellow beings arising out of love for them.[53] But of the cowards he says "cowards can never be moral.... Fearlessness is indispensable for the growth of the other noble qualities. How can one seek Truth or cherish love without fearlessenss."[54]

Gandhi says that perfect fearlessness is attainable only by him who has realised the Supreme which implies freedom from delusions. One can make progress towards the goal with strong determination and constant endeavour, with the cultivation of self-confidence.[55] It is by fearing God could one cease to fear man,[56] says Gandhi.

## Universal Religion

The study of many great religious scriptures helped Gandhi to find good precepts contained in them which are capable of attaining a religious and moral life. Many interpretations, commentaries and

---

51. D.M. Dutta, *The Philosophy of Mahatma Gandhi*, p. 102.
52. M.K. Gandhi, *From Yeravda Mandir*, p. 27.
53. D.M. Dutta, *The Philosophy of Mahatma Gandhi*, p. 103.
54. *Ibid*.
55. M.K. Gandhi, *From Yeravda Mandir*, p. 28.
56. *Speeches and Writings of Mahatma Gandhi*, p. 130.

practices have gone out of each religious tradition which have no moral and rational basis.

> A study of other religions is essential for the understanding of ones own and is a valuable constituent of one's general culture. It is true that no one can master all the scriptures of the world. We must work for a new spiritual reconciliation and outlook in the light of recent developments with the aim of living together in harmony. The great prophets reveal to us the new being.[57]

Gandhi was of the opinion that all great religions of the world are true and God-given. The diverse religions are similar to the branches of the same tree, but they tend to be imperfect due to the imperfect interpretation of human instrumentality.

> I believe in the fundamental truth of all great religions of the world. I believe that they are all God given, and I believe that they were necessary for the people to whom these religions were revealed. And I believe that, if only we could all of us read the scriptures of different faiths from the standpoint of the followers of those faiths, we should find that they were at bottom all one and were all helpful to one another.[58]

Religion is marked by discipline and moral practice. The different religions represent not truth but views or apprehensions of truth as men have believed. Varied historical expressions of the same truth could be found which is universal and timeless in its validity.[59]

Gandhi tested the different religious ideas and judged them by the lives and experiences of those who adopted them. Although there are many religions, Gandhi never subscribed to the fanatical view that there must be one religion. He believed in the equality of all religions and held that all religions in essence are one. Gandhi wanted that people should have a proper picture of what they want before they could have something to achieve. In this picture Gandhi

---

57. S. Radhakrishnan, *Religion in the Changing World*, p. 134.
58. *Harijan*, 16.2.1934, pp. 5-6.
59. S. Radhakrishnan, *Religion and Society*, p. 43.

visualised of equality of all religions and desired that every religion has its full equal place.[60] At the same time he strove hard to find a common factor for the promotion of the religious tolerance and pointed out:

> Religions are different roads converging upon the same point. What does it matter that we take different roads, so long as we reach the same goal?[61]
>
> I believe in the truth of all religions of the world. And since my youth upward, it has been a humble but persistent effort on any part to understand the truth of all the religions of the world; and adopt and assimilate in my own thought, word, and deed all that I have found to be best in those religions. The faith that I profess not only permits me to do so but renders it obligatory for me to take the best from whatsoever source it may come.[62]

Radhakrishnan emphasised the need to join in unity of the spirit embracing for richness in which religious realities have found expressions in other faiths which are not destroyed but cherished as valued expressions of one truth. The future of man is rewarding in the religious dimensions. He held that no one with a knowledge of the comparative history of religion could retain an exclusive belief in the tenets of his own sect. The need to enter into an inter-religious dialogue, unity should be an intense reality and religion which could be experienced is the religion of the future.[63]

For Gandhi religion is that which "binds man to God and man to man.[64] While explaining the meaning of religion, Gandhi stated that it is not Hindu religion, which he certainly praises, above all other religions but the religions which transcend Hinduism, and

---

60. *Harijan*, 4.5.1940, p. 17.
61. *Ibid.*, 16.2.1934, p. 7.
62. *Ibid.*
63. S. Radhakrishnan, *Religion in the Changing World*, pp. 133-4.
64. *Harijan*, 4.5.1940, p. 117.

change human nature and binds them indissolubly to the Truth and ever purifies.[65]

After a long study of different religions and deriving experience thereby, Gandhi arrived at the following conclusions:

1. All religions are true;
2. All religions have some error in them;
3. All religions are almost as dear to me as my own. Hinduism, inasmuch as all human beings should be as dear to one as one's own close relatives. My own veneration for other faiths is the same as that for my own faith; therefore no thought of conversion is possible. The aim of the Fellowship should be to help a Hindu to become a better Hindu, a Musalman to become a better Musalman, and a Christian a better Christian.[66]

In the modern context, religion has divided people instead of binding them together. Some religions divide humanity into hostile camps instead of uniting it by emphasising the individual significance rather than the social side of life. They give undue prominence to the personal development discouraging the growth of social sense and imagination. They give utmost importance to contemplation more than action and theory more than practice.[67] Any order built in the absence of moral values is immoral, irrational and unscrupulous.

The religious conflicts have been generated because of the misunderstanding of religious teachings.[68] Gandhi did not believe in the exclusive divinity of the Vedas. He also believed in the *Bible*, the *Koran*, and the *Zend Avesta* which, he stated, are as much divinely inspired as the Vedas. He declined to be bound by any interpretation, though it is scholarly, if it is in conflict with reason and morality. He tried to understand various scriptures of the orld

---

65. *Young India*, 12.5.1920, p. 2.
66. N.K. Bose (ed.), *Selections from Gandhi* 1957, pp. 258-9.
67. S. Radhakrishnan, *Religion and Society*, p. 50.
68. Ramjee Singh, *Gandhi and the Modern World*, p. 33.

by applying the test of *ahimsa* (non-violence) and truth laid down by the scriptures for interpretation. He rejected all which is inconsistent with the test of *ahimsa*, appropriating all that is consistent with it.[69]

The study of the *New Testament*, especially the 'Sermon on the Mount', went straight into his heart. He compared with *Gita* the verses from the 'Sermon on the Mount' of the *New Testament*: "But I say unto you, that ye resist not evil; but whosoever shall smite thee on the right check, turn to him the other also. And if any man take away thy coat let him have thy cloak too",[70] reminded him of Shamel Bhatt's popular saying: 'For a bowl of water, give a goodly need', etc. The young mind tried to unify the teaching of the *Gita*. 'The Light of Asia', and the 'Sermon on the Mount'. Renunciation, as the highest form of religion, appealed to Gandhi greately.[71] He found the concept of renunciation present in all the major religions.

> I have not been able to see any difference between the Sermon on the Mount and the Bhagavad Gita. What the Sermon describes in a graphic manner, the Bhagavad Gita reduces to a scientific formula. It may not be a scientific book in the accepted sense of the term, but it has argued out the law of love — the law of abandon as I would call it — in a scientific manner. The Sermon on the Mount gives the same law in wonderful language. The New Testament gave me comfort and boundless joy, as it came after the repulsion that parts of the old had given me. Today, supposing I was deprived of the Gita and forgot all its contents, but had a copy of the Sermon, I should derive the same joy from it as I do from the Gita.[72]

**Ends and Means**

The relevance and significance of Gandhian Philosophy lies in the

---

69. *Young India*, 27.8.1925, p. 293.
70. M.K. Gandhi, *The Story of My Experiments with Truth*, p. 49.
71. *Ibid.*
72. *Young India*, 22.12.1927, p. 426.

application of moral principles, viz., truth and non-violence to the problems confronted by the modern society. Throughout the life of Gandhi, he struggled to demonstrate only the moral means as his primary consideration. His insistence on the purity of means indicates the recognition of the moral law.

History recorded many politicians who tried to accomplish their ends by immoral and unscrupulous means. The classical, political dictum that 'end justifies means' is not compatible with the purity of means.

Machiavelli sanctioned the use of immoral means to the rulers to gain their political ends. He never doubted that moral corruption among the people would make good government impossible He offered double standard of morals — one for the ruler and another for the private citizen; as the ruler is empowered to do anything he likes because of the power he has and he is above the morality. Machiavelli was indifferent to morality, He was merely interested in a single end, i.e., the political power.[73] The classical political dilemma has always been "either to justify evil means by worthy ends or else to risk being overwhelmed by the triumph of evil over good".[74]

The term Good is used to signify something which is not a means to an end but something which is an end itself. Thus the term *summum bonum* which means the highest good is the supreme end aimed at.[75] To determine the truth or falsehood of a statement with regard to the character of a person or moral action, the terms such as vice, virtue, beauty, right, ought, good, bad, etc., are used to pass ethical judgement.[76]

If the means adopted is not moral, the end cannot be moral. Moral means should be used to make man morally better as the use of immoral means is morally not justifiable.[77] There has been an

---

73. George H. Sabain, *A History of Political Theory*, pp. 319-210.
74. Ramjee Singh, *The Relevance of Gandhian Thought*, p. 39.
75. John S. Mackenzie, *A Manual of Ethics*, pp. 1-2.
76. G.E. Moore, *Principa Ethica*, p. 1.
77. D.M. Dutta, *The Philosophy of Mahatma Gandhi*, p. 84.

inseparable nexus established between the means and ends as they should be equally pure. Some people give undue importance only to the end, but this was not acceptable to Gandhi. According to him, means must be as moral as the end. He pointed out that the end cannot justify the means.[78]

Gandhi stated that:

> For me, it is enough to know the means. Means and end are convertible terms in my philosophy of life.[79]

Gandhian dictum "means and ends are convertible terms" means the making of ends in the process. A true man who is committed to moral values will not remain fixated on either means or ends for their own sake. He will not permit himself or others to useful means with illusory justification.[80] While judging of the morality or a moral action, the motive of the doer or agent has to be taken into consideration. Whether the action is moral or immoral has to be judged on the basis of the motive that prompts it.[81]

Gandhi stated that if the means are taken care of, the goal could be reached sooner or later.[82] Means and ends are interdependent and equally necessary. When the means adopted are wrong the goal that is end even if it is pure, will not be reached. Even if it is reached, it cannot be realised as a pure end.

> Immoral means must ultimately have their effect on ends. If these desirable ends are necessary, moral means to achieve the ends are at least as necessary.[83]

Gandhi compared means with the seed and ends with the tree. The unbreakable and inseparable connection between means and ends exists as between the seed and the tree.[84] Gandhi did not accept

---

78. M.K. Gandhi, *Ethical Religion*, p. 40.
79. *Young India*, 26.12.1924, p. 424.
80. Erik H. Erikson, *Gandhi's Truth*, pp. 398-9.
81. M.K. Gandhi, *Ethical Religion*, p. 9.
82. M.K. Gandhi, *From Yeravda Mandir*, p. 9.
83. J.B. Kripalani, *The Gandhian Way*, p. 354.
84. M.K. Gandhi, *For Facifists*, p. 25.

violent means to achieve a goal. He did not like to bring about independence of India by violent means.

> If violence and untruth are necessary for the advancement of my country, let my country go under. I would not sacrifice these two for all World. . . . I do not seek to serve India at the sacrifice of Truth for I know that a man who forsakes Truth can forsake his country, and his nearest and dearest ones.[85]

For him non-violence is the means and the truth is the end.

> It is perhaps clear from the foregoing, that without ahimsa it is not possible to seek and find truth. Ahimsa and Truth are so intertwined that it is practically impossible to disentangle and separate him. They are like the two sides of a coin, or rather of a smooth unstamped metallic disc. Who can say, which is the obverse, and which the reverse? Nevertheless ahimsa is the means; Truth is the end. Means to be means must always be within our reach, and so ahimsa is our supreme duty. If we take care of the means, we are bound to reach the end sooner or later. When once we have grasped this point, final victory is beyond question whatever difficulties we encounter, whatever apparent reverses we sustain, we may not give up the quest for Truth which alone is, being God Himself.[86]

If morality is understood as an instrument of human development, the problem of means will not be understood. Even if a person is clear and definite about his goal, he cannot reach there without a proper path. So it is only in the context of means, the end is relevant.[87]

> I have, therefore, concerned myself principally with the conservation of the means and their progressive use. I know if we can take care of them, attainment of the goal is

---

85. Tendulkar, *D.G. Mahatma*, Vol. II, p. 32.
86. M.K. Gandhi, *From Yeravda Mandir*, pp. 8-9.
87. Ramjee Singh, *The Relevance of Gandhian Thought*, p. 42.

> assured. I fell too that our progress towards the goal will be in exact proportion to the purity of our means. This method may appear to be long, perhaps too long, but I am convinced that is the shortest.[88]

Scientific law states that every action will have reaction as every cause has its effect. The end is merely the result of a series of acts taken as means.[89]

According to Gandhi the means must be always within the human reach. Gopinath Dhavan interpreted purity of means by saying that man could only pursue or aim at, but he cannot determine the consequences which may be influenced by other factors. It is possible to control means but not goals.[90] Manu says that wealth and property gained through wrong means leads to its total destruction.[91] The opposite theory that end justifies the means leads to arrive at the conclusion that violent means that are dangerous and ethically unsound could be applied but this gives recourse to violence, untruth and other evils.[92] A victory won by violence and treachery will retain violence and other evils within its bosom.

So Gandhi embarked upon a revolutionary task of enunciating the principle of the integrity of means and ends which presupposes Truth and non-violence as the foundation of human life and social relationship.[93] This has bearing, on and relevance to on the human life even in this modern world.

## Religion and Truth

For Gandhi truth is the sovereign principle which is inclusive of

---

88. M.K. Gandhi, *Sarvodaya*, p. 6.
89. Ramjee Singh, *The Relevance of Gandhian Thought*, p. 43.
90. Gopinath Dhavan, *The Political Philosophy of Mahatma Gandhi*, p. 54.
91. *Manusmriti*, IV, p. 171.
92. Gopinath Dhavan, *The Political Philosophy of Mahatma Gandhi*, p. 55.
93. Ramjee Singh, *The Relevance of Gandhian Thought*, p. 45.

numerous other moral principles. Since his childhood the passion for truth was innate in him. The truth conceived by Gandhi signifies truthfulness in word, thought and deed.[94]

Gandhi pointed out that one thing was deep-rooted in him which is:

> the conviction that morality is the basis of things, and that truth is the substance of all morality. Truth became my sole objective. It began to grow in magnitude everyday, and my definition of it also has been ever widening.[95]

The discovery of truth requires self-examination and self-purification. One cannot claim to be truthful as long as he is under the influence of what Gandhi calls in the context of following the six deadly enemies namely, lust, anger, greed, infatuation, pride and falsehood of the ethics of the Indian tradition.[96]

Gandhi held that the word truth or *satya* is derived from *sat* which implies 'being'. It is only truth that exists in reality and nothing else. That is the reason why *sat* or 'Truth' is attributed to God. Gandhi pointed out that God is Truth but later on he changed this version and stated that it would be more appropriate and correct to say that Truth is God, rather than to say God is Truth.[97] In his saying, transition could be found from God is Truth, to Truth is God. He maintained that the uniform experience has convinced him to state that there is no other God than Truth.[98]

> To me God is Truth and love; God is ethics and morality. God is fearlessness. God is the source of light and life and yet above and beyond all these God is conscience. He is even the atheism of an atheist . . . . He transcends speech and reason.[99]

---

94. M.K. Gandhi, *The Story of My Experiments with Truth*, Introduction, p. xv.
95. *Ibid.*, p. 25.
96. M.K. Gandhi, *Hindu Dharma*, p. 240.
97. M.K. Gandhi, *From Yeravda Mandir*, p.1.
98. M.K. Gandhi, *The Story of My Experiments with Truth*, p. 382.
99. *Young India*, 5.3.1925, pp. 80-1.

Varrier Elwin made a correct statement about the Gandhian concept of truth. He observed that among the ultimate values of Platonism, viz., Goodness, Truth and Beauty — Truth is inclusive of other two values.[100] The attitude of Gandhi towards aesthetics has its basis in ethical and religious outlook which is truth centred.

While referring to the Art, Gandhi stated that there are two aspects of things, which are outward and inward. The outward has no meaning excepting to help the inward. "All true art is thus an expression of the soul. The outward forms have value only insofar as they are the expression of the inner spirit of man."[101]

Gandhi gave utmost importance to truth and said that "Truth is the first thing to be sought for and beauty and Goodness will then be added unto you."[102] For Gandhi the purity of life is the highest and truest art.[103]

> I see and find Beauty in truth or through Truth. All Truths, not merely true ideas, but truthful faces, truthful pictures, or songs, are highly beautiful. People generally fail to see Beauty in Truth, the ordinary man runs away from it and becomes blind to the beauty in it. Whenever men will begin to see beauty in Truth, then true Art will arise.[104]

The nature of Reality as realised by Gandhi is Truth. God could be experienced through Truth. The existence of God is felt in thought, word and deed. God exists because Truth exists. The other aspects of the God head namely beauty and goodness are not appealing to Gandhi as fundamental whereas truth for him implies beauty and goodness.[105]

Gandhi held that truth is the law of existence. There is no better duty (*dharma*) than truth. *Dharma* is that which holds together,

---

100. Surendra Varma, *The Metaphysical Foundation of Mahatma Gandhi's Thought*, p. 14.
101. *Young India*, 13.11.1924, p. 377.
102. *Ibid.*, 20.11.1924, p. 386.
103. *Harijan*, 19.2.1938, p. 10.
104. *Young India*, 13.11.1924, p. 377.
105. Benoy Gopal Ray, *Gandhian Ethics*, p. 5.

supports and upholds. *Dharma* is stated to be the foundations of the whole universe and upon it everything is founded. So *dharma* is called the highest good.[106] *Dharma* cannot be based on untruth and the law governing the human existence cannot be anything except Truth. In consonance with this Gandhi say that "nothing exists in reality except Truth".[107]

Truth is the knowledge acquired by identity or it is an integral experience of Reality. Ultimate Reality is intuitively known. When truth is experienced, all doubts and differences are removed all discords and discrepancies are vanished and the human life is transformed by the realisation of truth to experience bliss. According to Gandhi, there is no true knowledge in the absence of truth.

> Devotion to this Truth is the sole justification of our own existence. All our activities should be centred in Truth. Truth should be the breath of our life. . . . Without Truth it is impossible to observe any principles or rules in life.[108]

Philosophy does not mean the mere knowledge or wisdom about reality but it also implies the application of such knowledge in all spheres of the human endeavour. Theoretical knowledge which is not practicable is barren.

Gandhi was pre-eminently a practical man who judged theories and ideologies by the results they yielded in practice. This method indeed helps to resolve the differences.[109]

Radhakrishnan maintained that the real quality of religion is brought out by man's incessant search and unending quest to know the truth of things. There is need to keep up the pursuit of the truth until man is able to experience it.[110] Truth is indivisible reality and it is the end of all kinds of discipline. Truth in its totality must be regarded as one whole. The pursuit of the truth makes man

---

106. Bary and Hay, *Sources of Indian Tradition*, pp. 221-2.
107. M.K. Gandhi, *From Yeravda Mandir*, p. 1.
108. *Ibid.*, p. 2.
109. Gora, *An Atheist with Gandhi*, p. 35.
110. S. Radhakrishnan, *Search for Truth*, p. 9.

dignified and a really civilised human being.[111]

Gandhi held that truth resides in every human heart and everyone has to be guided by truth. But no one has right to coerce others to act in accordance with his own view of truth.[112] "The quest for truth is the summum bonum of life", says Dr. Radhakrishnan.[113]

Gandhi attempted to understand various religions of the world by applying the test of truth and non-violence. He rejected what is inconsistent with that test and appropriated all that is consistent with truth.[114] The test of truth is practical but it does not remain mere theoretical.[115]

> A devotee of Truth may not be anything in defence to convention. He must always hold himself open to correction and wherever he discovers himself to be wrong, he must confess it at all cost and atone for it.[116]

Tolstoy held that the miseries experienced by men in this world are due to the discord created for not following truth and adhering to falsehood at the same time. All the people could be united by the truth. If men seek the truth more sincerely nearer do they approach to union. As long as people pretend to be truthful and conceal the truth from themselves, no moral improvement can be possible.[117]

> That improvement can only take place when they recognize that their welfare lies solely in the union of all men in the truth, and are therefore ready to put above everything else the recognition and profession of that truth which has revealed itself to them.[118]

---

111. *Search for Truth*, p. 83.
112. *Harijan*, 24.11.1933, p. 6.
113. S. Radhakrishnan, *Religion in a Changing World*, p. 67.
114. *Young India*, 27.8.1925, p. 293.
115. S. Radhakrishnan, *Religion in a Changing World*, p. 27.
116. M.K. Gandhi, *The Story of My Experiments with Truth*, p. 58.
117. Leo Tolstoy, *The Kingdom of God is Within You*, p. 410.
118. *Ibid.*

There is need for every man to profess truth he is aware of and practice in his own life avoiding falsehood. The recognition of truth is the cause of all the manifestations of human life which does not depend upon the external phenomena but on inner qualities.[119] Those who knows the truth and acts with hypocrisy concealing evil injure not only themselves but also their victims. Tolstoy says,

> Hypocrisy in our time is supported by two things — Pseudo-religion and pseudo-science and has reached such colossal dimensions that were we not living in the midst of it, it would be impossible to believe that men could reach such a degree of self-deception. They have now reached such a strange condition and their hearts are so hardened that though they have eyes they see not and having ears they hear not, neither do they understand.[120]

Tolstoy further says:

> The recognition of truth which is the cause of all the manifestations of human life, does not depend on external phenomena but on certain inner qualities of a man not subject to his observation.[121]

Man has yet to perceive always truths not so far perceived and some truths are freshly illumined by the light of his reason demanding recognition.[122]

As man passes through life, he gains knowledge of a greater and greater degree of truth and frees himself more and more from error.[123] Truth brings out the path of human life and reveals the way that man must inevitably follow.[124] Gandhi in his search of truth found non-violence as the means to reach the truth which is the end. He felt that while the non-violence is the law of being, violence is the

---

119. *The Kingdom of God is Within You*, p. 411.
120. *Ibid.*, pp. 418-19.
121. *Ibid.*, p. 423.
122. *Ibid.*, p. 425.
123. *Ibid.*
124. *Ibid.*, p. 426.

law of destruction and brute. A brute tends to be violent because of the lack of understanding and realisation of truth.

## Religion and Politics

Religion and Politics are held to be two separate realms between which a gulf is fixed, each having its own standard of thought, feeling and conduct. But people need to have faith in the inner order so that they can build a stable order outside.[125]

Politicians generally do not take religion seriously in regard to the methods they adopt for the control of people by another, the economic exploitation of the poor and weaker sections of the community. They are clearly inconsistent with the values of religion which do not find correct expression. But for Gandhi human life is an integral whole.[126] If a man as a politician is not successful, it is because of the fact that he has kept religion and politics apart, without a proper understanding of the both. But Gandhi did not view religion apart from the rest of the human activity.[127]

> In the acid test of experience he (Gandhi) remains, not a Politician or a reformer, not a philosopher or a moralist, but someone composed of them all, an essentially religious person endowed with the highest and most human qualities and made more lovable by the consciousness of his own limitations and by an unfailing sense of humour.[128]

Gandhi made it a mission in his life to revolutionise politics.

Gopalakrishna Gokhale, an economist, Parliamentarian and Statesman influenced Gandhi profoundly who taught Gandhi to spiritualise politics. Gokhale gave the *mantra* that politics must be spiritualised in India, and he brought politics and religion together.

---

125. S. Radhakrishnan, *Religion and Society*, p. 50.
126. S. Radhakrishnan (ed.), *Mahatma Gandhi — Essays and Reflections on His Life and Work*, p. 1.
127. *Ibid.*, p. 3.
128. *Ibid.*, p. 2.

Gandhi says,

> Gokhale taught me that the dream of every Indian who claims to love his country should be not to glorify in language but to spiritualise the political life of the country and the political institutions of the country. He inspired my life and is still inspiring and in that I wish to purify myself and spiritualise myself. I have dedicated myself to that ideal.[129]

According to Radhakrishnan, truly religious man lives in between the frontiers of sacred and secular, between religion and politics, between being and non-being. People are not called upon to leave history, and get into the desert leading the lives of renunciation and recognition. Men of saintliness participate in the work of the world and work harder for the further progress. There is the road to fulfilment. Quality of the human life depends upon the religious values followed.[130]

Gandhi wrote:

> If I seem to take part in Politics, it is only because politics today encircles us like the coils of a snake from which one cannot get out, no matter how one tries. I wish to wrestle with the snake . . . I am trying to introduce religion into politics.[131]

Gandhi was compelled to enter into political field as he felt that he could not do the minimum social service without entering into politics. According to him, the political work must be looked upon in terms of the progress made in social and moral fields.[132]

Gandhi declared:

> For me politics bereft of religion is absolute dirt ever to be shunned. Politics concern nations and that which concerns

---

129. M.K. Gandhi, *In Search of the Supreme*, Vol. II, p. 3.
130. S. Radhakrishnan, *Religion in a Changing World*, p. 110.
131. *Young India*, 12.5.1920, p. 2.
132. *Harijan*, 6.10.1946, p. 341.

> the welfare of nations must be one of the concerns of a man who is religiously inclined.... Therefore, in politics also we have to establish the Kingdom of Heaven.[133]

Many considered Gandhi as a professional politician who bungles at critical moments. For some people politics is a profession. The politician is one who is trained to transact public business in an efficient manner and in another sense politics is a vocation in which the politician is one who is conscious of a mission to save the people and inspired them with faith in God and love for humanity. Gandhi is essentially a politician in arousing love of humanity. He has found faith on humanity, and he said that we could build a world of tomorrow without poverty and unemployment and without wars and bloodshed.[134]

Gandhi held that religion should pervade every texture of the human life. For him human life is an undivided whole and life can be never drawn between different compartments, social, political and religious, nor between ethics and politics. All act and react upon one another.[135]

According to Gandhi, religion does not mean exclusion of politics from its domain. In his view politics apart from the religion is dirt. Gandhi categorically wanted to bring religion into politics.

> For me the road to salvation lies through incessant toil in the service of my country and of humanity. I want to identify myself with everything that lives. In the language of the Gita, I want to live at peace with both friend and foe. So my patriotism is for me a stage on my journey to the land of eternal freedom and peace. Thus, it will be seen that for me, there are no politics devoid of religion. They subserve religion. Politics bereft of religion are a death trap because they kill the soul.[136]

---

133. *Young India*, 18.6.1925, p. 214.
134. S. Radhakrishnan, *The Mind of Mahatma Gandhi, Foreword*, p. x.
135. *Harijan*, 30.3.1947, p. 85.
136. M.K. Gandhi, *My Mission*, *Young India*, 3.4.1924, p. 112.

The central principles of Gandhian political philosophy is that the fundamental religious and ethical values, common to all great religions, have to be incorporated in the political philosophy. The religious basis of Gandhian politics means the supremacy of the concept of the moral right of conscience in the place of divine right of rulers.[137] Basically Gandhi felt that the religious ethics of piety, forgiveness, meekness, humility and universal tolerance should guide the human action.[138]

In his first letter addressed to Tolstoy, Gandhi stated that:

> . . . a law which I and many other considered to be degrading and calculated to unman those to whom it was applicable. I felt that submission to law of this nature was inconsistent with the spirit of true religion.[139]

Further, Gandhi said:

> Politics divorced from religion, has absolutely no meaning. . . . Politics are a part of our being. We ought to understand our national institutions. We may do this from our infancy. . . . But we want also the steady light, the infallible light of religious faith.[140]

V.P. Verma wrote that Gandhi never sanctioned any political exploitation of religion as he was not concerned with growth of organised churches or narrow-minded sects. His support to the Khilafat movement during 1920-22 was only out of the humanitarian consideration, but it was not out of political bargaining.[141] Gandhi said that social and political plans for the modern India should be laid on the solid basis of true religious and moral consciousness as

---

137. V.P. Verma, *The Political Philosophy of Mahatma Gandhi and Sarvodaya*, pp. 71-2.
138. *Ibid.*, p. 73.
139. *Letter of Gandhi addressed to Tolstoy* on 1-10-1909.
140. *M.K. Gandhi's speech at Madras (1916) Speeches and Writings* (3rd edn.), p. 162.
141. V.P. Verma, *The Political Philosophy of Mahatma Gandhi and Sarvodaya*, p. 74.

Religion binds man to God and man to man.[142] On the other hand, Gandhi declared religions are not for separating men from one another, but they are meant to bind them.[143]

The religion-based politics of Gandhi has laid utmost stress on the moral values to set his politics on right action with an object to keep politics apart from the evils such as corruption, injustice, expediency and Machiavellian policies which separate the political expediency from morality. For Machiavelli, end justifies the means and he sanctioned the use of immoral means by the rulers to achieve their ends which indicates the double standard of morals — one for the ruler and another for the citizens.[144] But Gandhi on the contrary held that the means must be as important and as moral as the end. He pointed out that end cannot justify the means.[145]

Gandhian political thought makes submission to the supreme moral law and takes precedence over other systems. He treated all religions equal without giving any preference to any particular religion over the other.[146] His tendency helps to avoid the possible religious fundamentalism and upholds religious tolerance and promotes inter-religious understanding. In the modern times we need a religion which contributes to the national integration for the progress and mutual cooperation and peace-keeping politics aimed at the service of the mankind but not the religion which separates people or a religion which supports fundamentalism resulting in bloodshed.[147] Radhakrishnan says,

> Religion is the discipline which touches the conscience and helps us to struggle which evil and sordidness, saves us from greed, lust and hatred, releases moral power, and

---

142. *Harijan*, 4.5.1940, p. 117.
143. *Ibid.*, 8.6.1940, p. 157.
144. George H. Sabin, *A History of Political Thought*, p. 319.
145. M.K. Gandhi, *Ethical Religion*, p. 42.
146. V.P. Verma, *The Political Philosophy of Mahatma Gandhi and Sarvodaya*, p. 77.
147. Ramjee Singh (ed.), *Aspects of Gandhian Thought*, p. 91.

imparts courage in the enterprise of saving the world. As a discipline of the mind, it contains the key and the essential means of coping with evil which threatens the existence of the civilised world. It implies the submitting of our thinking and conduct to the truths of spirit.[148]

---

148. S. Radhakrishnan, *Religion and Society*, p. 42.

# 3

# Social Problems — Gandhian Solutions

THE human society witnessed several changes in the passage of time through evolution and revolution. History made evidential record of all these changes towards progress. Social philosophy is broader in scope. Every society cherishes certain goals, values, ideals and norms. The relevance of the Gandhian social philosophy lies in his conceptualising the social issues and making them relevant and dynamically operative to the modern world.

No social idea is final. Every idea is subject to the acid test of human experience, and underwent changes from time to time. Gandhi made a thorough study of these social issues and tested them on rational and moral grounds to make them relevant and significant to the present and the future generations to come.

## Origin of the Caste

The caste structure is stated to be an institution, developed and grown over centuries.

> Caste as it now is an institution which has grown and developed through many centuries, but since it is so firmly rooted in India, and since it is found nowhere else, it would appear almost certain, on the face of it, that its first beginnings are to be sought in India and not outside.[1]

S. Radhakrishnan held that the caste divisions are based on

1. J.H. Hulton, *Caste in India*, p. 182.

individual temperment which is not unchangeable. In his view there was only one caste during the earlier times. All were either brahmanas or all were shudras. In a Smriti text it was written that through purification one becomes a brahmana though born as shudra. People were divided into different castes depending on their needs and actions.[2]

In the words of Risley, caste is:

> a collection of families or groups of families bearing a common name which usually denotes or is associated with specific occupations, claiming common descent from a mythical ancestor, human or divine, professing to follow the same professional callings and are regarded by those who are competent to give an opinion as forming a single homogeneous community.[3]

Several theories were formulated about the origin of caste. While some theories are occupational or racial, others are attributed to colour and to the doctrine of *karma*. "The question of caste is held to be not of blood but of function" says Nesfiled, "for the Indian race is practically same in blood, character and traditon."[4]

In the *Bhagavad Gita*, chapter IV, verse 13, Lord Krishna stated:

> The order of the four Varnas was created by Me according to the different gunas and karma of each; yet know that though, therefore, author, thereof, being changeless I am not the author.[5]

The word *varna* should not be mistaken for the English word colour but it might be nearer to the meaning conveyed by the term 'true

---

2. S. Radhakrishnan, *Religion and Society*, p. 129.
3. H.H. Risley, *The People of India*, p. 67.
4. J.C. Nesfield, *The Caste System in N.W. Provinces and Oudh*, p. 90.
5. M.K. Gandhi, *The Bhagavad Gita*, p. 123 (As Interpreted by him) These *gunas* or qualities are described under three categories, *sattvika*, *rajasika* and *tamasika*.

colour'. *Varna* does not relate to the physical colour or physical appearance but to the mental qualities. The qualities or *gunas* find symbolic expression in terms of colour or *varna* which is compatible with explanation given in the *Bhagavad Gita*.[6] All the members of the four castes should be treated equally without any distinction or difference.[7] Gandhi has no hesitation in rejecting scriptural authority of a doubtful character if it supported a sinful institution. *Varnashrama* was not a system of watertight compartments.[8]

K.M. Panikkar maintained that the four-fold castes are merely a theoretical division of society to which the tribes and the family groups are affiliated. As per the census there are more than 3,000 castes, with innumerable subdivisions among them. Thereby the four-fold division stands only as a mere fiction. Among the innumerable sub-castes existing in the Indian society each caste claims to have belonged to one of the four. All the castes are theoretically within the frame of the main four-fold castes.[9] The essential principles underlying the caste are as follows:

1. Unchangeable inequality based on birth
2. the gradation of professions and their inequality, and
3. restrictions on marriage outside one's own group:.[10]

Jawaharlal Nehru stated that each person was divided and fixed up with a bundle of duties and responsibilities within his narrow sphere in the graded hierarchy without the conception of society as a whole and no attempt was made to make him feel his solidarity with the society. This idea is held to be perhaps largely a modern development which could not be found in any ancient society. The emphasis on individualism and exclusiveness on graded castes is much evident in India. Caste became poisonous in the subsequent ages and it is not alone the lower castes who suffered most from it, but the higher castes also. Caste has become a weakening factor and

---

6. T.K.N. Unnithan, *Gandhi and Free India*, p. 158.
7. S.R. Bakshi, *Gandhi and Status of Harijans*, p. 38.
8. Joan V. Bondurant, *Conquest of Violence*, pp. 169-70.
9. K.M. Panikkar, *Hinduism and the Modern World*, pp. 21-2.
10. *Ibid.*

the rigidity in the caste structure could also be found paving the way for the rigidity of mind and suppressing the creative energy of the race. Thus, caste has permeated every quarter of the Indian society and began to have control over the individual and social behaviour affecting the institution of marriage and family ties.[11]

## Caste and Untouchability

In India caste exists with the evil manifestation of untouchability which Gandhi fought tooth and nail. This element is present in some form or the other in the world. In the West there is colour prejudice and racial apartheid between the black and the white and there has been class struggle, i.e., between the working class and capitalists, haves and have-nots in the world.

Equal love of all the people brought the problem of untouchability early in his life. When his mother said that he cannot touch the boy doing scavenging, he questioned back and from that day revolt began in his life.[12] He himself was subject to humiliation and racial discrimination and became a victim of colour prejudices.[13, 14]

---

11. Jawaharlal Nehru, *The Discovery of India*, pp. 95-6.
12. *Harijan*, 24.12.1938, p. 393.
13. A first class seat was booked for Gandhi at Durban, when he was travelling in a first class compartment. An official said to him that he should go to the van compartment for the reason that he happened to be a coloured man. When Gandhi refused to leave the first class compartment voluntarily for he was entitled to travel by first class compartment, he was pushed out. This was the humiliation he was meted out with, while travelling from Durban.

    M.K. Gandhi, *The Story of My Experiments with Truth*, pp. 80-1.
14. Gandhi who was illegally pushed out of the first class compartment at Pietermaritzburg was remembered after more than 100 years. He was posthumously honoured by the South African President, Mr. Nelson Mandela who said that the country has atoned for its shame. The grandson of Gandhi, Mr. Gopala Krishna Gandhi, the Indian High Commissioner to South Africa received, 'freedom of pietermaritzburg' award on behalf of Gandhi from Mr. Mandela at a function held in the historic city on 25th April 1997.

cont. →

Gandhi considered the individual as the unit and the reformation of the society has to start from the individual. For him 'individual is the supreme consideration'. He stood against the irrational traditional customs which have no moral basis. He found untouchability as cancer eating away of the vitals of Hinduism.[15] He said that 'if untouchability lives, Hinduism must die'.[16]

Gandhi wrote:

> This monster of untouchability has invaded every form of society in India; and the idea behind this message is that there should be not only no untouchability between Hindus and Hindus, but that there should be no untouchability whatsoever between Hindus, Christians, Mussulmans, Parsis and the rest. I am convinced that if this great change of heart can be brought about among millions of Savarna Hindus and if their hearts can be purified — as certainly they will be purified — we should live in India as one people trusting each other and without any mutual distrust or suspicion. It is untouchability with all its sub-forms that separates us from one another and makes life itself unlovely and difficult to live.[17]

He held that it would be wrong to destroy caste because of the outcast. So outcasteness altogether has to be destroyed. He felt it to be an excrescence to be removed if the whole system is not to perish. Untouchability has entered into the caste system as an unwanted evil.

Untouchability is the product therefore, not of the caste

---

→ Mr. Mandela while addressing a big gathering at the function stated:

"Today we are righting a Century old wrong. This station once one of the world's most notorious symbols of discrimination, intolerance and oppression, today proclaims a message of dignity, restored."

*The Hindu*, Daily, 27.4.1997, p.7.

15. Pyarelal, *The Epic Fast*, p. 311.
16. *Harijan*, 28.9.1947, p. 349.
17. *Ibid.*, 26.1.1934, p. 4.

> system, but of the distinction of high and low that has crept into — Hinduism and is eroding it. The attack on untouchability is thus an attack upon this 'high and lowness'. The moment untouchability goes, the caste system itself will be purified, that is to say according to my dream, it will resolve itself into the true Varnadharma, the four divisions of society, each complementary of the other and none inferior or superior to any other, each as necessary for the whole body of Hinduism as any other.[18]

According to Gandhi, *varna* is intimately, if not indissolubly, connected with birth. The observance of the law of the *varna* means to follow the part in accordance with the hereditary and traditional calling of the forefathers. The performance of the hereditary functions have to be done as a matter of duty, carrying with the earning of his livelihood. Gandhi accepted the idea of *varna* for realising an ideal of egalitarian society which promotes mutual love and cooperation but he refused to accept any sense of distance or subordination or humiliation among the *varnas*.

Gandhi envisaged a casteless, classless and egalitarian society as against the caste-ridden society. He attempted to give a rational interpretation of the functions of caste division of the ancient times. Unfortunately the Indian society has degenerated into caste-ridden social disorder.

Gandhi pointed out:

> Thus the function of a Brahmana is to study and to teach the science of Brahman (or spiritual truth). He performs the function as he cannot do otherwise, as it is the law of his being, that secures him his livelihood, but he will take it as a gift from God. A Kshatriya will perform the function of protecting the people in the same spirit, accepting for his livelihood whatever the people can afford to give him. A Vaishya will pursue wealth-producing occupations for the welfare of the community, keeping for himself enough for his own maintenance and rendering the balance to the community in one shape or other. A Shudra will perform

18. *Harijan*, 11.2.1933, p. 3.

> physical labour in the same spirit of service. Varna is determined by birth, but can be retained only by observing its obligations. One born of Brahmana parents will be called a Brahmana, but if his life fails to reveal the attributes of a Brahmana when he comes of age, he can not be called a Brahmana. He will have fallen from Brahmanhood. On the other hand, one who is born not a Brahmana but reveals in his conduct the attributes of a Brahmana will be regarded as a Brahmana, though he will himself disclaim the label.[19]

Although Gandhi was a reformer undoubtedly, he did not like to give a rough handling to the social patterns and institutions and social experimentation.[20] Gandhi gave an impression that he was in defence of caste system in 1920 for he was found to be a conservative as he upheld other matters for radical changes except the phenomenon of the caste because of his profound influence of Hindu philosophy. He supported the principle so long as it was in conformity with *varnashrama-dharma* but opposed when it degenerated with its evil manifestation of untouchability. He did not subscribe to the fanatical view that a Brahmana born of a Brahmana remains ever a Brahmana by virtue of his birth, but it is only when he reveals the characteristics and noble qualities of Brahmana could be called a Brahmana.

Though he himself called *sanatana* Hindu, yet he asserted: "Caste has nothing to do with religion. It is harmful both to spiritual and national growth."[21] Subsequently in 1946 he stated that "caste is an anachronism".[22] These statements are evident to establish the fact that there is evolution in his thought process in comparison to his earlier sayings on caste.

---

19. *Harijan*, 28.9.34, pp. 260-1.
20. V.P. Verma, *The Political Philosophy of Mahatma Gandhi and Sarvodaya*, p. 109.
21. *Harijan*, 6.3.1937, p. 27.
22. *Hindustan Times*, 15.4.1985.

### His Views on inter-dining and inter-caste marriages

As far as his views on inter-dining and inter-caste marriages are concerned, they have progressively undergone transformation. It was during 1921 that he stated that inter-dining and inter-caste marriage would deprive the man of his status that his birth has given. According to him, *varnashrama-dharma* has not been effected by inter-dining and inter-caste marriage.

A Brahmana remains as a Brahmana eventhough he dines with his shudra brother when he does not leave his duty of sharing his knowledge with others. The restrictions relating to the matter based upon the marriage and dining do not depend upon the notion of superiority or inferiority. When a Hindu refuses to dine with another outcaste person with the sense of superiority, he misrepresents his *dharma*.[23] Subsequently, he said that he was personally of the opinion that restrictions on inter-caste dining and inter-caste marriage do not constitute a part of Hinduism. He pointed out that he would welcome the parties or functions attended by the touchables and untouchables which he considered as a healthy sign.[24]

In 1933 Gandhi wrote:

> Inter-dining and inter-caste marriage is in no way essential for the promotion of the spirit of brotherhood or for the removal of untouchability.[25]

In the year 1935 he stated that there should be no prohibition on inter-caste marriage or inter-dining in *varnashrama-dharma*. He wanted a change in the outlook of the people.[26] He felt that caste system generates the feeling of superiority or inferiority in the

---

23. *Young India*, 6.10.1921, p. 371.
24. Pyarelal, *Epic Fast*, pp. 314-15.
25. *Harijan*, 29.4.1932, p. 2.
26. *Ibid.*, 16.11.1935, p. 316.

    The Elaya Perumal Committee observed that "Untouchability is not a separate institution by itself, it is a corollary of the institution of the caste system of Hindu Society."

minds of those people belonging to the caste ridden society.[27]

The Indian constitution guarantees equal treatment for all the people irrespective of caste, creed or religion.

> Untouchability is abolished by the Constitution of India and enforcement of any restriction, disabilities or limitations on the ground of 'untouchability' is an offence punishable by law whereas caste system remained untouched.[28]

So the most important function of Hindu thought is to re-examine the customs and traditions and to modify each one of the taboos it insisted upon in the name of religion from the standpoint of social usefulness.[29]

Gandhi wrote:

> Classless society is the ideal, not merely to be aimed at but to be worked for and in such society, there is no room for classes or communities.[30]

Gandhi used to encourage and bless the inter-caste marriages. He said that the boys or girls who want to marry, cannot be married at Sevagram Ashram where he stays, unless one of the parties is a Harijan. He did not find any problem in this and what all is needed is change of outlook.[31]

The attitude of social affection helps to reform the society and to establish a classless and casteless society bridging the gulf between the haves and have-nots to promote integrity, equality, brotherhood, communal unity and harmony which are relevant to the modern times.

The relevance of the inter-caste marriages have been recognised in the modern society. Inter-dining has become very common these

---

27. R.K. Kshira Sagar, *Untouchability in India — Implementation of the Law. Report of the Committee on Untouchability*, p. 1 (1969).
28. *Ibid.*, p. 26.
29. K.M. Panikkar, *Hinduism and the Modern World*, p. 91.
30. *Harijan*, 17.2.1946, p. 9.
31. N.K. Bose (ed.), *Selections From Gandhi*, p. 268.

days. It is the policy of the government to give incentives to the inter-caste married couples and extend all possible support to them and provide them with better job opportunities and give preferential treatment in all respects to encourage the marriages of this nature and establish social equalitarianism and also to shed the differences and discriminations arising out of the caste-ridden society.

However there is a lot of change in the social customs and traditions. Some people are coming out of the caste-ridden society and marching ahead with progressive views. The nation is progressively marching from the barriers of caste-ridden society to realise casteless and classless society and social equality.

## Status of Women and their Problems in the Society

Gandhi thoroughly studied the position of women in the past, the struggles that they had undergone for their individuality, their place and their roles in the social structure. He evolved new methods for their social upliftment basing on the values of morality, equality and social justice.

Gandhi defined the ignoble role of women in the traditional past. He integrated the old with the modern to bring out something new to uphold the women and their position in the society. Women remained within the frame of the social structure without any voice, and were confined to the network of the social relations to be called as daughters, wives and mothers for the past several centuries without any role to play. Today woman is no less important than man, and has acquired a new dimension and she has to play a vital role in the modern society in all the spheres.

The age-old social customs and traditions adopted in the Indian society had greatly brought down the status of women. Certain social taboos laid down in the past impeded the woman's progress, and restricted her moments to function independently

> women's movements the world-over, have gathered momentum to move national Governments to alter their legislation, increase resource allocations to enhance the status of women and mainstream them in the course of development. The women's movement in India has played a vital role in this direction. The Constitution of India

founded on a base of equality has moved to an affirmative position of empowering women to give them a share in the decision-making processes. The Government of India have further extended this process to programme implementation through the Indira Mahila Yojana.[32]

## Exploitation of Women

Women constitute almost half of the population. They are conditioned themselves to think unsuitable for the positions of skill and authority. Jobs have been classified under men or women categories rather than that of the individual best suited for the purpose regardless of sex.[33]

In the male dominated society, women are the losers in the division of labour. Women are mostly appointed in unskilled menial or poorly paid occupations when compared with men. Generally women are denied the opportunity to use their individual talents to their best advantage in their work.

> The benefits of those abilities are therefore lost not only to the women concerned but to their employment's and hence to the economic well-being of the country in which they live and work.[34]

It has been felt that women throughout the centuries have been less paid than men particularly in the modern industrial sector. The following quotation is an ample proof for this:

> The statute of 12, Richard II, 1388, states that because the wages of said labourers have not been put in certainty before these times, it is agreed that and assented that the belief of husbandry takes 13s.4d. a year, and his clothing once a year at most, the master hind 10s; the cater 10s; the shepherd 10s; the oxherd 6s.8d; the cowherd 6s.8d.; the

---

32. *Foreword, Fourth World Conference on Women held in Beijing*, China, 1995, Government of India, Human Resource Development.
33. Ross Davies, *Women and Work*, p. 13.
34. *Ibid.*, p. 14.

> swineherd 6s.; the woman labourer 6s.; the dairy maid 6s.; the ploughman 7s. at most, and every other labourer and servant according to his degree.[35]

In the employment sphere, women have been discriminated in regard to payment of wages in the rural sector and their promotional job opportunities have been blocked in the urban sector.

Throughout the history discriminatory treatment was accorded to women which aroused great concern among the socially conscious sections of the society. Woman has been labelled as weaker sex and subordinated to man throughout the history, Shakespeare said "Frail'ty thy name is women".[36] Alexander Pope held that every woman is at best a contradiction.[37] In the words of St. Augustine woman is a creature, neither decisive nor constant.[38] Alfred Tennyson commented,

> Women for the earth, man to command and woman to obey. God made the woman for man.[39]

Aristotle said,

> The female is a female by virtue of a certain lack of qualities, she is naturally defective.[40]

Woman was meted out with ill-treatment by Manu, the earliest exponent of the Indian laws. He equalled woman with that of a slave. The epitome of his laws is the submission of woman to man which is still the sanctioned code of conduct ascribed to woman and it is by and large acceptable to woman.[41] According to Manu, woman is always dependent on somebody — "on the father, the husband or

---

35. *Report of the War Cabinet Committee on Women in Industry*, HMSO, 1919.
36. William Shakespeare, *Hamlet*, 1.2.146.
37. Alexander Pope, *Moral Essays Epistle*, 2, 215.
38. St. Augustine, *Confessions*.
39. Alfred Tennyson, *The Princess*, 2nd Song, 5, 427.
40. *Simone de Beauvoir*, Introduction, xvi.
41. Prithvi Nath Tikoo, *Indian Women*, p. 13.

the son".[42] He deprived women of their education and this trend continued over several centuries despite the renaissance that exerted profound influence in the socio-economic, political and religious scenario.

## Women and Observance of Purdah

Seclusion of women and *purdah* observed since the recent centuries is stated to be the cause for the fall of the progress of the nation. Nehru pointed out,

> I am even more convinced that the complete ending of this barbarous custom is essential before India can have a progressive social life.[43]

Nehru further says:

> That it injures women is obvious enough, but the injury to man, to the growing child who has to spend much of its time among women in *purdah*, and to social life generally is equally great.

To keep the women in seclusion which is otherwise called as *purdah* stands as a barrier to their progress in all the fields. The observance of this custom entails not keeping the women away from the social or political life only but also to deny her opportunities to mix up with the rest of the society. This system deprived her of educational opportunities and her involvement in other social activities and thereby preventing the development of her personality in the society.

Gandhi stood against the evil practice of *purdah*. He called it a vicious and barbarous custom which kept the Indian women backward and he wanted to tear it down with one mighty effort. The evil effect of *purdah* was clearly demonstrated during the first general elections since Independence which were based on universal

---

42. Jawaharlal Nehru, *The Discovery of India,* p. 118.

    Woman depends upon her father till she is married and she depends upon her husband till his death and she depends upon her son in her old age.

43. *Ibid.*, p. 243.

adult suffrage. The existence of *purdah* was stated to be a handicap to exercise their franchise which is their political right in full measure.[44] The situation is improving with the awareness of women through education and gradual realisation of their position in society.[45]

Gandhi held that the institution of *purdah* being adopted in India is of recent origin. He referred to the age-old Hindu epic *Ramayana* where the proud Draupadi and spotless Sita lives without the observance of *purdah* system.

Gandhi pointed out:

> Gargi could not have held her discourses from behind the Purdah. Nor is the Purdah universal in India. It is unknown in the Daccan, Gujarat and the Punjab. It is unknown among the peasantry, and one does not hear of any untoward consequences of the comparative freedom which women in these provinces and among the peasantry enjoy. Nor will it be just to say that the women or men in the other pārts of the world are less moral because of the absence of Purdah system.[46]

Gandhi asserted that people must test on the anvil of reason everything that is capable of being tested by it and reject that which does not comply with reason even if it appears to be ancient. He stated that the humanity would remain diminished as long as women are caged and confined to their houses.

> The Purdah system, the economic dependence, non-existence of widow-remarriage, the custom of polygamy and numerous other customs hampered the woman to develop her personality and raise her status in society. She had to perform domestic functions under social constraints which had made her life cramped, narrow and fruitless so far as the modern world and its new developments were concerned.[47]

---

44. A. Appadorai (ed.), *Status of Women in South Asia*, p. 92.
45. T.K.N. Unnithan, *Gandhi and Free India*, p 141.
46. M.K. Gandhi, *Women and Social Justice*, p. 96.
47. S.R. Bakshi, *Gandhi and Status of Women*, Preface.

Gandhi raised his voice against the *Purdah* system among the women. By doing so his idea was to make the women realise that they were not meant simply for the household work but also to stand for the better, higher causes of society. He was critical of the *purdah* system for this custom retarded the development of the personality of the women.

Gandhi pointed out:

> Chastity is not a hot-house growth. It cannot be protected by the surrounding wall of the purdah. It must grow from within and to be worth anything, it must be capable of withstanding even unsought temptation.[48]

### The Awakening of Women

*Satyagraha* has brought about the political awakening and quickened the pace of national life in other spheres also. Thus, women were largely emancipated from their bonds and could bear their due share in the national life.[49] Woman is considered to be the embodiment of sacrifice and suffering. Her entry into the public life should result in purifying it and in restraining the unbridled ambition of men.[50]

The practice of non-violence involves the avoidance of the suppression of women. Woman has as much right as man in the matter of shaping her own destiny in a plan of life based on non-violence.[51] Gandhi was more concerned for the welfare of women. He stated that the largest part of the human effort for promoting the regeneration of women should be directed towards removing the blemishes represented in the *shastras* as necessary requisite ingrained in the characteristics of women.[52] He held that it is the privilege of the awakened women to spot out the age-long evils and

---

48. *Young India*, 3.2.1927, p. 37.
49. Gopinath Dhaven, *The Political Philosophy of Mahatma Gandhi*, p. 273.
50. S.R. Bakshi, *Gandhi and Status of Women*, p. 124.
51. M.K. Gandhi, *Constructive Programme,* p. 14.
52. M.K. Gandhi, *Women and Social Injustice*, p. 4.

eradicate them.[53] When the rebellion of women against the man's injustice is non-violent it would be nevertheless more effective. Gandhi says,

> To call women the weaker sex is a libel, it is man's injustice to women. If by strength is meant, brute strength, then indeed; is woman less brute than man. If by strength is meant moral power; then woman is immeasurably man's superior, Has she not greater intuition, is she not more self sacrificing, has she not greater powers of endurance, has she not greater courage? Without her, man could not be. If non-violence is the law of our being, the future is with women. . . . Who can make a more effective appeal to the heart than woman?[54]

## Women and Education

Due to the injuctions laid down by Manu, the study of Vedas was restricted for women. Ever since, the Indian women have systematically been deprived of education. This had narrowed down their outlook and completely suppressed their interest for their quest for knowledge.

It was in the year 1936 Gandhi raised a question about the boys and girls who completed their courses in the colleges but they were unable or unwilling to resist the evil manifested in custom of compulsory marriage with dowry which affects their future. He questioned the value of education that was imparted to them. He maintained that there was something basically lacking in the system of education, that made the educated to be insensitive to evil customs.

Gandhi stood for proper education for women and believed that in proportion to the education they receive, they would become sensitive to the glaring inequalities which they are subject to.[55] The absence of education for women is felt to be responsible for their low

---

53. *Young India*, 17.10.1929, p. 34.
54. *Ibid.*, 10.4.1930, p. 121.
55. Hemalata Swarup, *Women Politics and Religion*, p. 227.

status in the society.[56] Gandhi pointed out that there was no justification for men to deprive or deny women of their equal rights on the ground of their illiteracy.

Gandhi states:

> Education is essential for enabling women to assert these natural rights to exercise them wisely, and to work for their expansion again true knowledge is unattainable by the millions who lack such education.[57]

The principle of gender equality has been advocated since long time. The nineteenth and twentieth centuries witnessed a succession of wome's movements all over the world against the burning social issues pertaining to women's education and widow remarriages. The Indian National Congress in 1931 upheld the fundamental rights and resolved to adopt gender equality as a finding principle. The progress of the nation is integrally linked with the advancement of women and their status in the society.[58] Gender discrimination is one of the forms of deprivation. Due to the lack of education and information and low levels of literacy, the situation of deprivation on women has increased. Thereby women have been deprived of social and political power and also the power of knowledge.[59]

> An education system to work as catalyst for the socio-political awakening of women needs serious restructuring and reorientation of its values and ideals. Education pattern if properly sensitive to women, can to a considerable extent help in redefining the role of women in the society and polity. It needs to become 'neutral' to socio-religious norms, and establish a new set of values and norms for the progress of society. Then only can it become 'agent' for improving the status of women, making them active

---

56. N.J. Usha Rao, *Women in a Developing Society*, p. 9.
57. M.K. Gandhi, *Women and Social Injustice*, p. 5.
58. *Fourth World Conference on Women held in Beijing* — 1995, Government of India, p. 4.
59. *Ibid*., p. 6.

participants in the process of social and political development.[60]

## Women and Legal Equality

Gandhi held that women should labour under no legal disability, not suffered by man. He should treat the daughters and sons on the same footing of perfect equality. The education that has been imparted to a woman helps to realise her strength and she would naturally resent to glaring inequalities to which she is subjected to.[61] Gandhi was of the opinion that mere removal of the legal inequalities would remain a mere palliative. He found that the root of the evil lies much deeper than most of the people could realise. It has its basis in man's greed for power and fame. Man always desired power and he hankers after posthumous fame based on power which cannot be had if property is progressively cut up into pieces and if all the posterity become equal co-sharers.[62]

The Indian National Congress, which was guided by Gandhi, had always worked for raising the status of women and to improve her social conditions. After Independence, the Congress Party which assumed political power has undertaken several legislative measures for the emancipation of women. These serve as an indication of the impact of the Gandhian ideals.[63]

According to Jawaharlal Nehru, every effort should be made by the state and the private agencies to remove all social and customary barriers which retard the full development of the individual.

> Apart from full protection of all such rights of the individual and the group, it was common ground that every effort should be made by the state as well as by private agencies to remove all invidious social and customary barriers which came in the way of the full development of the individual as well as any group and the educationally and

---

60. Hemalata Swarup (ed.), *Women Politics and Religion*, p. 110.
61. M.K. Gandhi, *Women and Social Injustice*, p. 12.
62. *Ibid.*
63. T.K.N. Unnithan, *Gandhi and Free India*, p. 149.

> economically backward classes should be helped to get rid of their disabilities as rapidly as possible. This applied especially to the depressed classes. It was further laid down that women should share in every way with men in the privileges of citizenship.[64]

The struggle for securing legal equality has been one of the major concerns of the women's movement in the country. By, passing appropriate laws and by involving an effective machinery to implement these laws, discrimination could be effectively reduced. The women's organisation recently viewed that gender equality in laws could be pursued as a desired objective.[65]

Gandhi was aware of the various social customs observed by women and their state of mind. He stood against the evil social practices, viz., child marriages, the deplorable living conditions of women in the society, the practice of *sati*[66] and the possession of more than one wife by a single man and numerous other obnoxious customs which were to be tackled, Gandhi wished to seek public opinion in these matters. He was not opposed to legislation in such matters with more stress on the culmination of public opinion.

## Widow Remarriages

Gandhi showed a great concern over the plight of the millions of women who became widows. He wished them to remarry and lead a happy life. He was opposed to the system of enforced widowhood. He thought that every widow has as much right to remarry as every widower. While the voluntary widowhood is a priceless boon in Hinduism, enforced widowhood is a curse. He always wished to gain the support of enlightened public opinion.

Gandhi stated with all emphasis:

> The curse of every widow who is burning within to remarry but dare not for fear of a cruel custom, descends upon

---

64. Jawaharlal Nehru, *The Discovery of India*, p. 383.
65. *Fourth World Conference on Women held in Beijing*, 1995, p. 104.
66. Before the advent of the British to India, *Hindu Women used to immolate herself (set on fire) on her husband's funeral pyre.*

> Hindu society so long as it keeps the widow under an unforgivable bondage.[67]

Gandhi held that voluntary widowhood, consciously adopted by woman who experienced the affection of her partner, adds grace and dignity to life and sanctifies the home. Widowhood imposed by religion or custom cannot be borne, defiles home and degrades religion. He stated that the reform should be brought about in case of those who suffer from the enforced widowhood.

> The reform must begin by those who have girl widows taking courage in both their hands and seeing that the child widows in their charge are duly and well married — not remarried. They were never really married.[68]

### Evil Practice of Dowry

Gandhi stood against the evil practice of dowry system. He called it as 'the hateful system of dowry', 'marriage by purchase', 'a degrading practice' and so on. According to him, there is inherent evil in the dowry system for those that are involved in it as it results in bondage. Human being under this system is reduced to a mere commodity in the process of buying and selling followed by bargaining. This badly affects the human relationships.

He pointed out:

> The system has to go. Marriage must cease to be matter of arrangement made by parents for money. The system is intimately connected with caste. So long as the choice is restricted to a few hundred young men or young women of particular caste the system will persist on matter what is said against it. The girls or boys or their parents will have to break the bonds of caste if the evil is to be eradicated. All this means education of a character that will revolutionise the mentality of the youth of the nation.[69]

---

67. A.T. Himgorani (ed.), *To the Women*, p. 132
68. *Young India*, 5.8.1926, p. 276.
69. *Harijan*, 23.5.1936, p. 117.

Gandhi called for the formation of a strong public opinion to discredit the dowry system. He advocated even for the excommunication, of those who received dowry. In order to counteract these differences, he urged the parents of those girls to ignore the caste and other differences. He pointed out,

> Any young man who makes dowry a condition of marriage discredits his education and his country and dishonours womanhood.[70]

Gandhi further pointed out:

> A strong public opinion should be created in condemnation of the degrading practice of dowry and youngmen who soil their fingers with such ill gotten gold should be excommunicated from society. Parents of girls should cease to be dazzled by English degrees and should not hesitate to travel outside their little castes and provinces to secure true gallant young men for their daughters.[71]

In our country, it has become common to have dowry deaths. Some of the brides are subjected to harassment and humiliation and some are set on fire. Behind all these ghastly events, the prime cause is stated to be dowry, the degrading practice. This heinous act mocks at the norms of human values and dignity.

In order to counter the threat of violence, harassment, humiliation of a bride and dowry death, the Fourth World Conference holds the following amendment to be relevant.

> In the present context two significant amendments to the Indian Penal Code are relevant. Firstly, Section 304-B defines dowry deaths as being one where a woman dies of burns or other injuries within seven years of her marriage and there is evidence of cruelty and harassment by the husband 'for or any relative of her husband for or in connection with any demand for dowry'. Secondly, the harassment in itself can be cause of considerable agony, anguish and trauma for married woman was taken

70. *Young India*, 21.6.1929, p. 207.

71. *Ibid.*

> cognizance of in Section 498-A which extended a prison sentence to a husband or relative accused of cruelty.[72]

There have been anti-dowry movements organised by the progressive organisation of women in Hyderabad. Subsequently Delhi focuses the movement against Dowry and the violence inflected upon the women in the marital home. The groups that play a vital role in the campaign in Delhi include Stree Sangharsh, and Mahila Dakshata Samiti. A joint front called the Dahej Virodhi, Chetna Manch later on was formed. Under this group several party and non-party groups joined and worked. The anti-dowry campaign has attempted to bring about social pressure to isolate the offenders from the community.[73]

## The Problem of Prostitution and AIDS

Some women under certain conditions due to some causes are forced to take up prostitution as a means of their livelihood. Gandhi was realistic to admit that the men would be as fallen as the women if this prostitution spreads and flourishes. He never believed that the possible solution could be merely by finding suitable jobs for these brothers for their living. He regarded prostitution as a social disease 'a moral Leprosy' promoted by men without any ethical or moral standards. He stated that the evil practice of prostitution should be declared illegal. But he was never optimistic about the total eradication of this evil practice, for the reason that the evil practice exists clandestinely in almost all the countries despite the enforced law. So Gandhi wanted that a vigorous public opinion should be raised to avoid this evil.[74]

Gandhi observed:

> The proper method of dealing with brothels is for the women to carry on a double propaganda, (a) amongst women who sell their honour for a livelihood, and (b)

72. *Fourth World Conference on Women held in Beijing* during 1995, p. 101.
73. *Ibid*., pp. 128-9.
74. *Harijan*, 15.9.1946, p. 310.

> amongst men whom they must shame into behaving better towards their sisters whom they ignorantly or insolently call the weaker sex.[75]

The modern world is confronted with the grave problem of AIDS (Acquired Immune Deficiency Syndrome). This deadly disease is caused by the unnatural methods of human indulgence in sex. The grave situation in the modern world arises to the utmost out of AIDS rather than world terrorism or nuclear proliferation.

Drs. Fauci and Love of the National Institute of Allergy and Infectious Diseases write that AIDS is characterised by a profound defect in cell-mediated immunity which lead to opportunistic infections and unusual malignancies. The virus selectively infects a particular subject of white blood cells accounting for profound defects in immunity.[76] AIDS is fatal which slowly destroys the immune system of body and thereby making a person vulnerable to a host of infectious diseases. Seale described AIDS as "the molecular biological equivalent of nuclear war against man".[77]

AIDS cases were registered under such categories who are homosexuals, bisexuals, and children of AIDS parents and it is also commonly found among some prostitutes. So there is need for the programme of sex education. Gandhi stated that an useful solution to the grave problem could be focused in the scheme of sex education advocated by Gandhi. Systematically evolved sex education should be imparted to the people to overcome and control their sexual passions and to have mastery over their self.[78]

## Women and Social Justice

Gandhi recognised clearly that woman has a vital role to play in the matter of the reconstruction of the society. He fought for the woman's rights in order to bring about social justice to realise

---

75. *Harijan*, 4.9.1937, p. 233.
76. Rus Walton, *Biblical Solutions to Contemporary Problems*, pp. 21-2.
77. *AIM Report*, April 1987.
78. *Harijan*, 21.11.1936, p. 322.

equality. He held that woman should have same liberty and opportunity for self-development as man. Gandhi said,

> I make no distinction between man and woman. Woman should feel just as independent as man. Bravery is not man's monopoly.[79]

Gandhi further said:

> Man and woman are equal in status but not identical. They are peerless pair being complementary to one another; each helps the other so that without the one the existence of the other cannot be conceived and therefore it follows as a necessary — corollary, from these facts that anything that will impair the status of either of them will involve the equal ruin of both.[80]

### Women and Their Role in Society

Gandhi held that man and woman are equal and their problems must be one and the same in essence. Since both have the same feelings, both are complementary to each other. Both are interdependent and they cannot live without the other's active life.[81]

In his address on 20th February 1918, Gandhi dealt in detail with the problems faced by women and their regeneration.

He stated in his speech that:

> Woman is the companion of man, gifted with equal mental capacities. She has the right to participate in every minutest detail in the activities of man and she has an equal right of freedom and liberty with him. She is entitled to a supreme place in her own sphere of activity as man is in his. This ought to be the natural condition of things and not as a result only of learning to read and write.[82]

---

79. *Harijan*, 5.1.1947, p. 478.
80. M.K. Gandhi, *Women and Social Injustice*, p. 5.
81. *Harijan*, 24.2.1940, p. 13.
82. *Speeches and Writings of Mahatma Gandhi*, p. 425.

Recently the Southern State of Andhra Pradesh witnessed a series of struggles against the sale of arrack (country liquor) with the support of the State Government. The struggle gained momentum and spread rapidly to other parts of the state, drawing the attention of the public and became a major issue. Banning arrack sales in Andhra Pradesh State is one of the important items included in the manifesto on the basis of which the State Government could come to power. The new Chief Minister immediately banned the arrack sales in the state.[83]

The political awakening and the spirit of sacrifice and service to fight against the social evils through non-violent resistance could be attributed to this revolutionary step, the women had taken in their struggle against the sale of the arrack which is same as the *satyagraha* movement initiated by Gandhi wherein women in large numbers participated in picketing the liquor shops in Bihar.

## The Evil Effects of Alcoholism

Gandhi with a great insight recognised the fact that practice of non-violence results in the indomitable human will. *Bhagavad Gita* states that, he that controls his senses, controls the attachment to the senses which leads to attraction and attraction leads to passion which breeds recklessness resulting in the loss of the memory and keeping of evil in the mind. So control over the sensual enjoyment arising out of sensual attachment is of prime importance. So there is need to strengthen man's will to be guided in accordance with the dictates of his conscience to have control over his senses.

The soft drinks and beverages such as coffee and tea, smoking and consumption of alcohol in any form did not escape the attention of Gandhi.[84] Gandhi warned the people from the misapprehension of drink and tobacco. Drink is comparatively lesser evil than tobacco. He held that "if cigarette is Beelzebub, then drink is Satan". Drunkenness causes great havoc and the peril caused by it has been recognised by the people. The drink causes pathetic condition to the people and ruin their lives. Most of the people's earnings go to alcohol devoid of any

83. *Economic and Political Weekly*, January 16-23, pp. 87-90.

84. Tendulkar, *D.G. Mahatma*, Vol. II, p. 371.

grace in their lives. Under this evil influence of liquor, most of the intoxicated people fall flat on the ground and roll in the gutter for getting their respectable position in the society.

Gandhi pointed out:

> The condition of labour as a result of taking alcohol is also pitiable. That, as a result of such bitter experiences, I have become a staunch opponent of alcohol. . . . In a nutshell, alcohol ruins one physically, morally, intellectually and economically.[85]

Gandhi was greatly moved for the suffering experienced by the wives of drunkards. He was indignant about the crimes rampant because of the indulgence of the evil drink. He held that the drink is more a disease than a vice such as thieving, prostitution and other vices. He had much concern for the miseries brought upon the homes of labourers arising out of the drinking habit. This habit completely destroyed the human values. He was very clear about his position against the evil habit of drinking alcohol.

> Alcohol makes a man forget himself and while its effects last he becomes utterly incapable of doing anything useful. Those who take to drinking, ruin themselves and ruin their people. They lose all sense of decency and propriety.[86]

Gandhi stood against those who favour to take limited and regulated consumption of alcohol or who believe it to be useful. He did not find any weight or rationality in such arguments. The habit of alcohol consumption leads to other evils such as prostitution resulting in venereal infection, paralysis and so on.

Dr. C.E. Riggs stated:

> Alcohol promotes prostitution and prostitution is the main source of venereal disease. Individuals under the influence of alcohol are more liable to expose themselves to venereal infection, as alcohol attacks and paralyses the higher levels of the nervous system, such as caution, judgement, and self

85. M.K. Gandhi, *Key to Health*, pp. 35-6.

86. *Ibid.*, p. 38.

> restraint. Fear of disease which is an important restraining factor, under the influence of alcohol is likely to be cast to the winds.[87]

Apart from all these evils associated with the habit of alcohol, it badly affects the health. The man who drinks heavily and eats little could not digest the little he ate, and developed hemorrhages.[88] The statistical data in the major cities of the USA relating to the death rate from alcoholism indicate that it is responsible directly or indirectly for much infant mortality. The life of the child is badly affected through hereditary, inadequate food, carelessness and ignorance arising out of intoxication.

The cultivation of alcoholic habit results in ruining the health of a person:

> Between Chronic alcoholism and vitamin deficencies, there is a direct interaction; it has been found that the vitamin intake attendant upon inebriety is insufficient and that changes occur in vitamin assimilation and utilisation resulting from liver damage and gastric anomalies in chronic alcoholics.[89]

The excessive intake of alcohol causes general diseases which often entails destitution. The drink is capable enough to lead to sickness and thereby to unemployment and from there to poverty and so on.[90] Gandhi stated that no country however richer and prosperous it could be, could hardly afford to drink for drink brings nations to the verge of ruin and sometimes topples them over the drink.[91]

It was under the leadership of the Indian National Congress that the prohibition on liquor and opium was included as a part of the Non-cooperation Movement of 1920-22. Gandhi made his crusade against drinks and drugs and urged the government for prohibition

---

87. Nihal Singh, *Dry America*, p. 110.
88. *Ibid.*
89. Herman Leavy, *Drink*, p. 8.
90. *Ibid.*, p. 29.
91. M.K. Gandhi, *Drink, Drugs and Gambling*, p. 9.

on all of these. The Congress men and women rallied in his support and obstructed the auction of licences to liquor dealers and picketed the liquor shops at the same time. The movement gained momentum and spread all over the country. As a result many people gave up the drinking habit and consequently the revenue from the liquor fell, to the great inconvenience of the government.

Gandhi realised that moral regeneration has to be brought about from within but not by the mere prohibition or through legislation. He hoped that through prohibition, people could be prevented from drinking as the closing down of the liquor shops helps to get rid of the temptation. He knew it pretty well that the great misery followed by poverty of the broken families was due to the cultivation of the evil habit of drinking. He pointed out:

> I ask you to accept my evidence that the country as a whole is sick of the drink curse. Those informative men who have become slaves to the habit require to be helped against themselves.[92]

## The Significance of Prohibition

Gandhi suggested that prohibition is only the remedy to abolish the evil arising out of the drink. He held that complete prohibition was to be introduced not merely alone on the matter of drinking alcohol in any form but also in the use of other intoxicants such as bhang, *ganja*, tobacco and opium.[93]

Warren G. Harding, the President of the United States of America made the following statement about the advantages of the prohibition.

> In every community men and women have had an opportunity now to know what prohibition means. They know that debts are more promptly paid, that men take home the wages that once were wasted in saloons that families are better clothed and fed and more money finds its way into the Savings Bank. The liquor traffic was

---

92. *Drink, Drugs and Gambling*, p. 3.

93. M.K. Gandhi, *Key to Health*, pp. 32-6.

> destructive of much that was most precious in American life. In the face of so much evidence on that point, what conscientious man would want to let his own selfish desires influence him to vote to bring it back.[94]

Prohibition forbids the sale of intoxicants for consumption by law which results in a great moral awakening leading to the closure of liquor shops. The indispensable beginning of this movement ends in the complete weaning from drink. Such a consummation cannot be brought about by the State Government alone.[95] People have to rise their voice against this evil and campaign against drink and drugs.

Prohibition is proved to be a great stimulant for the promotion of business. Indeed even the most sanguine optimist would not have dared to predict that its effect upon trade and commerce would have been so far reaching.[96] When the people abstain from the consumption of liquor they could engage themselves in their work such as farming, stock raising and other industries and their standard of living rises with their increased prosperity.[97] There has been a notable change with those persons who used to spend their leisure time at the saloon. Now they stay at home during the evening times with their families and spend their time happily during their holidays in painting, gardening or otherwise beautifying their homes and surroundings. Domestic discord has disappeared and they take better care of their growing children.[98]

Gandhi measured the progress of the individual, society or the nation in terms of morality. According to him, the moral loss is greater than the financial loss. Those that are addicted to the drinks are degraded morally, socially and economically in the society. He remarked that they forget the distinction between wife, mother and sister and indulge in crimes. In their sober moments

---

94. *Statement Issued on the eve of the Presidential Election* during Nov. 1920.
95. M.K. Gandhi, *Drink, Drugs and Gambling*, p. 25.
96. Nihal Singh, *'Dry' America*, p. 70.
97. *Ibid.*, p. 90.
98. *Ibid.*, pp. 93-4.

they feel ashamed of their crimes.[99] Gandhi noticed that while the well-placed men could be protected by the police all over the world, the drunken poor are punished.[100] Gandhi advocated punishment to such of those who manufacture the liquor and those drunkards who could not give up the drunk despite the repeated warnings.

> And so long as I do, I must advocate the summary punishment of those who manufacture fiery liquid and those even who will persist in drinking it not withstanding repeated warnings. I do not hesitate forcibly to prevent my children from rushing into fire or deep waters. Rushing to red water is far more dangerous than rushing to a raging furnace or flooded stream. The latter destroys only the body, the former destroys both body and soul.[101]

Prohibition registered a remarkable improvement in the health condition of the people. Unlike in the past, when the hospitals were equipped fully with the patients for the treatment of delirium tremrs, now they are not used. The intoxicated patients have disappeared and number of patients is on decrease.[102]

On the other hand, the general elections used to be controlled by the commercialised liquor business which has been abolished by the prohibition element and restored a free and fair election. As it has been pointed out,

> Democracy depends upon a clean ballot and a free electorate. Both these are impossible when the political boss uses the saloon as a functioning point in the interests of bad government and corrupt politics.[103]

The restoration of liberty to the old ballot and establishing of the purity of elections could be made possible thereby.[104]

---

99. M.K. Gandhi, *Drink, Drugs and Gambling*, p. 10.
100. *Ibid.*, p. 10.
101. *Ibid.*, p. 14.
102. Nihal singh, *Dry America*, p. 104.
103. *Ibid.*, p. 146.
104. *Ibid.*, p. 145.

Gandhi did not hesitate for the consequent loss of revenue from the sale of the liquor due to the prohibition in force. He stated that it could be adjusted by cutting down the military expenditure. In order to accommodate the unemployed workmen who are left idle by the closing of factories, he advised to open the model farms nearby the factories. The state government could take over those factories from the owners and could profitably run the factories under the required conditions.[105]

Gandhi termed the revenue coming out of the drink and drugs as "a form of extremely degrading taxation". He held that all taxation to be healthy must return tenfold to the taxpayer in the form of the services required by him. If the excise duty is examined, it makes people to pay for their own corruption in the moral, mental and physical spheres. It is a dead weight to such of those who could not bear it. So Gandhi pointed out:

> The loss of revenue is only apparent. Removal of this degrading tax enables the drinker, i.e., the taxpayer to earn and spend better. Apart therefore from the tremendous gain, it means a substantial economic gain to the nation.[106]

Gandhi made an appeal to the women of Gujarat to help the campaign in connection with the prohibition movement. They were advised to visit the places where the liquor was sold by the liquor sellers. If they could not be successful in their endeavour, they should approach the drinkers and do their best in convincing them to abstain from the intoxicants.[107] Under the leadership of Gandhi, the liquor shops in Bihar were picketed. Gandhi had great faith in the abilities of women. He stated that women in a way could make even greater contribution than men to a non-violent war, if they could realise their inherent strength. He stated that the women "will succeed in shaming the drinkers into leaving the shops".[108] This statement has come to be literally true with this movement started by the poor rural women during 1992 in Nellore District of

---

105. *Young India*, 26.6.1931, p. 155.
106. M.K. Gandhi, *Drink, Drugs and Gambling,* p. 29.
107. *Ibid.*, p. 64.
108. *Ibid.*

Andhra Pradesh, India, which gathered a great momentum in the several neighbouring districts. When the women united, they emerged as a great force and within a few months the movement spread all over the 800 villages. It is because of the struggle that the women could gain a large measure of control and could transform their relations with men. They effectively confronted the State Government and destabilised its economy by enforcing the closure of village liquor shops. Behind this movement, no party provided an ideological framework or strategic plan. The women comprehended their daily predicaments associated with their work, family, economy, health, education, etc. Closure of the liquor shops became their nodal point. They initiated action to have control over them. The women were successful in their endeavour in mobilising against the sale of liquor and made it a major issue in the elections during 1994. The State Government could come into power only on the condition of banning the liquor sales in the State. Subsequently the liquor sales have been banned in the State.[109] Later again the prohibition was lifted because of change of the government.

## Value Oriented Education

Among the several resources available education could be termed as the most vital resource at the disposal of mankind. More energy has to be devoted to achieve education in a systematic and useful manner. Education plays a key role in all aspects of the human life.

In order to make education meaningful, Gandhi held that it must be related to conditions of the human life. There is need to restructure or shape the education to raise the standards of the people.[110] His education is an all-round drawing of the best in child, man, body, mind and spirit. Real education consists in drawing the best out of the individual and he held that there is no book better than the book of the humanity.[111] The education which does not enable the common masses to equip themselves in the struggle of their life to bring out strength of character, a spirit of philanthropy

109. *Economic and Political Weekly*, 1-1-1993, pp. 16-23.

110. M.K. Gandhi, *True Education*, p. 38.

111. N.K. Bose (ed.), *Selections from Gandhi*, p. 251.

and the courage of a lion is not worth to be named education.[112]

## Education and Moral Values

In order to make education meaningful and purposive, it must not overlook any area of human development. It is not merely adequate to produce the good individuals but it has to make the individuals who are conscious of their social responsibility as the integral elements of the society in which they live.[113]

Gandhi did not believe in the system of education which does not lay more stress on the inculcation of the moral values. He had an ideal education to be realised by experience and he wanted to experiment with this true system of education. He upheld character in education and regarded character building as the proper foundation of education. If the foundation is firmly laid, the children could learn all other things themselves or through the assistance of their friends.[114] His educational ideas were taught after a deep understanding and thorough check depending on their consequences that contribute for the human progress and moral regeneration. He turned out to concreteness from abstraction and from the inadequacy of such of the fixed ideas and from the closed system which claim to be absolute and final. As a man of action believing in the values, he turned towards concreteness of facts and reality.

The reconstructionist in education contends that much of mankind today suffers from institutional disequilibrium followed by moral confusion and uncertainty. There is need to make a search for such of the values which stand as the highest priorities of education. It would not be adequate merely to be content with the values for education does not merely involve values, but education has a good purpose and end. So it is the obligation of the people and teachers to critically analyse the values and find out their relevance.[115]

---

112. Anil Dutta Mishra (ed.), *Gandhian Approaches to the Contemporary Problems*, p. 331.
113. *Ibid.*, p. 333.
114. M.K. Gandhi, *The Story of My Experiments with Truth*, p. 251.
115. Joe Park (ed.), *Selected Readings in the Philosophy of Education*, p. 126

The world of today has been split into warring camps. The resources and the energies of the countries of the world are wasted in their destructive tendencies, while hate and destruction are disvalues conspicuously found in the human life than the values such as love and cooperation which are constructive. In order to achieve a goal such as world civilisation, there is need for the people of all colours, creeds, races and nations to join together to promote peace and unity under the banner of international world order.[116]

Education is held to be a powerful medium of social change in the emerging world civilisation. In order to channellise the inherent abilities, realisation of the potentialities is necessary. Education has to be related to the human life and it is an essential characteristic. Education has to be value oriented. The significance of education depends upon the realisation of the values and actualising them in the human life.

In order to make education purposive and meaningful, it should invariably cover the entire gamut of the human life providing opportunities for the development in the socio-economic-religious, moral, mental and physical spheres. Gandhi laid the foundation for such type of education which he called as 'Nai Talim' popularly known as 'Basic Education'. His concept of basic education is based on the firm conviction that an equitable social order can be established with the development of the human personality. The student can undertake some productive work while learning.

Man cannot lead a life which has no values. E.F. Schumacher pointed out that education is the transmission of ideas of value related to the human life which enable man to choose between one thing and the other. Leading a life without purpose or meaning is a disgrace and this life loses its charm.[117]

John Dewey held that it is the business of the intelligent theory of education to enquire into the causes for conflict. There is need to introduce a new order of conceptions which lead to a new mode of practice. He referred to the contending educational idea of development from within which is based upon the natural

---

116. *Selected Readings in the Philosophy of Education*, p. 128.
117. E.F. Schumacher, *Small is Beautiful*, p. 77.

endowments and the development of education from without which is the substitution of habits acquired under external pressure.[118]

The modern education lacks the capacity to discriminate between right and the wrong to bridge the gulf between theory and practice. The education needs to have some resemblance between thought and action. The concepts such as equality, liberty and freedom should not remain as mere ideals but they have to be realised in action. True wisdom lies in its practice. Gandhi aimed at the human transformation rather than the mere acquisition of knowledge. For Gandhi the significance of the practical life lies in the realisation of the values which is termed the core as of his true education.

In the modern times the moral values are corrosive and the people are more susceptible to the evil rather than good because of the degeneration of the moral standards. Education helps to make the people realise about the evils that have crept in the society which tend to make the society unstable and immoral. According to Dr. Ramjee Singh,

> An operationally viable value system would be lasting through educational orientation.[119]

There has been an intimate relationship between the process of experience and education. The constructive development depends upon the correct idea of experience.[120] Experience and education cannot be directly equated with each other as some experiences are not educative.[121] So there is need to choose the experience that proves fruitful and creative to the subsequent experiences.[122]

> Unless the problem of intellectual organisation can be worked out on the ground of experience, reaction is sure to occur toward externally imposed methods of organisation.[123]

118. John Dewey, *Experience and Education*, p. 1.
119. Ramjee Singh, *Gandhi and the Modern World*, p. 225.
120. John Dewey, *Experience and Education*, p. 7.
121. *Ibid.*, p. 13.
122. *Ibid.*, p. 17.
123. *Ibid.*, p. 107.

**Basic Education**

"Education is that which liberates" was the ancient aphorism. As it was before, it remains true even today. Education does not mean to have the mere spiritual knowledge and liberation does not signify only spiritual liberation after death. It is also the acquisition of knowledge which includes all training which is useful for the service of mankind and liberation is freedom from all manner of servitude even in the present life.[124] Gandhi held that children must be taught about the dignity of labour as the largest part of the human life is devoted to earn livelihood.[125] In his viewpoint, the literary education should follow the education of hand.

> It is a superstition to think that the fullest development of man is impossible without a knowledge of the art of reading and writing that knowledge undoubtedly adds grace to life but it is no way indispensable for man's moral, physical or material growth.[126]

Gandhi held that the true education involves a proper exercise and training of the bodily organs, hands, feet, eyes, ears, nose, etc. An intelligent use of the bodily organs of the child helps the child to improve his intellect. The education has to proceed from the physical and spiritual faculties of the child. It is a fallacy to suppose that they can be developed independently. Gandhi recognised the significance of the education followed by an useful handicraft to be taught to every child. Such system of education is purposive and. meaningful which brings about revolutionary changes in the socio-economic, religious and political spheres with far-reaching consequences.

> By education I mean an all-round drawing out of the best in the child and man-body, mind and spirit. Literacy is not the end of education nor even the beginning. It is only one of the means whereby man and women can be educated. Literacy in itself is no education. I would therefore begin

124. *Harijan*, 10.3.1946, p. 38.

125. *Ibid.*, 8.9.1946, p. 306.

126. *Ibid.*, 8.3.1935, p. 28.

> the child's education by teaching it a useful handicraft and enabling it to produce from the moment it begins its training. . . . I hold that the highest development of the mind and the soul is possible under such a system of education. Only every handicraft has to be taught not merely mechanically as is done today, but scientifically, i.e., the child should know the why and the wherefore of every process.[127]

The core of suggestion of Gandhi is that the handicrafts are to be taught not merely for the productive work but to develop the intellect of the individuals.[128] Gandhi stated that an intellect developed through the medium of socially useful labour will stand as an instrument of service and it will not go out of the path.[129]

> The notion of education through handicrafts rises from the contemplation of truth and love permeating life's activities. Love requires that true education should be easily accessible to all, and should be of use to every villager in his daily life. Such education is not derived from, nor does it depend upon books. It has no relation to sectional religion. If it can be called religious it is universal religion from which all sectional religions are derived. Therefore it is learnt from the Book of life which costs nothing and which cannot be taken away from one by any force on earth.[130]

Gandhi held that the object of the basic education is to transform the village children into modern villagers.[131]

> My plan to impart primary education through the medium of village handicrafts like spinning and carding, etc., is thus conceived as the spearhead of a silent social revolution fraught with the most far-reaching consequences.[132]

---

127. *Harijan*, 31.7.1937, p. 197.
128. *Ibid.*, 11.9.1937, p. 256.
129. *Ibid.*, 8.9.1946, p. 306.
130. *Ibid.*, 21.12.1947, p. 480.
131. M.K. Gandhi, *The Constructive Programme*, p. 18.
132. *Harijan*, 9.10.1937, p. 293.

The concept of basic education (Nai Talim) is based on the fundamental assumption that an equilibrated social order can be built up only with full development of the human personality. 'Collective and cooperative brotherhood of man' is the correct means to achieve this rather than the isolated human behaviour. The development of the human personality is not an end in itself but constitutes only an integral part of the common good of society.[133]

In order to achieve progress, people have to be prepared for the change. Education is a powerful means of social change. To achieve this, channellising of the inherent potentialities is necessary. Unless education is related to the human problems and human life as its essential characteristic, it loses its charm.

The educational approach of Gandhi is sustainable for all-round development of the individual and the society. His concept of education makes people self-supporting and educate. He made the people conscious of their social responsibilities as they constitute the integral elements of the society. His concept of basic education is an important measure to avoid the crises in the society arising out of the growing unemployment and lack of coherence between the education imparted and the jobs the people secured.

Basic education makes provision for participation of its members on equal terms in the educational process of learning while doing some productive work. This brings about a social change and makes the individuals economically sound. This method needs to be followed with commitment, honesty and integrity.

> A double standard of reality, one for our own private and more or less concealed interests, and another for public and acknowledged concerns, hampers, in most of us, integrity and completeness of mental action.[134]

John Dewey termed the traits of the good method of the individual as straightforwardness, open-minded, will to learn, integrity of purpose and acceptance of the responsibility.[135]

---

133. T.K.N. Unnithan, *Gandhi and Free India*, p. 179.
134. John Dewey, *Democracy and Education*, p. 177.
135. *Ibid.*, p. 179.

For Gandhi the real education is self-sufficiency. He held that if education is made compulsory for the rural people, it ought to be made self-supporting also. Education has to be value-oriented and not merely academic in nature.

The significance of education in the modern times lies in the part to be played by morality. This has been recognised widely by the people. For Gandhi the goal of education is character building. Human transformation is the aim of Gandhi. Man has to realise higher values of life. When education is value-oriented, it continues to be perennially relevant. The Draft National Policy on Education during 1967 laid stress on "the cultivation of moral and social values. The educational system must produce young men and women of character and ability, committed to national service and development."[136] The national policy of education during 1979 emphasised on Gandhian ideas and experiments which have stressed the need for moral education as forming part of the content through interrelated curricular and co-curricular programmes in all subjects and it should be the responsibility of all teachers and entire institution.[137]

The aim of education is not merely the preparation for employment but it has also to make the individual realise his noble ideas and enable him to perform them in his life. The moral ideas and ideals tend to quicken the moral life of the people and bring about dynamism and purity in social life.[138]

Education is a process of bringing up, moulding or shaping into the standard form of social activity. Gandhi pointed out that the scheme of education is to facilitate the acquisition of knowledge connected with their main occupations.[139] He advocated that National Education has got to play a great role as a part of self-rule. The present educational system has to be changed and overhauled.

---

136. *National Policy of Education*, New Delhi, Ministry of Education, 1968, p. 2.

137. *Draft National Policy on Education*, 1979, New Delhi, Ministry of Education, p. 2.

138. Hardayal, *Thoughts on Education*, p. 50.

139. M.K. Gandhi, *True Education*, p. 38.

Gandhi wanted the National Education to be evolved on the following lines:

1. Education must be imparted through the mother tongue.
2. There must be accord between the education a child receives at school and the environment of the home.
3. It must be so planned as to meet the needs of the majority of the people.
4. The teachers in primary classes must be competent men of good character right from the first class.
5. Education must be free.
6. Over all controls must be in the hands the people.[140]

Gandhi held that the best teachers have to be procured to impart education for the children who lead a highly exemplary life to be set as good models. In the ancient times, the students received their education from the teachers who were learned and men of great wisdom. Education should neither be politicalised nor commercialised and it must be freely available to all. The teacher should not depend merely upon the textbook alone to impart education to his students but he has to teach from the human experience to make original contribution to education. He held that the failure in the educational system cannot be ascribed to the lack of soundness in the system, but it is due to the defect in the implementation of its policies and programmes.

The future of the individual and the progress of the nation wholly depends upon education. Alvin Toffler says that in order to avoid the possible future shock, a new system of education has to be evolved. To achieve this, a search for the new objectives and methods well suited to the future is necessary rather than to rely on the past.[141]

> What counts for each nation in the long run are products of mind — work; scientific and technological research . . . the education of the workforce . . . sophisticated software . . .

---

140. *True Education*, pp. 40-1.

141. Alvin Toffler, *Future Shock*, p. 398.

> smarter management . . . advanced communications . . . electronic finance. These are key sources of tomorrow's power, and among these strategic weapons none is more important than superior organisation — especially the organisation of knowledge itself.[142]

As an educationist, Gandhi judged those attitudes that are conducive for the continued growth of the society and avoided such of the elements that are detrimental to the progress. He never lost sight of the manifold problems and the challenges the nation is confronted with and he had the foresight of the future. He took future into consideration at every stage and made innovations in the educational process to make education meaningful and purposive, useful and relevant to the needs of the modern society and also the future requirements of the society. The modern society recognised the significance of the job-oriented courses and it lays more stress on these courses to be started to widen the scope for better professional opportunities for the people.

142. Alvin Toffler, *Power Shift*, p. 161.

# 4

# Economic Reorganisation — A Gandian Perspective

GANDHI was a true economist who can be termed as the economist of the masses. His crusade against exploitation, poverty, and the disorganised socio-economic order. He stood for raising the deteriorating moral values relying on Trusteeship as an economic policy which was evolved by him in the process, with his thorough understanding of the traditional religious teachings, innumerable experiences in alleviating the human suffering.

The modern challenges and the international strains of capitalism and communalism alike inspired Gandhi to evolve a new economic philosophy.[1] In the opinion of Gandhi production is to be determined by social necessity but not by personal whim or greed. This stands against exploitation of any kind. The approach of Gandhi towards the economic order is revolutionary and essentially constructive but not violent and evolutionary but not static.[2] His ideas of trusteeship opened a new vista of employer-employee relationship providing a new basis for class collabaration.[3]

## Trusteeship

When Gandhi was pursuing his legal studies in England, he obtained the idea of trusteeship. Incidentally he found the same idea present in the *Gita* also. He tried to apply this idea as a solution

1. *Gandhi Marg*, 39, p. 327.
2. *Ibid.*, p. 329.
3. *Ibid.*, p. 331.

to the economic inequalities which beset the society. He felt that inequalities existing in the society cannot be removed unless the rich and the poor are morally conscious, aware of their duties, and realise their defects and weaknesses. An appeal to reason and love helps to create such awareness and an atmosphere conducive for self-purification. Gandhi found economic inequalities in the society. He felt that non-violence could play a great rôle for establishing economic equality.

> Economic Equality is the master key to non-violent independence. Working for economic equality means abolishing the eternal conflict between capital and labour. It means the levelling down of the few rich in whose hands is concentrated the bulk of the nation's wealth on the one hand, and the levelling up of the semi-starved naked millions on the other.... A non-violent system of government is clearly an impossibility, so long as the wide gulf between the rich and the hungry millions persists. . . .
>
> A violent and bloody revolution is a certainty one day unless there is a voluntary abdication of riches and the power that riches give and sharing them for the common good.[4]

Acquisition of wealth could be possible only under certain moral conditions of the society, basing on the attainability of honesty for practical purposes.[5]

> Inequalities of wealth, unjustly established, have assuredly injured the nation in which they exist during their establishment; and, unjustly directed, injure it yet more during their existence. But inequalities of wealth, justly established, benefit the national in the course of their establishment; and nobly used, aid it yet more by their existence.[6]

---

4. M.K. Gandhi, *Constructive Programme*, pp. 20-1.
5. John Ruskin, *Unto This Last*, p. 3.
6. *Ibid.*, pp. 34-5.

The modern economics gives utmost importance to the capital. But for Gandhi, the labour is far superior to capital He held that without labour, gold, silver and copper are useless burden for it is labour which extracts the precious ore from the bowels of the earth. No society can thrive and progress following the methods of hatred or violence in any form. It is immoral for the capitalists to rob the fruits of the worker's labour. Instead of asking for the fulfilment of their legitimate demands, it is equally immoral for labourers to paralyse industries and tyrannise the capitalists with their exaggerated demands. Gandhi was not against the capitalists but against capitalism. He wanted to bring about a total transformation in the economic sphere through his non-violent method. Gandhi wanted a union between capital and labour and a harmonious co-operation between these two.

> By the non-violent method we seek not to destroy the capitalist, we seek to destroy capitalism. We invite the capitalist to regard himself as a trustee for those on whom he depends for the making, the retention and the increase of his capital. Nor need the worker wait for his conversion. If capital is power, so is work. Either power can be used destructively or creatively. Either is dependent on the other. Immediately the worker realises his strength, he is in a position to become a co-sharer with the capitalist instead of remaining his slave.[7]

Gandhi's regulated trusteeship did not recognise any right of private ownership of property but aimed at the provision of means of transforming the present existing capital order of society into an egalitarian society.[8] Gandhi held that the capitalists will have to be the trustees for the welfare of the labouring classes working under them for, capital is meant for the material and moral welfare of the labourers.[9] Gandhi believed that it would be possible to appeal to

---

7. *Young India*, 26.3.1931, p. 49.
8. Niharanjan Ray (ed.), *Gandhi, Theory and Practice Impact and Contemporary Relevance*, p. 8.
9. *Young India*, 20.8.1925, p. 285.

the reason and love, to persuade the capitalists to make them realise that capital in their hands represents the fruit of the labour of the people and it, is treated as such.

> I am inviting those people who consider themselves as owners today to act as trustees, i.e., owners, not in their own right, but owners in the right of those whom they have exploited.[10]

Gandhi stated that when a person comes with a fair amount of wealth either by way of legacy or by means of trade and industry, he should be aware of the fact that all wealth does not belong to him, and what belongs to him, is right to have an honourable living, no better than that enjoyed by millions of others. The rest of his wealth should belong to the community to be used for the well-being and welfare of the community. The person should know about the evils and dangers of the accumulation of wealth. He should see that it is in the larger interests of the community rather than for personal comforts. Then capitalists would exist as trustees. When that happy day dawns, the difference existing between capital and labour would be obligatory. The labour will have ample food and sanitary dwellings and all necessary education with proper medical assistance.

Gandhi enunciated the theory of labour when the socialist theory was placed before the country regarding the positions held by *zamindars* and the ruling chiefs. Gandhi wanted the privileged classes to outgrow their greed, sense of position and to come down to the level of the labour who earn their daily bread. Since the labourer has the power to work, he has to realise that he is a better owner of his own, than the wealthy man who is the owner of his wealth.[11]

In his theory of trusteeship, Gandhi stated that there is no makeshift, and certainly no camouflage. He was confident that this theory would survive other theories as it has religious sanction behind it. When the possessor of wealth has not acted up to this

---

10. *Young India*, 26.11.1931, p. 369.
11. *Harijan*, 3.6.1939, p. 145.

theory, it does not prove its falsity but proves the weakness of the wealthy.[12]

## Trusteeship as a practical formula

The following formula was drawn up by Kishore Lal Mashruwala and Narahari Parikh which is simple and practical, approved by Gandhi with a few changes.

1 Trusteeship provides a means of transforming the present capitalist order of society into an egalitarian one. It gives no quarter to capitalism, but gives the present owning class a chance of reforming itself. It is based on the faith that human nature is never beyond redemption.

2. It does not recognise any right of private ownership of property except so far as it may be permitted by society for its own welfare.

3. It does not exclude legislative regulation of the ownership and use of wealth.

4. Thus under state-regulated trusteeship, an individual will not be free to hold or use his wealth for selfish satisfaction or in disregard of the interests of society.

5. Just as it is proposed to fix a decent minimum living wage, even so a limit should be fixed for the maximum income that would be allowed to any person in society. The difference between such minimum and maximum incomes should be reasonable, and equitable and variable from time to time so much so that the tendency would be towards obliteration of the difference.

6. Under the Gandhian economic order the character of production will be determined by social necessity and not by personal whim or greed.[13]

Gandhi examined how equal the distribution of wealth could be brought about through non-violence. According to Gandhi, the first

---

12. *Harijan*, 16.11.1939, p. 376.

13. *Ibid.*, 25.10.1952, p. 301.

step towards it is that one who has made this ideal realised into practice as to make necessary changes in his personal life. He has to reduce his wants to the minimum, keeping in view of the poverty of the nation. There won't be any place for speculation. He has to be self-restrained in every sphere of his life. When he could make all this possible in his own life, then only he would be in a position to preach this ideal among his associates and neighbours. The root of the doctrine of the equal distribution lies in the trusteeship of the wealthy for their superfluous wealth. The doctrine of equal distribution can be realised non-violently. Resorting to violence to make the wealthy dispossessed of their possessions would not benefit the society. Society will become poorer for it would lose the gifts of the talented persons who know the method of accumulating wealth. So Gandhi found non-violent way to be evidently superior. The rich man will make use of the possession of his wealth to the extent reasonably he requires for his personal needs and would act as trustee for his remaining possessions for the welfare of the society. Herein honesty of the trustee is assumed.

In the event of the rich refusing to become the trustee of the poor in the true sense of the term, allowing the poor to be crushed and die of hunger, Gandhi found the solution to this riddle by relying on non-violent, non-cooperation and civil disobedience as the right and infallible means. There is need for the poor to realise the fact that the rich cannot accumulate their wealth without the cooperation of the poor in the society. If this fact is spread among the poor, they would learn to free themselves by non-violent means from the inequalities which crushed them and kept them on the verge of starvation.[14]

Gandhi held that it is not merely wealth but one's physical strength, talents and intelligence which must be utilised for the service of all. "His doctrine of trusteeship means the use of all one has, for the good of all."[15] His economic order is based on individual non-possession.[16]

---

14. *Harijan*, 20.8.1940, p. 260.
15. Prof. K. Satchidananda Murty, *Indian Philosophy Since 1498*, p. 111.
16. *Ibid.*

**Economic Equality**

By economic equality Gandhi means approximate but not absolute equality.

> Economic equality must never be supposed to mean possession of an equal amount of worldly goods by everyone. It does not mean, however, that every one will have a proper house to live in, sufficient and balanced food to eat, and sufficient Khadi with which to cover himself. It also means that the cruel inequality that obtains today will be removed by purely non-violent means.[17]

Gandhi prescribed that a *satyagrahi* has to lead a life of voluntary poverty, and strictest honesty and care has to be taken while handling the public funds, which is an indispensable condition for the growth of a healthy life.[18] And for any good cause *satyagrahi* must be willing "to give up his life and his possessions".[19] Gandhi says,

> I shall bring about economic equality through non-violence, by converting the people to my point of view. . . . I will not wait till I have converted the whole society to my view but will straight away make a beginning with myself. . . . For that I have to reduce myself to the level of the poorest of the poor.[20]

Gandhi admitted that there are inequalities existing in the society but he held that the essential equality has not to be missed. His idea of society is based on the conviction that

> while we are born equal meaning that we have a right to equal opportunity, all have not the same capacity. It is in nature of things, impossible.[21]

---

17. *Harijan*, 18.8.1940, p. 253.
18. M.K. Gandhi, *Satyagraha*, p. 73.
19. *Harijan*, 25.3.1939, p. 64.
20. *Ibid.*, 31.3.1946, p. 64.
21. *Young India*, 26.3.1931, p. 49.

He was of the opinion that the people who are talented would have more advantage to earn more and they would utilise talents for the welfare of all the people.

> I would allow a man of intellect to earn more, I would not cramp his talent. But the bulk of his greater earnings must be used for the good of the State, just as the income of all earnings of sons of the father go to the common family fund. They would have then earnings only as trustees.[22]

This could be done if a man identifies himself with the poor and through him will all mankind in a spirit of renunciation by broadening his outlook and rising himself above the self. Economic equality in his conception is:

> Economic equality of my conception does not mean that everyone will literally have the same amount. It simply means that everybody should have enough for his or her needs.[23]

If a single man demands as much as a family, it is tantamount to the violation of economic equality. What Gandhi wanted was that:

> Everyone must have a balanced diet, a decent house to live in, facilities for the education of one's children and adequate medical relief.[24]

Gandhi stated that he would bring about economic equality through appealing to the reason of the people, by harnessing the forces of love that stand against hatred and finally converting them to his point of view by making a beginning with himself straightaway by reducing himself to the poorest of the poor.

## Equitable Distribution

The ideal of Gandhi — equal distribution cannot be realised. He therefore worked out for equitable distribution.[25] Here the Marxian

---

22. *Young India*, 26.11.1931, p. 368.
23. *Harijan*, 31.3.1946, p. 63.
24. *Ibid.*
25. *Young India*, 17.3.1927, p. 86.

definition 'to each according to his need' was considered by Gandhi as the real definition of economic equality.[26] Gandhi says,

> The real implication of equal distribution is that each man shall have the wherewithal to supply all his natural needs and no more. For example, if one man has a weak digestion and requires only a quarter of a pound of flour for his bread and another needs a pound, both should be in a position to satisfy their wants. To bring this ideal into being, the entire social order has got to be reconstructed. A society based on non-violence cannot nurture any other ideal. We cannot perhaps be able to realize the goal, but we must bear it in mind and work unceasingly to near it. To the same extent as we progress towards our goal, we shall find contentment and hapiness.[27]

## Industrial Civilisation — A Gandhian Attitude

The writings of Ruskin and Tolstoy about the economic history of India under the British Regime helped Gandhi to form the idea about industrialisation.[28] John Ruskin time and again raised his voice against the degrading social and moral conditions of the labour during the nineteenth century and the exploitation and enslavement of man by the machine. Similarly, Tolstoy held that the hateful industrialisation reduced the people to the deplorable state of slavery. Like Ruskin and Tolstoy, Gandhi also felt industrialisation as a great menace to realise the basic moral ideals of the human society.

There were two trends in the Indian National Congress during the beginning of the twentieth century — one was represented by Gokhale who believed in the Parliamentary form of Government wherein the village was expected to occupy the same position as the local bodies in England, whereas the other trend represented by Annie Besant, Bipin Chandra Paul and C.R. Das, believed in

---

26. *Harijan*, 31.3.1946, p. 63.
27. *Ibid.*, 25.8.1940, pp. 260-1.
28. Nirmal Kumar Bose, *Studies in Gandhism*, pp. 23-4.

upholding the village as the primary and basic unit of political set-up. Gandhi was confined to the latter trend and successfully tried to reverse the course of the national movement towards the village. So he challenged the very basis of modern civilisation which was solely responsible for impoverishing the Indian villages.[29]

Industrialisation flourishes in the atmosphere where the production of the vast quantities of raw materials and the wide market for the sale of finished goods are present. To serve both the purposes, the availability of the resources and the market of the foreign countries become necessary. Developed countries exploit the underdeveloped countries. "Colonial expansion, imperialism, commercial monopoly, repeated war with other rival industrialised countries, diplomatic mechanisms for keeping down the economic and political growth of the rivals as well as of the myths of cultural, racial, and religious superiorities of the exploiters — all follow in a ceaseless train, demoralising to the whole world.[30]

The growth of the large-scale industries depends upon the investment of large capital and the employment of a good number of labourers which breeds equally the problems of the relations between capital and labour. Gandhi with disgust and horror could see openly the violent rebellions of labourers in other countries against the violence of the capitalistic industrialists and found the same story being repeated in India in some industrial areas. So he thought that it would be unwise for India to try to establish and increase industrialism inviting all the troubles that had already set upon the industrialised countries.[31]

The blind use of machines without any sense and technological advancement erodes moral fibre and badly effects the value system. So Gandhi vehemently opposed the growing use of machines. He knew that heavy industrialisation would result in exploitation. The beauty of human life is not felt.

He knows that it lays down the seeds of exploitation within

---

29. Ramjee Singh, *Gandhi and the Modern World*, p. 153.
30. Dhirendra Mohan Datta, *The Philosophy of Mahatma Gandhi*, p. 112.
31. *Ibid.*, pp. 112-13.

> as well as outside the country; it breeds violence, class conflict and misery; it provides unwanted leisure to a few by robbing it from majority, it gives unemployment, slumps, uneven distribution of wealth, wars and imperialism. It makes a few to ride on millions; it demands a huge social cost by uprooting innocent people from their homes and villages, spoiling their health and intelligence and depriving them of joy in their work and even in life.[32]

The growth of big cities especially in India are attractive to the crowds. Many people drifted to the cities to improve their living conditions which finally resulted in breaking their family ties.

> But when the woman goes out to industrial work like her husband, and the children spend most of their day at school, the economic tie between husband and wife is enormously weakened. It is probable that, with the growth of industrialisation the practice of eating in public eating-houses will increase, and house-work will be reduced to a minimum. The children will have first their midday meal, and then all meals, at school; thus the peculiar work which has hitherto been done by wives will cease more and more. Under these circumstances, marriage as it has existed since men took to agriculture is likely to come to an end. Women will prefer to preserve their independence, and not rely upon the precarious bounty of an individual man.[33]

The healthy social relations and neighbourly feelings had mostly gone and the individuals are lost in crowds. Man is reduced to a mere tool and his personality is lost. Life is reduced to a mechanical drudgery and escape is sought in gross sensual pleasures like drinking, gambling and all other vices that follow from them: The whole process of industrialisation appeared to Gandhi as a monstrous process of mechanisation, dehumanisation and demoralisation.[34]

---

32. Ramjee Singh, *Gandhi and the Modern World*, p. 156.
33. Bertrand Russell, *The Prospects of Industrial Civilization*, pp. 44-5.
34. Dhirendra Mohan Datta, *The Philosophy of Mahatma Gandhi*, p. 113.

The classical economists like Adam Smith and Ricardo, Mill and Marshall made people to think that industrialisation, free play of forces, private ownership and minimum interference by the Government would improve matters. But it was not so. Sisomondi revolted against this policy and criticised the growing use of machines and Karl Marx fought against the capitalism. So the classical doctrines were revised by Marshall, Keynes, etc., whether the capitalists are socialists or capitalists, they all stood for material advancement as they thought that material progress and human happiness go together. So both of them laid stress on industrialisation, large-scale production, growing mechanisation, automation and multiplicity of wants.[35]

Gandhi vehemently opposed the modern industrial civilisation. He measured the progress in terms of moral values and real human happiness. The real progress does not lie in the material progress. Thousands of people work in the factories or mines at the risk of their lives to make their living. They are made to take up dangerous work for the sake of millions. He held that this type of civilisation is self-destroying.

In the words of Bertrand Russell

> What is called civilisation may be defined as the pursuit of objects not biologically necessary for survival.[36]

The industrial civilisation is a disease as it is all evil. Gandhi measured the industrial civilisation in terms of the human welfare and stated that people should not suffer exploitation on account of this. People are in the mad rush in search of their pleasure and go on multiplying their wants. Modern civilisation does not take morality or religion into consideration. As Bertrand Russell stated quantity is valued more than quality and mechanism is more valued than its uses.

## Place of Man in the Industrialisation

The modern industrial civilisation has reduced man to a mere cog,

---

35. Ramjee Singh, *Gandhi and the Modern World*, p. 156.
36. Bertrand Russell, *The Prospects of Industrial Civilization*, p. 39.

atrophying his limbs. What Gandhi wanted was that

> whilst this machine age aims at converting men into machines, I am aiming at reinstalling man turned machine into his original estate.[37]

For Gandhi man is the measure and "the supreme consideration is man".[38]

The modern machinery is evil as "machinery is like a snake-hole which may contain from one to a hundred snakes".[39] This civilisation is self-defeating. The air and water have become polluted and the health of the people has badly suffered. In this regard Gandhi says,

> Honest physicians will tell you that where means of artificial locomotion have increased, the health of the people has suffered.[40]

Mass production which is the result of heavy industrialisation tends to isolate the individual.[41] So Gandhi objected to the craze for machinery.

> What I object to is the craze for machinery, not machinery as such. The craze is for what they call labour saving machinery. Men go on saving labour till thousands are without work and thrown on the open streets to die of starvation. I want to save time and labour not for a fraction of mankind but for all.[42]

Gandhi has no consideration for machinery which is meant either to enrich the few at the cost of the many or to displace the useful labour of many.[43] He took the socio-economic conditions and the problem of

---

37. *Harijan*, 29.8.1936, p. 228.
38. *Young India*, 13.11.1924, p. 378.
39. M.K. Gandhi, *Hind Swaraj*, p. 96.
40. *Ibid.*
41. Ramjee Singh, *Gandhi and the Modern World*, p. 158.
42. *Young India*, 13.11.1924, p. 378.
43. *Harijan*, 22.6.1935, p. 146.

unemployment of the country into consideration and stated:

> Mechanisation is good when hands are too few for the work intended to be accomplished. It is an evil where there are more hands than required for the work, as is the case of India. The problem with us is not how to find leisure for the teeming millions inhabiting our villages. The problem is how to utilise their idle hours, which are equal to the working days of six months in the year.[44]

## Concentration of Wealth

If the economic consequences of the industrialisation is examined, industrial revolution if it is on the right direction, is the fountain spring of prosperity. Because of the mass production, the commodities may be available at the cheaper rate. But, on the other hand, it would contribute to the problems associated with unemployment, international market competitions, etc.[45] As common people cannot afford to have the large-scale machinery, only a few rich could afford to have the heavy machinery and the concentration of wealth will be in the hands of those few at the exploitation of many. But Gandhi was opposed to it. "Abundance of money particularly in the hands of a few, is a highly dangerous phenomenon."[46]

Gandhi pointed out

> I want the concentration of wealth, not in the hands of a few, but in the hands of all. Today machinery merely helps a few to ride on the backs of millions. The impetus behind it all is not the philanthropy to save labour, but greed. It is against this constitution of things that I am fighting with all my might. . . .[47]

Gandhi held that the organisation of machinery for the purpose of

---

44. *Harijan*, 16.11.1934, p. 316.
45. Ramjee Singh, *Gandhi and the Modern World*, p. 158.
46. *Kurukshetra*, October 1994. Annual Number, p. 10.
47. *Young India*, 13.11.1924, p. 378.

concentrating wealth and power in the hands of a few and for the exploitation of many was altogether wrong. Machinery in the present age is of this type.[48] Machinery has to be of such type that should promote the total human welfare and solve the human problems such as unemployment. But the present use of machinery tends to concentrate its wealth more and more in the hands of a few in total disregard of the impoverished millions who are deprived of their food and basic requirements of life.

As B.N. Ganguli observes

> What, in his view, threatened the social structure of a rural civilisation was the extreme pull of centripetal forces operating from beyond the village communities owing to the increasing centralisation of the foci of economic and political power.[49]

E.F. Schumacher stated that the industry is the pace-setter of the modern life.[50]

## Type of Machinery Needed

It has to be noted that Gandhi was not totally opposed to machinery but the machinery has to promote the human welfare and subserve the interests of all. He stated,

> Machinery has its place; it has come to stay. But it must not be allowed to displace necessary human labour.[51]

The machines in the modern times are capable of performing the work of more people. When the unemployed persons are more, the use of machines that deprives the people of their employment, adds more to the problem of unemployment. So in a country like India, where the problem of unemployment is growing by leaps and bounds, the choice of the type of machinery should be such that,

---

48. *Young India*, 17.9.1925, p. 321.
49. B.N. Ganguli, *Gandhi's Social Philosophy Perspective and Relevance*, p. 148.
50. E.F. Schumacher, *Small is Beautiful*, p. 18.
51. *Young India*, 5.1.1925, p. 377.

they do not add any further to the existing problem of unemployment. So the type of machinery has to be chosen according to the need and location, to set-up appropriately.[52]

The technology that has to be selected has to be non-exploitative and its purpose has to uplift every human being without encouraging centralism. According to Ramesh K. Diwan the following four conditions must be fulfilled. They are :

1. The operators must have full control of the technology.
2. The technology must not replace the worker.
3. The technology must increase the productivity of the workers, and
4. It must be productive of goods and services that are needed by the worker.[53]

E.F. Schumacher who presented his economic views on Gandhian lines stated that people could show interest in the evolution of small-scale technology which is relatively non-violent technology and a 'technology with a human face', so that people may enjoy while working[54] and make their lives meaningful and purposive.

Gandhi believed that some key industries are necessary but they have to be undertaken by the state for the benefit of the people.

He pointed out:

> The heavy machinery for work of public utility which cannot be undertaken by human labour has its inevitable place, but all that would be aimed by the state and used entirely for the benefit of the people.[55]

In the modern times, the revival of the rural industries is the need of the day as they are non-exploitative. The production has to be

---

52. *Gandhi Marg*, Vol.IV, October 1982, p. 644.
53. *Ibid.*, p. 643.
54. E.F. Schumacher, *Small is Beautiful*, p. 18.
55. *Harijan*, 22.6.1935, p. 146.

undertaken by the masses but not the mass production by the heavy industries. The economic policies have to be laid for the total human welfare but not to stand for the benefit of a few. A distinction has to be maintained between the wants and needs and people have to lead a need based life but not a life based on the multiplicity of their wants. The heavy industries which a few could manage to increase their riches out of their greed has to be replaced by love, service and sacrifice. While the heavy industries could be undertaken by a few which stand for the benefit of a few whereas the rural industries stand for the greatest good of all and their welfare. People who lead want based life cannot think of higher values of life as they go on multiplying their wants and satisfy their pleasures and the need based life which is austere and simple helps to think of higher values of life. So Gandhi stated, "High thinking is inconsistent with complicated material life."[56]

## Meaning and Scope of Rural Development

Since the times immoral, India has been a land of villages (and the same system is being continued). In the Vedic Age, village was the basic unit of administration, and a reference to *Gramani*, i.e., a village leader was made in the ancient *Rigveda*. More than 800 million people in India live in rural areas. Any programme of socio-economic development that bypasses rural people and rural areas is bound to be a failure.[57] Rural Development is the absolute need of the day.

S.C. Jain remarks:

> Rural Development is part of a larger process of development of national society. It is legitimate that it contributes to the overall goals of national development, growth, employment, equity, development of industries and services for self-reliance in defence, environmental conservation and so on.[58]

---

56. *Harijan*, 1.9.1946, p. 285.
57. Katar Singh, *Rural Development Principles, Politics and Management*, p. 17.
58. S.C. Jain, *Rural Development, Institutions and Strategies*, p. xii.

The term rural development is of much importance. It is widely acclaimed in the developed and developing countries of the world. It connotes overall development of rural areas with a view to improve the quality of life of rural people. It is a comprehensive and multi-dimensional concept encompassing the development of agriculture and allied activities such as village and cottage industries and crafts, socio-economic infrastructure, community services and facilities. Above all, it is the utilisation of human resources in rural areas.

While giving the meaning and scope of rural development, Katar Singh pointed out:

> As a phenomenon, it is the result of interactions between various physical, technological, economic, socio-cultural, and institutional factors. As a strategy, it is designed to improve the economic and social well-being of a specific group of people — the rural poor. As a discipline it is multidisciplinary in nature representing an intersection of agricultural, social, behavioural, engineering and management sciences.[59]

Rural development is defined as

> a process of developing and utilising natural and human resources, technologies, infrastructure facilities, institutions and organisations and development policies and programmes to encourage and speed up economic growth in rural areas to provide jobs and to improve the quality of rural life towards self-sustenance.[60]

Apart from the geographic location, culture and historical stage of development of society, three basic elements are stated to be considered which constitute the true meaning of development.

These are as follows:

1. *Life-Sustenance*: People have certain basic needs without which it would be impossible or very difficult to survive.

---

59. Katar Singh, *Rural Development, Principles, Policies and Management*, p. 18.
60. *Ibid.*, pp. 18-19.

These basic necessities include food, clothes, shelter, healthcare and security, when any of these is absent or in critically short supply, we may state that a condition of 'absolute underdevelopment' exists. Provision of these 'life sustaining' requirements to everybody is a basic function of all economies whether they be capitalist, socialist, or mixed. In this sense, we may claim that economic growth (increased availability of basic necessities) is a necessary condition for the improvement of the 'quality of life' which is development.

2. *Self-respect*: Every person and every nation seeks some basic form of self-respect, dignity, or honour. Absence or denial of self-esteem indicates a lack of development.

3. *Freedom*: In this context freedom refers to political or ideological freedom and freedom from social servitude. As long as a society is bound by the servitude of men to nature, ignorance, other men, institutions, and dogmatic beliefs, it cannot claim to have achieved the goal of 'development', servitude in any form reflects a state of under development.[61]

Reduction or elimination of poverty, inequality and unemployment is considered to be an important sign of economic development. Economic development has to be perceived as a multi-dimensional process which involves the recognisation and reorientation of the entire economic and social systems and radical changes in institutional and administrative structures.[62]

The following objectives are absolutely needed for all the societies for their development.

1. To increase the availability and widen the distribution of basic life-sustaining articles such as food, clothes, shelter, health care and security.

2. To raise standards of living, including in addition to higher purchasing power, the provision of more jobs, better

---

61. *Rural Development, Principles, Policies and Management*, pp. 19-20.

62. *Ibid.*, p. 20.

education, and greater attention to cultural and humanistic values.

3. To expand the range of economic and social choice to individuals by freeing them from servitude and dependence.[63]

Although expectations differ from person to person and region to region, the expectations of a marked improvement in material conditions of life is general, throughout the world. People expect to have a better diet, clothes, accommodation, education, a secured life, and freedom from servitude. These expectations have become revolutionary, sweeping over the Third World countries.[64] The economy of developing countries like India cannot possibly fulfil these expectations in the immediate future. There is bound to be unrest arising out of discontentment between the rising expectations and economic reality resulting in disillusionment, demoralisation, agitation and political upheaval. This situation makes rapid agricultural and economic development which is a national imperative.[65]

If the term development is examined, it can be a cause and a consequence of change. Development not only influences but it is also influenced by the change. Change takes place in physical, technological, economic, social, cultural, attitudinal, organisational and political spheres. While some developments may result in some change somewhere sometime, all changes do not lead to the real development. A change may contribute either for good (development) or for bad (retrogression).[66]

Katar Singh states that the development of the peoples necessarily implies rebellion. At an appointed time in history, men decide to act against these conditions which retard their freedom.

> Unless we participate actively in the rebellion against these social structures and economic organisations which

---

63. *Rural Development, Principles, Policies and Management*, p. 21.
64. *Ibid.*
65. *Ibid.*, p. 22.
66. *Ibid.*

> condemn men to poverty, humiliation and degradation, we become irrelevant and become identified with injustice and persecution.[67]

He further says:

> Those who control a man's livelihood control a man. His freedom is illusory and his equal humanity is denied when he depends upon others for the right to work and the right to eat. Equally, a nation is not independent if its economic resources are controlled by another nation. Political independence is meaningless if a nation does not control the means by which its citizens can earn their living.[68]

Some development that occurs may not be sufficient to maintain the socially desirable level of living in the country. There is need to realise that planning is capable of making a positive contribution if it facilitates the achievement of development in a more rapid and efficient way than the natural method for development. It is clear that the development effort cannot be limited to the Government alone but must be equally shared by the private, cooperative, corporate and other non-governmental organisations and agencies. Above all the effort has to be shared by the people themselves. Planning by the Government should also coincide with the efforts of the individuals and non-governmental organisations.[69]

> A plan is a blue print for action — it points out a precise way to reach a pre-determined goal or a set of goals within a pre-determined period of time with the means that are available with the planner and under the prevailing circumstances, planning is a process of formulating a plan.[70]

Rural Development should be looked upon as a joint venture of public, corporate, cooperative and private sectors. A systematic approach should be followed to bring about all round and balanced

---

67. *Rural Development, Principles, Policies and Management*, p. 23.
68. *Ibid.*
69. *Ibid.*, p. 29.
70. *Ibid.*, p. 265.

development of the economy. Since the Government alone cannot effectively tackle all the problems of rural development, voluntary agencies, cooperatives, corporations and entrepreneurs can all play an important role in the process of development. Defining the roles of other agencies, and to coordinate and if necessary to regulate their activities and provision of infrastructure facilities and services which cannot be provided by other agencies, constitute the role of the Government. The Government should help the rural poor in an organised manner within the frame-work of the institution that is capable enough to give access to the nation's economic and political systems.[71]

## Mahatma Gandhi and Rural Development

To such of those nations which are highly urbanised and which believe that urbanisation is the sign of progress, the theme of rural development may appear irrelevant. But same is not the case with Gandhi. The experiments conducted by him with the establishment of self-reliant *ashrams* in South Africa and India convinced him of the fact that the villages can become the nurseries for rearing a new humanity on self-reliant, non-exploitative, truthful and healthy living lines. Nowhere did Gandhi see any need to discard the foundation of village life to build up an urban euphoria. He was more particular of retaining the base.[72] He declared that "if the villages perish, India will perish too".[73]

Gandhi strove hard to create a society based on equality in the social, economic and religious spheres. He felt that this ideal cannot be realised in a society based on materialism. He upheld the need based life but not the life based on the multiplicity of wants. Gandhi pointed out that the human civilisation and their culture depend not upon multiplying our wants, self-indulgence, but upon the restriction of their wants — self-denial. It is an attempt to substitute money values for life values.[74]

71. *Rural Development, Principles, Policies and Management*, pp. 314-15.
72. S.C. Jain, *Rural Development Institutions and Strategies*, p. 127.
73. *Harijan*, 29.8.1936, p. 226.
74. Lewis Mumford, *Techniques and Civilization*, p. 23.

> People were so pre-occupied with their daily cares and the pursuit of material welfare that they never gave thought to the dangers threatening humanity. It is an oppressive, breath-taking age in which we live filled with haste, insecurity and discord.[75]

Economic progress holds good to the extent of its sufficiency and beyond that, it is held to be evil, destructive and uneconomic, says E.F. Schumacher. Man has to do the job that is something real, purposive, useful and creative at the same time for himself and to his industry. When the owner or the worker is not identified morally, with the source of income, the principle of continuity does not apply for "no institution can survive in a moral vaccuum".[76]

To be compatible with the decentralised, village-based economy, industry has to be small-scale and traditional, employing a non-violent, non-alienating technology that would allow labourers to acquire a maximum of human dignity and moral substance.[77]

> The goal of Gandhian basic development strategy is to increase the proportion of labour-intensive activities in the investment mix in order to reduce urban unemployment and rural under-employment. Any improvement in the job market hinges on the creation of new opportunities for employment and self-employment exceeding the growth of the labour force.[78]

Gandhi realised that social life will be dominated by violence if social aim is predominated by economic motive.[79] He stood against the modern industrialisation and aimed at economic regeneration of India in a decentralised pattern. He held that

> The revival of the village is possible only when it is no more

75. Adenaur, *Dr. Statesman*, 21.12.1961.
76. Tannebaun, *The Philosophy of Labour*, p. 106.
77. Mark A. Lutz & Kenneth Lux, *Humanistic Economics — The New Challenge*, p. 305.
78. *Ibid.*, p. 305.
79. J.S. Mathur (ed.), *Economic Thought of Mahatma Gandhi, Introduction*, p. xxxv.

> exploited. Industrialisation on a mass scale will necessarily lead to the passive or active exploitation of the villages as the problem of competition and marketing comes in.[80]

He wanted the villages to be free from the influence of industrialisation. He did not believe in the idea that industrialisation is indispensable. He was of the opinion that India could lead an ennobled life by developing cottage industries to have a peaceful life in the world. His challenge of industrialisation is marked by an encounter between the factory civilisation and handicraft civilisation.

Gandhi pointed out that the importation of dried milk for village children might be good enough from a humanitarian point of view, but it would make a monstrous inroad into the economic freedom of the village.[81] The revival of rural industries, according to him, is possible in the absence of exploitation, for industrialisation on a mass scale leads to exploitation and competition to market their finished goods. So there is need to make the village self-contained which should be able to manufacture its finished goods for the use of the people. If this tendency is maintained, there would be no problem and objection for the villagers to use even the up to date machinery that they could make and afford to use, but they should not be used as a means to exploit others.

> If I can convert the country to my point of view, the social order of the future will be based predominantly on the Charkha and all that implies. It will include everything that promotes the well-being of the villagers.[82]

## Revival of Rural Industries

The expansion of rural industries and services should be the appropriate strategy for the developing countries. This would diversify as the rural economy and contribute for the further development of agriculture. Providing inputs to agriculture and

80. *Harijan*, 29.8.1936, p. 226.
81. *Ibid.*, 21.3.1936, p. 43.
82. *Ibid.*, 27.1.1940, p. 428.

process large varieties of agricultural produce. Rural industries create new opportunities for gainful employment, particularly to the under-employed during the lean periods in the absence of agricultural operations.[83]

Emphasising the significance and the role of rural industries, the United Nations Committee for Development and Planning affirmed:

> Industrialisation should be viewed primarily as a means of improving the condition of work and living standards of poverty-stricken masses the world over, and not merely as a means of producing a wider variety of production by application of modern technology. If this is not kept in mind, efforts to industrialise many leave the lives of the majority of the people untouched.[84]

Gandhi seeks to revive such village industries which are capable of being revived. He held that the revival of the village is possible only when it is no more exploited. The establishment of village industries to solve the problem of growing unemployment is relevant to the modern world especially to India.

> Industrialisation on a mass scale will necessarily lead to passive or active exploitation of the villagers as the problems of competition and marketing come in. Therefore, we have to concentrate on the village being self-contained, manufacturing mainly for use.[85]

Gandhi held that the real planning of the nation consists in the best utilisation of the whole manpower and the distribution of the raw products of the country in her numerous villages instead of sending them outside and rebuying finished articles at fabulous prices.[86]

---

83. R.P. Misra, *Rural Industrialization in the Third World Countries*, pp. 142-3.
84. *United Nations Publications*, p. 8.
85. *Harijan*, 28.9.1946, p. 226.
86. *Ibid.*, 23.3.1947, p. 79.

## The Significance of Khadi as a Village Industry

Gandhi gave utmost importance to *khadi* as a village industry in the programme of the economic building and national reconstruction. His wide coverage of the Indian villages and the personal contact he established with the vast masses who are neglected, living below the poverty line with abject poverty scattered all over the nation made him realise the significance of the revival of the village industries. He felt that this was the only way open for the revival of the entire economic, social and cultural life in the villages and also to serve the suffering millions in the impoverished state. The growing problem of unemployment could be solved by establishing the small-scale industries. Among the major economic problems confronting the Indian nation in particular and the world in general, the problem of unemployment takes precedence over the other problems like a canker corroding the entire gamut of the economy.

> This introduction of village industries as the media of instruction will have far-reaching educational, cultural and economic consequences. It will dispel the distaste and the contempt for physical labour — an evil which has penetrated deep into the present system of education.[87]

Gandhi wanted to remove the lethargy and shake off the inertia and also from the feeling of helplessness to make the people self-sufficient through hand spinning. He expected them to learn to rely on themselves as mills could not achieve this, for they employ only a small fraction of the people. In the mill production the employees are not self-dependent for they are dependent on the employer for wages, raw materials and machinery. *Khadi* alone teaches the village population to depend on their own efforts to improve themselves to be self-dependent. Therefore, *khadi* is not merely of economic importance but is also of a cultural value. It is an infusion of new life into the individual to make him self-dependent and resourceful. Hand spinning when universalised, Gandhi felt, would teach the population about the dignity of labour. The degenerated

---

87. Vithaldas Kothari (ed.), *Why Khadi and Village Industries?*, p. 5.

88. M.K. Gandhi, *Khadi, Why and How?*, Preface, pp. iii-iv.

form of caste system was fostered by the aristocratic tradition and there also existed a gulf between the rich and the poor. If hand spinning was carried on by all, the gulf would be bridged and in its place a bond of unity would be established between the masses, all classes, all castes and creeds. This was the social value that Gandhi found in hand spinning. Gandhi realised — that industrialism with its need for raw materials and markets, led to imperialism, international strife and war. At the same time *khadi* is an attempt to revive the economy which is self-sufficient restricting primarily to the needs of the village. All these reasons which are economic, cultural, social and political that led Gandhi to establish the Khadi movement. Gandhi laid the foundations of a non-violent economic and social order to bring about peace and happiness to the entire mankind.[88]

Gandhi formulated the following proposition to fully show that *khadi* must hold the field for any length of time that people could think of:

> Khadi is the only true economic proposition in terms of the millions of villagers until such time if ever, when a better system of supplying work and adequate wages for every able bodied person above the age of sixteen, male or female is found for his field, cottage or even factory in everyone of the villages in India; or till sufficient cities are built up to displace the villages so as to give the villagers the necessary comforts and amenities that a well regulated life demands and is entitled to.[89]

Gandhi was convinced that the revival of hand spinning and hand weaving would make the largest contribution to the economic and the moral regeneration of the country. He felt the need of a simple industry to the millions to supplement agriculture. In the past spinning was the cottage industry. If millions are to be saved from starvation, they must be able to reintroduce spinning in their homes and every village must repossess its own weavers.[90] B.N. Ganguli says,

---

89. M.K. Gandhi, *Khadi, Why and How?*, Preface.

90. *Young India*, 21.7.1920, p. 4.

> The real reason why Gandhi regarded the spinning-wheel and the handloom as a counter-prise against modern machinery was that he considered the former as the means to mass employment where other means did not exist. "Unemployment and idleness of millions", Gandhi argued, "must lead to bloody strife. Khadi is the only alternative to this and not the so-called socialism which presupposes industrialism." Modernisation, industrialisation and mass production that the socialists wanted were at best slow processes. They were not calculated to remove mass poverty and unemployment; rather they tended to create pockets of prosperity that merely accentuated the surrounding poverty and privation. Gandhi did not think that this was socialism. Therefore, he said that "the socialism that India can assimilate is the socialism of the spinning-wheel".[91]

Gandhi envisaged several advantages and uses of the spinning wheel:

1. It supplies the readiest occupation to those who have leisure and are in want of a few coppers.
2. It is known to the thousands.
3. It is easily learnt.
4. It requires practically no outlay of capital.
5. The wheel can be easily and cheaply made. Most of us do not yet know that spinning can be done even with a piece of tile and splinter.
6. The people have no repugnance to it.
7. It affords immediate relief in times of famine and scarcity.
8. It alone can stop the drain of wealth which goes outside India in the purchase of foreign cloth.
9. It automatically distributes the millions thus saved among the deserving poor.

---

91. B.N. Ganguli, *Gandhi's Social Philosophy Perspective and Relevance*, p. 311.

10. Even the smallest success means so much immediate gain to the people.

11. It is the most potent instrument of securing cooperation among the people.[92]

The *charkha* (spinning-wheel) serves the poor and needy and, in addition, it also restores the villages to their rightful place, abolishing the distinction between the high and the low.[93] The spinning wheel stands as a symbol of commercial peace but not of commercial war.[94] Gandhi held that mills cannot grow up like mushrooms as *charkha* can and the failure of the *charkha* has not been felt by anybody.

Highlighting the significance, the role and hope of the spinning-wheel of the masses,

Gandhi pointed out:

> The spinning-wheel represents to me the hope of the masses. The masses last their freedom such as it was, with the loss of the Charkha. The Charkha supplemented the agriculture of the villages and gave it dignity. It was the friend and solace of the widow. It kept the villagers from idleness. For the Charkha included till the anterior and posterior industries — ginning, carding, warping, sizing, dyeing and weaving. These in their turn kept the village carpenter and the blacksmith busy. The Charkha enabled the seven hundred thousand villages to become self-contained. With the exist of the Charkha went the other village industries, such as the oil press. Nothing took the place of these industries. Therefore, the villages were drained of their varied occupations and their creative talent and what little wealth these brought them.[95]

While organising the *khadi* production, the science of *khadi* in

---

92. *Young India*, 21.8.1924, p. 277.
93. *Harijan*, 13.4.1940, p. 85.
94. *Young India*, 8.12.1921, p. 406.
95. *Harijan*, 13.4.1940, p. 85.

some respect works on lines diametrically opposite to that of ordinary business. Gandhi referred to Adam Smith, the great economist and the writer of the outstanding book *The Wealth of Nations* in which he mentioned about certain principles governing the economic phenomena. Adam Smith went on describing certain other things which constitute the 'disturbing factor' preventing the economic laws from having a free play. Chief among those disturbing factors is found to be the human element. On the contrary the entire gamut of *khadi* economics rests on the human element. Adam Smith's pure economic motive is human selfishness constitutes the disturbing factor which needs to be overcome.[96] Gandhi says,

> Khadi to me is the symbol of unity of Indian humanity, of its economic freedom and equality and therefore, ultimately in the poetic expression of Jawaharlal Nehru, 'the livery of Indian freedom'.

Moreover,

> Khadi mentality means decentralisation of the production and distribution of the necessaries of life. Therefore, the formula so far evolved is, every village to produce all its necessaries and a certain percentage in addition for the requirements of the cities.[97]

Today machine industries being run with electricity have gradually been usurped by the cottage industries which produce the basic products needed for daily life. This resulted in the large-scale unemployment. The consumers are habituated to prefer the machine made goods to hand-made goods. This situation has forced the exploited unemployed labour to offer their goods at lower prices. This has evolved into a system of politics and economics sustained by such exploitation of weaker masses. This tendency paved the way for the further accentuation of the unemployment position and also gave rise to numerous other sources of exploitation.[98] People

---

96. *Harijan*, 21.9.1934, p. 253.
97. M.K. Gandhi, *Constructive Programme*, p. 12.
98. Vithaldas Kothari (ed.), *Why Khadi and Village Industries?*, pp. 6-7.

need to have enough job opportunities so that they may be able to earn their daily bread to be free from hunger and want and remain self-sufficient.

*Khadi* and village industries assume great importance in Indian nation.

> Khadi and village industries are and ought to be in the forefront of this new order. They are the true national industries of India. Only by reviving and promoting these industries shall we be able to bring true economic independence to the millions of our countrymen and build a joint national family based on peace, harmony and love.[99]

## Equal Distribution of Wealth

There has been considerable progress in the economic fields which remains as a valuable asset. Yet the problems and liabilities have become far more serious and menacing. In order to promote the interests and lust for power of a few individuals, the polity and some institutions have been destroyed. The economy is badly affected, passing through a prolonged phase of stagnation and inflation. The moral fabric of the society is reduced to pieces.[100]

As John Ruskin pointed out:

> In equalities of wealth, unjustly established, have assuredly injured the nation in which they exist during their establishment, and unjustly directed, injure it yet more during their existence. But inequalities of wealth, justly established, benefit the nation in the course of their establishment, and nobly used, aid it, yet more by their existence.[101]

Gandhi reduced all religions to morality as their common denominator and made morals as a determining factor. So economy in the Gandhian context cannot be stated without referring to the

99. Vithaldas Kothari (ed.), *Why Khadi and Village Industries?*, p. 8.
100. J.D. Sethi: *Gandhi Today*, Forward, p. viii.
101. John Ruskin, *Unto This Last*, pp. 34-5.

concept of equality. There can be no fundamental rights without observing fundamental duties.[102]

By the implication 'equal distribution' Gandhi meant that each man shall have the supply of the basic needs and nothing more else. He says,

> Everyone must have a balanced diet, a decent house to live in, facilities for the education of his children and adequate medical relief.[103]

Vasant Sathe pointed out:

> Gandhian economics, rightly understood, therefore, tries to seek a synthesis and what can be described as the middle path in the modes of economic production and distributive activity. If considered in the correct context and perspective, the Gandhian method of decentralised means of production as well as distribution would automatically prevent the growth of a centralised mode of ownership, control of the means of production as well as the resulting capital formation.[104]

Gandhi advocated the idea of decentralisation of economic activity at the village level with a view to achieving the welfare of especially those who live there. In the view of Gandhi, decentralisation does not mean division of economic activities including industries. The following are the basic ingredients:

(a) Village as the most desirable unit of planning.

(b) Self-reliance of the villages for their basic necessaries like food, shelter, clothing, education and also justice in case of local disputes, law and order within the village.

(c) Village and cottage industries including small-scale industries to provide employment for those who do not get absorbed in agricultural activity.

---

102. J.D. Sethi: *Gandhi Today*, Forward, p. 32.

103. *Young India*, 13.10.1921, p. 325.

104. *Kurukshetra*, October 1994, Annual Number, p. 8.

(d) Cooperation among the villagers in all matters relating to their everyday social, economic and political life.[105]

## Rural Development

E.F. Schumacher in his book *Small is Beautiful* stated that the role and significance of the individual is undermined in the economics of today, and it is held to be the main problem. He prescribes new alternatives to the existing economic situation to have a new vision of the future which is promising and progressive.

Three main targets in the economic plane are the promotion of equitable and equal distribution of economic resources, provision of wider employment opportunities, and to secure the best use of capital and labour. Every village has to be self-sufficient and has to grow its own food and produce its own clothing. Several measures have to be taken up in the field of agricultural relations, land reform and cooperative farming. Much importance has been attached to the decentralised small villages and cottage industries.[106]

> Gandhi undertook the first step of relieving the peasants from the burden of revenue by suggesting improvements in terms of settlement and by assigning new roles to the intermediaries. Economic equality and self-sufficiency were to be the ultimate result of the economic pursuits through the application of the principles of trusteeship, cooperation and reintroduction of handicrafts like spinning and weaving.[107]

Gandhi held that the message of spinning wheel has to be viewed for leading a simple life and render service to the mankind. It helps to keep the mankind at the proper pace from the state of exclusiveness and exploitation without reducing him to a mere cog in the machine.

> . . . the message of spinning wheel is much wider than its circumference. Its message is one of simplicity, service of

105. G. Thimmaiah (ed.), *Studies in Rural Development*, p. 202.
106. Savita, *Gandhi and Social Policy in India*, pp. 38-9.
107. *Ibid.*, p. 42.

> mankind, living so as not to hurt others, creating an undissoluble bond between the rich and the poor, capital and labour, the prince and the peasant. The larger message is naturally for all . . . it is not an attempt to spiritualise the machinery — because that seems to me an impossible task — but to introduce, if it is at all possible, a human or humane spirit among the men behind the machinery. . . . The movement of the spinning wheel is an organised attempt to displace machinery from the state of exclusiveness and exploitation and to place it in its proper state.[108]

## Cooperative Farming in the Villages

There are two schools of thought about cities and villages. One wants to divide the world into villages and other into cities, but the nature of villages and cities are entirely different. While one depends on machinery and industrialisation, the other depends on handicrafts. Gandhi preferred the latter.

Gandhi had the belief which is based on his firm conviction that agriculture provides the only unfailing and perennial support to the people of this country. He was of the opinion that improvements could be brought about to enable the cultivator to make some income for himself from the land. He suggested to improve the condition of the people through rehabilitation of agriculture, cattle-breeding and other village industries.[109] B.N. Ganguli says,

> Gandhi thought that if the Indian economy as well as the Indian polity, if it has to be restructured from the bottom outwards (rather than upwards in a pyramidal structure) it would be necessary to refashion the village communities as an "ideal type and readapt them to the modern methods of 'co-operative' operation.[110]

Gandhi firmly believed that people will not derive the full benefits

108. *Young India*, 1927, p. 321.

109. M.K. Gandhi, *Khadi Why and How?*, 1959, p. 181.

110. B.N. Ganguli, *Gandhi's Social Philosophy Perspective and Relevance*, p. 147.

of agriculture until they take up cooperative farming as it is not possible for an individual farmer to look after the welfare of his cattle properly in a scientific manner. Apart from other causes, lack of collective effort has been a principal cause of the deterioration of the cattle. "The world today is moving towards the ideal of collective or cooperative effort in every department of life", says Gandhi. He held that even the individual could safeguard his independence through cooperation while the individual effort in the cattle farming has led to selfishness and inhumanity, the collective effort could abate both the evils.[111] Gandhi elaborates his notion of cooperation in these following words:

> My notion of cooperation is that the land would be held in cooperation by the owners and tilled and cultivated also in cooperation. This would cause a saving of labour, capital, tools, etc. The owners would work in cooperation and own capital, tools, animals, seeds, etc., in cooperation. Cooperative farming of my conception would change the face of the land and banish poverty and idleness from their midst. All this is only possible if people become friends of one another and as one family. When that happy event takes place there would be no ugly sore in the form of a communal problem.[112]

It is only when a new society based on cooperation through the persuasive power of non-violence, non-cooperation and love are built, and the foundation of individuality could be preserved. The real and abiding progress could be assured to the whole world.

## Village Life

Gandhi stated that the villagers should develop a high degree of skill so that articles prepared by them could command ready market outside. When the villages are sufficiently developed, there will be no dearth in them of men with a high degree of skill and artistic talent. If the present situation is taken into consideration, the villages are dung heaps and if properly designed for the progress,

111. M.K. Gandhi, *Village Swaraj*, pp. 104-7.

112. *Harijan*, 9.3.1947, p. 59.

they will be like tiny gardens of Eden where highly intelligent live, whom no one could deceive or exploit. There is need to reconstruct the villages on these lines right now on permanent basis.[113]

In the villages some flour mills, rice mills, etc., have displaced the village labour, impoverishing the villagers, being encircled by the moneyed men. Gandhi stated that if this process continues for a longer time, the villages would be destroyed without any further effort.[114] The problem confronting the villages is how to find work for the millions of the villages. These people are fast losing interest to work even to think or live. They are leading a living death. This was the condition of the villagers during 1936 when Gandhi was well acquainted with villagers and their problems. The Government has to find self-employment schemes with financial assistance and check for the proper utilisation of the funds for these deserving poor and needy villagers.

## A Balance between the Rural and Urban Life

When people living in the rural areas are unemployed or underemployed and there is no hope for employment in the rural areas, they migrate into big cities. The rural unemployment is due to the population explosion also. Thereby rural unemployment becomes urban unemployment. As long as the process of development is confined mainly to the big cities where it is easy to establish new industries, the competition from these industries will further disrupt and destroy, the new agricultural production in the rest of the country, causing additional unemployment outside and further accelerating the migration of destitute people into cities which cannot absorb them. So it is necessary to make effort to bypass the big cities to be directly concerned with the creation of an agro-industrial structure in the rural and small town areas as an important part of the development. For a poor man it is better to be even poorly paid than to remain idle.[115]

---

113. *Harijan*, 10.11.1946, p. 394.
114. *Ibid.*, 20.6.1936, p. 145.
115. E.F. Schumacher. *Small is Beautiful*, p. 161.

Gandhi pointed that:

> It is only when the cities realise the duty of making an adequate return to the villages for the strength and sustenance which they derive from them, instead of selfishly exploiting them, that a healthy and moral relationship between the two will spring up. And if the city children are to play their part in this great and noble work of social reconstruction, the vocations through which they are to receive their education ought to be directly related to the requirements of the villages.[116]

The restoration of proper balance between city and rural life is perhaps the greatest task in front of the modern man. It is not merely a matter of raising agricultural yields to avoid world hunger. Unless the whole level of rural development is raised, no possible answer could be found to the evils of mass unemployment and mass migration into cities. This requires the development of an agro-industrial culture to facilitate variety of occupations.

Gandhi stated that:

> This cry of 'back to the village' some critics say, is putting back to the hands of the clock of progress. But it is really so? Is it going back to the village or rendering back to it what belongs to it? I am not asking the city-dwellers to go to and live in the villages. But I am asking them to render unto the villagers what is due to them. Is there any single raw material that the city-dwellers can obtain except from the villager? If they cannot, why not teach him to work on it himself, as he used to before and as he would do now but for our exploiting inroads?[117]

Gandhi wanted the transformation of society by shifting the centre of gravity to the villages till everyone was employed and become self-sufficient. Gandhi did not foresee any possibility of full employment in urban areas for the rural masses who migrate to the cities. He had the knowledge of urban problems such as the problem

116. *Harijan*, 9.10.1937, p. 293.

117. *Ibid.*, 7.12.1934, p. 340.

of unemployment the menace of slums, etc. If the rural population was not in full employment, there will be a threat. Changes within the rural areas play a decisive role and for starting any social activity village is the best place.[118] Gandhi says,

> I would say that if the village perishes, India will perish too. It will be no more India. Her own mission in the world will get lost. The revival of the village life is possible only when it is no more exploited.[119]

The great importance that Gandhi attached to the emulation of the rural character and the need for the regeneration of rural life as stressed by him could be noticed. The approach of Gandhi basing on decentralisation of economic activity at the village level is to achieve the welfare of those who live there. He stated that the society based on non-violence can only consist of groups settled in villages in which voluntary cooperation is the condition of dignified and peaceful existance.[120] Gandhi seeks to revive villages which are no more exploited.

> You cannot build non-violence on a factory civilisation, but it can be built on self-contained villages.... Rural economy as I have conceived it eschews exploitation altogether and exploitation is the essence of violence. You have, therefore, to be rural-minded before you can be non-violent and to be rural-minded you have to have faith in the spinning-wheel.[121]

Gandhi remarked that industrialisation has been so planned as to destroy the village crafts. So Gandhi specifically stated that he was not against machinery or industrialisation but against the acquisitive spirit of modern industries. Significantly enough, Gandhi made a distinction between the role of machinery of the European civilisation which undermined and dominated Indian civilisation and the role of machinery which proved itself to be useful. While the

---

118. J.D. Sethi, *Gandhi Today*, p. 108.
119. *Harijan*, 29.8.1936, p. 226.
120. *Ibid.*, 13.1.1940, pp. 410-11.
121. *Ibid.*, 4.11.1939, p. 331.

former was not acceptable, the latter has to fulfil certain conditions to be acceptable.

Gandhi referred to the urban industrial culture which had been corroding the simplicity of village life. He wanted to reduce the urban and village disparities. On several occasions Gandhi clarified about his concept of village self-sufficiency and stated that he did not advocate the isolation of villages but stood against the demoralising and dangerous effects of urban cultures dominating the villages. The optimum utilisation of local resources cannot take place in the countries which are densely populated when they have been implanted with the sophisticated technologies which do not respond to the local factors.

Gandhi visualised a society wherein man and machine together would promote the basic human values on the basis of which he could construct a new society. Although Gandhi was in the habit of answering every question, he was diffident to answer about the future of the nation except in the context of value system on which it would be based.

> In the state of the future, it will subserve the villages and their crafts. I do not share the socialist belief that centralisation of the necessaries of life will conduce to the common welfare when the centralise industries are planned and owned by the state. The socialistic conception of the West was born in an environment reeking with violence. The motive lying behind the Western type and the Eastern is the same — the greater welfare of the whole society and the abolition of the hideous inequalities resulting in the existence of millions of have-nots and a handful of have's. I believe that this end can be achieved only when non-violence is accepted by the best minds of the world as the basis on which a just social order is to be constructed.[122]

## Swadeshi

*Swadeshi* is a spirit of restricting the use and service of surroundings

---

122. *Harijan*, 27.1.1940, p. 428.

at the exclusion of the remote.[123] Gandhi held that a votary of *swadeshi* would dedicate himself to the service of his immediate neighbours as his first duty involving the exclusion or even sacrifice of the interests of the rest which would be rather apparent. Gandhi held that by pure service of one's neighbours, it could never result in disservice to those who are far away. When a person on the other hand runs to the ends of the earth to offer his service being lured by the 'distant scene' fails in his duty towards his neighbours.[124]

B.N. Ganguli says,

> From the economic angle Swadeshi meant economic self-reliance, economic independence, reconstruction of the rural economy, laying the foundation of an Indian economy on the basis of a new kind of consumers, preferences, going back to the masses of the rural population and organising them to fight the evils of poverty and foreign oppression.[125]

*Swadeshi* is the most significant concept. A modern name for this would be 'self-reliance' or economic independence. It is a positive force to fight neo-colonialism which has an increasing grip over the Indian economy and society.

> For Gandhi, politics and political power were value oriented, both in personal life and group action. To him distribution of political power was as important as its accumulation. His whole theory of economic decentralisation was designed to bring about a proper distribution of political power. He was not against state power but insisted on much greater dedication, personal austerity and exemplary behaviour on the part of those who wielded state power. For example, in respect of his trusteeship concept, when it was pointed out that the trustees may not behave like good trustees, he answered by saying that the take over by the state was the next logical step.[126]

---

123. G.A. Natesan, *Speeches and Writings of Mahatma Gandhi*, p. 336.
124. M.K. Gandhi, *From Yeravda Mandir,* p. 62.
125. B.N. Ganguli, *Gandhi's Social Philosophy Perspective and Relevance*, p. 281.
126. J.D. Sethi, *Gandhi Today*, p. 16.

According to Gandhi *swadeshi* meant three things. First *swadeshi* is the self-reliance of the basic units of society, the village or other natural communities wherein production is for use up to a point but not for exchange. Production for exchange comes in the next circle. The contact between one village and the other and also between villages and cities is established through the production for exchange; with the limits of production for use. The production and use aspect of *swadeshi* has been designed against the domination of villages by cities.

Gandhi held that people must boycott the foreign yarn for the sake of the starving masses living in enforced idleness to enable them to spin and weave in their cottage for their living. Gandhi was afraid that several indigenous (*swadeshi*) commodities in the market are in the danger of disappearance due to lack of patronage. Further the law of country's progress demands its inhabitants to give preference for the products locally made.[127]

Gandhi says,

> My nationalism is as broad as Swadeshi. I want India's rise so that the whole world may benefit. I do not want India to rise on the ruin of other nations. If, therefore, India was strong and able, India would send out to the world her treasures of art and health-giving spices, but would refuse to send out opium or intoxicating liquors although the traffic may bring much material benefit to India.[128]

To avoid the possible exploitation either by India or of India, *swadeshi* has to be extended to India and other nations. The concept of *swadeshi* is of more significance to the modern world. It is disastrous for one-half of the world should live in gross poverty and the other in gross affluence basing on the artificial stimulation of demands. The selected few who are after the power in search of economic independence finally ended in setting the models of economic dependence.[129]

---

127. *The Collected Works of Mahatma Gandhi*, XL Feb-March, 1929, p. 435.
128. *Young India*, 8.1.1925, p. 18.
129. J.D. Sethi, *Gandhi Today*, pp. 38-9.

> A true votary of *swadeshi* will never harbour ill-will towards the foreigner; he will not be actuated by antagonism towards anybody on earth. Swadeshism is not a cult of hatred. It is a doctrine of selfless service that has its roots in the purest ahimsa, i.e., love.[130]

The self-reliance and self-sufficiency in *swadeshi* is not in isolation. *Swadeshi* is not to be confused with the narrow sense of protecting small-scale indigenous industries but to be used in a much broader sense. This relates to the most important question viz., the transfer of technology. The transfer of technology could be transfer between the nations and transfer within a nation.[131]

Gandhi says,

> Swadeshi is a universal law. A man's first duty is to his neighbour. This does not imply hatred for the foreigner or partiality for the fellow-countrymen. Our capacity for service has obvious limits. We can serve even our neighbour with some difficulty. If every one of us duly performed his duty to his neighbour, no one in the world who needed assistance would be left unattended. Therefore one who serves his neighbour serves all the world. As a matter of fact there is in Swadeshi no room for distinction between one's own and other people. To serve between ones own and other people. To serve one's neighbour is to serve the world. Indeed it is the only way open to us of serving the world.[132]

Through *Swadeshi*, Gandhi warned the leaders of the nations against the imperialist exploitation of one nation by another in their trade and other links of economic importance which necessitate the maintenance of military to protect their economic interests.[133] *Swadeshi* movement was intended to organise the rural masses into economically and socially self-dependent. But is not a boycott movement to be undertaken by way of revenge.

130. M.K. Gandhi, *From Yeravda Mandir*, p. 66.
131. J.D. Sethi, *Gandhi Today*, p. 129.
132. V.G. Desai (tr.), *Ashram Observances it Action*, 1959, pp. 67-8.
133. J.D. Sethi, *Gandhi Today*, p. 130.

Schumacher pointed out that people must understand the human problem and explore the possibility to evolve a new lifestyle following the new methods of production and new patterns of consumption. It is a lifestyle designed for permanence. Schumacher stated that in agriculture and horticulture people could interest themselves in the perfection of production methods which are biologically sound, increase the soil fertility and produce health, beauty and permanence. Productivity then would take care of itself. In the industry people could take interest in the evolution of small-scale industry. It is relatively non-violent technology and 'technology with a human face' to enable people to enjoy themselves while working rather than to work merely for their salary. Industry is stated to be the pacesetter of modern life. People can enter into partnership with management and even forms of common ownership.[134]

Man's cultivation and expansion of needs is the anti-thesis of wisdom, freedom and peace. Every increase of needs tends to increase the dependence of the individuals on outside forces over which he cannot have control and results in the increase of existential fear. It is only by reduction of needs that the individual can promote a genuine reduction of these tensions which are stated to be the ultimate causes of strife and war.

The economics which promotes permanence implies a profound reorientation of science and technology and to incorporate wisdom into their very structure. The scientific and technological solutions poison the environment or degrade the social structure and man himself.

What the people really requires from the scientists and technologists is new methods and equipment which are as follows:

- cheap enough so that they are accessible virtually to everyone.
- suitable for small-scale application.
- compatible with man's need for creativity

The three characteristics are stated to be non-violent. A

134. E.F. Schumacher, *Small is Beautiful*. p. 18.

relationship of man to nature guarantees permanence. If these three are neglected, things are bound to go wrong.[135]

The machines which are cheap and within the reach of everyone need to be developed. This means that their cost must commensurate with the level of incomes in the society. If the cost of the proposed machines tends to be significantly higher, the society is more likely to enter into serious problems such as undue concentration of wealth and power in the hands of a privileged few with an increasing problem of 'drop outs' standing on the way for the integration of society constitute an every growing threat, structural unemployment, mal-distribution of the population due to excessive urbanisation and general frustration and alienation with soaring crime rates, and so forth.[136]

Though the small-scale industries are numerous, they are less likely to be harmful to the natural environment rather than the large-scale ones. The greatest danger arises from the heavy industries and their ruthless application on a vast scale such as the application of nuclear energy.[137]

> Man's true life does not consist in the business of filling his belly and clothing his body, but in art and thought and love, in the creation and contemplation of beauty and in the scientific understanding of the world. If the world is to be regenerated, it is in these things, not only in material goods, that all must be enabled to participate.[138]

Gandhi was aware of the fact that industrialisation was inevitable. But he evolved a mechanistic conception of the society. He thoroughly studied, experienced and analysed the various forces, evils, drawbacks of the industrialised modern society in comparison to the society of the pre-industrial times. He examined the society to find out whether it could adjust morally or not and investigated how far could the industrialisation promote the individual freedom and

---

135. *Small is Beautiful*, pp. 29-30.
136. *Ibid.*, p. 31.
137. *Ibid.*
138. Bertrand Russell, *The Prospects of Industrial Civilization*, p. 50.

happiness. The economic philosophy that hurts the moral well-being of an individual, a society or a nation could be termed as immoral and sinful. He measured the progress of the society or nation in terms of morality and human welfare. So Gandhi aimed at the rural industries and the village development to uplift the people who are in the impoverished state for their well-being and total welfare.

# 5

# Gandhian Approach to the Contemporary Political Issues

## The Meaning and Scope of Political Philosophy

THOUGH the terms political theory and political philosophy are used interchangeably, there has been a recognisable and significant difference between these two as far as the theoretical work of the political scientists and political philosophers are concerned. Ofcourse, there is a discernible distinction between what is social and political. These two terms, viz., political theory and political philosophy in the wider sense are inclusive of the social studies, embracing everything of the activities of man in relation to society.[1]

Similarly Gandhi also did not make any distinction and made no wall of separation between social, economic, religious and political, but gave a concrete expression in a comprehensive manner. For him the human life is a synthetic whole which cannot be divided into watertight compartments, viz., social, economic, religious, moral, etc. To Gandhi all facts of human endeavour are interconnected.[2]

Gandhi also felt that harmonious balance has to be maintained

---

1. D.D. Raphael, *Problems of Political Philosophy*, p. 1.
2. *Hirijan*, 30.3.1947, p. 85.

   Cf. While challenging the notion of 'Political Power' is meant to assert the primary of the social over the political.

   Raghavan Iyer, *The Moral and Political Thought of Mahatma Gandhi*, p. 56.

among the moral, social economic and political spheres to avoid the possible domination of one sphere over the other and destroy its identity with the other.[3]

> Some of the time honoured subjects of political philosophy, such as the nature of the state, sovereignty and the grounds of political obligation, clearly belongs to the sphere of the political, but others, such as authority, liberty, equality and justice, have a wider application and are best considered as belonging to the sphere of the social in the sense of the term which includes the political.[4]

Generally it has been said that politics deals with the pursuit and capture of power. The political theory laid down by Gandhi challenges the substantial presuppositions of the main stream of political theory.

Commenting on the outstanding contribution of Gandhi to the political thought, Dr. Joan V. Bondurant pointed out:

> Gandhi did not proceed from any specific political ideology and yet the significance for political theory of his action on the practical field of politics, is inestimable. The contribution has been not alone to the development of a social and political method. It extends further into the realm of political thought and challenges the substantial presuppositions of the mainstream of political theory.[5]

It is in this context that the challenge of Gandhi to the modern political thought bears significance and relevance. The approach he made in the domain of politics is stated to be moral and this gains utmost significance in the modern age of power politics. He conceived a broader notion of politics and stood against any dichotomy between the public and the private.

---

3. *Gandhi Marg*, Vol. 18, No. 2, July/Sept. 1996, p. 214.
4. D.D. Raphael, *Problems of Political Philosophy*, p. 20.
5. Joan V. Bondurant, *Conquest of Violence, The Gandhian Philosophy of Conflict*, p. 189.

**Welfare State**

The modern notion of welfare state is based on the conviction that the state is responsible to provide the basic and minimum requirements and the welfare for all. The individual has to rise above the basic minimum.[6] State is considered to be distinctive in being a compulsory association while the other associations are voluntary.[7] The primary function of the state is to redress the grievances and prevent conflicts and to keep order and take the security measures. In this context two types of security are involved, viz., security within the community and security against external sources.[8] It is the business of the state to protect the liberty of each individual. The interference of the state in this regard has to be minimal and limited to prevent other individuals or group of individuals to come in conflict with the freedom of the individuals.[9]

> In a democracy the individual will is governed and limited by the social will which is the state which is governed by and for democracy. If every individual takes the law into his own hands there is no state, it becomes anarchy, i.e., absence of social law or state. That way lies destruction of liberty. Therefore, you should subdue your anger and let the state secure justice.[10]

The state is constituted with three powers, namely, legislative, executive and judiciary. The legislative frames laws, statutes, rules and regulations, the executive implements the laws giving effect to it and the judiciary examines the validity of laws and interprets them.[11] In the modern state the rules framed by it are stated to be supreme. Gandhi stated that the will of the individual is governed and limited by the social will which the state represents.

Austin and Weber hold that the state has to be effective and

---

6. D.D. Raphael, *Problems of Political Philosophy*, p. 48.
7. *Ibid.*, p. 44.
8. *Ibid.*, p. 46.
9. *Ibid.*, p. 47.
10. *Harijan*, 28.9.1947, p. 350.
11. D.D. Raphael, *Problems of Political Philosophy*, p. 50.

strong enough to improve its rules and the means thereof to be effective is secured by wielding the physical force. It is generally recognised to be as legitimate.[12] Unless the state is efficiently tyrannous, the citizens may have a good reason to disobey the laws framed by the state if they are proved to be morally repugnant and by doing this, they remove the essential characteristic of the state.[13] When there is an obvious clash between the demands of the state and the moral obligations of the people, they are restrained by the possible consequences of the disobedience, people are prompted to obey the state if its policies are just and moral.

**Democracy**

While the perverted forms of rule such as monarchy and oligarchy and aristocracy promote the interests of a select few, democracy aims at the promotion of the interests of majority for it is called the rule of the people in contrast to other forms of the government. "In democracy the people's will must rule", says Gandhi.

Abraham, in his address delivered at Gettysberg, defined "democracy as government of the people, by the people and for the people".[14] A democrat believes that every adult who exercises his franchise is capable enough to exercise the power of self-direction and all should be given the equal opportunity to exercise their self-directions.[15]

In the words of Gandhi:

> Democracy must in essence. . . mean the art and science of mobilising the entire physical, economic and spiritual resources of all the various sections of the people in the service of the common good of all.[16]

But a democrat has to be invariably a born disciplinarian which

---

12. Anthony Quinton (ed.), *Political Philosophy*, p. 6.
13. *Ibid.*, p. 8.
14. D.D. Raphael, *Problems of Political Philosophy*, p. 146.
15. *Ibid.*, p. 142.
16. *Harijan*, 27.5.1939, p. 143.

could be only when he is habituated normally to yield willing obedience to all laws whether human or divine. He has to be utterly selfless. He should not think of self or party except that of democracy.[17]

## Majority and Minority in Democracy

In a democracy, government by all the people implies arriving at unanimous decisions but this is not possible in the political matters. So democracy in its practice has to follow the opinion of the majority. For all practical purposes, the majority rule should necessarily seek to serve the interests of all, although it is not in agreement will all. Otherwise the danger of the majority rule becoming the tyranny of majority is not ruled out.[18]

It is evident that the will of the majority is the will of the majority but does not represent the will of 'the people'.[19] Gandhi held that in the matter of conscience, the law of majority has no place.[20] The democracy represented by the disciplined and enlightened people is the finest thing in the world. When a democracy is represented by the prejudiced, ignorant, and superstitious, it will lead to chaos and may be self-destroying.[21]

Bertrand Russell was of the opinion that it is a mistake to suppose that the majority is necessarily right in certain political matters.[22] Gandhi held that the opinion of the minority has to be taken into consideration. Gandhi was a great critic of the majority system in the democracy.

He pointed out:

> The rule of majority has a narrow application, i.e., one should yield to the majority in matters of detail. But it is

17. *Harijan*, 27.5 1939, p. 136.
18. D.D. Raphael, *Problems of Political Philosophy*, p. 146.
19. Anthony Quinton (ed.), *Political Philosophy*, p. 177.
20. *Young India*, 4.8.1920, p. 4.
21. *Ibid.*, 30.7.1931, p. 199.
22. Bertrand Russell, *Political Ideas*, p. 45.

> slavery to be amenable to the majority, no matter what its decisions are. Democracy is not a state in which people act like sheep under democracy, individual liberty of opinion and action is jealously guarded. I, therefore, believe that the minority has a perfect right to act differently from the majority.[23]

Gandhi was not contented with the mere formal adherence to the external mechanism of the parliamentary system of government. He stood for a democratic form of government where the liberty of the individual, freedom of opinion and action could be zealously guarded. The minority would not be coerced but only convinced, persuaded and respected.

Gandhi says,

> The rule of majority when it becomes coercive, is as intolerable as that of a bureaucratic minority. We must patiently try to bring round the minority to our view by gentle persuation and argument.[24]

He held that the majority should exhibit their magnanimity to persuade the minority even though self-suffering. Thereby the tyranny of the majority could be avoided.[25] Democracy, in order to represent the government of the entire community, cannot afford to be intolerant. The tyranny of the majority must come to an end.[26] Gandhi did not consider a majority decision to be valid and sacrosanct and upheld the opinions of the minority when they are just and moral. He stated that it is a slavery to be amenable to the majority without taking its decision into consideration.

Gandhi pointed out:

> True democracy is not inconsistent with a few persons representing the spirit, the hope and the aspirations of

---

23. *Young India*, 2.3.1922, p. 129.
24. *Ibid.*, 21.1.1922, p. 54.
25. V.P. Varma, *The Political Philosophy of Mahatma Gandhi and Sarvodaya*, p. 239.
26. Ramjee Singh, *The Relevance of Gandhian Thought*, p. 67.

> those whom they claim to represent. I hold that democracy cannot be evolved by forcible methods. The spirit of democracy cannot be imposed from without. It has to come from within.[27]

Gandhi held that the rule of majority should not suppress the opinion of even an individual if it is sound. This would be the view of real democracy.[28] He was of the opinion that it would be another delusion to behave that a large number of delegates are in any way help to the better conduct of the business or that it safeguards the democratic principle.

Gandhi says,

> Fifteen hundred delegates jealous of the interests of the people, broad-minded and truthful, would any day be a safeguard for democracy than six thousand irresponsible men chosen anyhow. To safeguard democracy the people must have a keen sense of independence, self-respect and their oneness and should insist upon choosing as their representatives only such persons as are good and true.[29]

## Notion of Political Power

Bertrand Russell in his book *Political Ideas* stated that the present institutions rest upon two things, viz., property and power. The problem is that both these are very unjustly distributed though they are of great importance to promote the happiness of the individual.[30] There is need to have the diffusion of power in the politico-economic sphere instead of concentrating in the hands of the officials, owners of the industries and the rich. Hobbes stated that man seeks power to have control over others for his self-preservation being apprehensive of danger from all sources.[31] He presented the pursuit of power as the basic human characteristic.

---

27. *The Bombay Chronicle*, 18.9.1954.
28. *Mahatma*, Vol. VI, p. 354.
29. M.K. Gandhi, *The Story of My Experiment with Truth*, p. 369.
30. Bertrand Russell, *Political Ideas*, p. 14.
31. Hobbes, *Leviathan*, Introduction, p. xix.

Gandhi resisted injustice and the abuse of power to usher in a new socio-politico-economic order. Gandhi went beyond in challenging the conventional view of nature and domain of politics, and in widening, the concept of power. He destroyed the dichotomy between the private and the public, moral and religious values and political norms, ethical norms and political expediency.[32] He gave a different interpretation to the concept of power.

Gandhi says,

> To me political power is not an end but one of the means of enabling people to better their condition in every department of life, political power means capacity to regulate national life through national representatives. If national life becomes so perfect as to become self-regulated, no representation becomes necessary. There is than a state of enlightened anarchy. In such a state everyone is his own rules. He rules himself in such a manner that he is never a hindrance to his neighbour. In the ideal state, therefore, there is no political power more because there is no state. But the ideal is never fully realised in life. Hence the classical statement of Thoreau that the government is best which governs the least.[33]

Gandhi tried to challenge the very notion of power, which acquired great significance in the modern world similar to that of the kind of importance and autonomous character that some medieval philosopher gave to universal essence which they believe to constitute reality.[34] Gandhi describes power is of two kinds, viz., power obtained by the fear of punishment and the other by arts of love. The power based on love is more effective and permanent than that of the power derived from the fear of punishment.[35] He held that when the power is superimposed, it needs always the help of

---

32. Raghavan Iyer, *The Moral and Political Thought of Mahatma Gandhi*, p. 40.
33. *Young India*, 2.7.1931, p. 162.
34. Raghavan Iyer, *The Moral and Political Thought of Mahatma Gandhi*, p. 54.
35. *Young India*, 8.1.1923, p. 15.

police and military. But the power generated from within should have no use of them.[36]

Gandhi stood against the increase of the power of the state.

He pointed out:

> I look upon an increase in the power of the state with the greatest fear because, although while apparently doing good by minimising exploitation, it does the greatest harm to mankind by destroying individuality, which lies at the root of progress.[37]

It has been said that power corrupts and the absolute power corrupts absolutely. Gandhi referred to an over-estimated segment of politics as a whole. In the ideal state as visualised by Gandhi, there is no political power because there is no state. But such type of ideal state has yet to be realised in life.[38] When power is concentrated, a political union could be achieved instead of diffusion among the various agencies.[39]

The state has a power which is distinct, but its effectiveness depends upon the ability to draw other forms of power in its support. In corollary to this statement, Gandhi maintains that if the individuals could recognise the power in their hands and use it constructively to secure the social good or engage in non-violent resistance against the unjust laws and forcible measures of the state, the monopolistic effectiveness of state power, would be reduced and its coercive authority would be morally and materially undermined. Thereby the purification of power politics becomes possible. In this context, Gandhi gave utmost importance to the constructive programme.[40]

The furthering of the pursuit of non-violence and truth results in weakening of the coercive role of the state. The greater the

---

36. *Harijan*, 4.9.1937, p. 233.
37. *The Modern Review*, October 1935, p. 412.
38. *Young India*, 2.7.1931, p. 162.
39. Raghavan Iyer, *The Moral and Political Thought of Mahatma Gandhi,* p. 55.
40. *Ibid.*

decentralisation of power in any society, the greater would be the chances for the collective pursuit of non-violence and truth.[41]

In the modern society, the individual is a victim of social and economic forces. He has little control over him. On the other hand, the life in the community has developed a sense of community. The individual is felt to be a distinct personality living with other personalities with the possibility of development as the highest personality.[42] If the political and economic power is combined and vested in the hands of the state, it destroys the individuality and the individual initiative.

Gandhi advocated the limitation of state power. He laid more emphasis on controlling rather than the increase of the authority of the state. It is for the reason that the modern state seizes power and thereby the role of the individual is reduced to nothing.

## Non-Violent Democracy vs Centralisation

Gandhi held that true democracy is based on non-violence. If the state rules on violence, such type of rule could be termed as a totalitarian regime. The object of state is to restrict or limit the social violence committed by the individuals through the employment of force and violence. The violence of the individual is prevented and controlled by the superior violence and force exercised by the state. In the opinion of Gandhi, state is nothing but the manifestation of violence. So Gandhi said, "What I disapprove of is an organisation based on force which a state is."[43] Hobbes maintained that there can be no state without authority.[44]

Since the state is born of violence and force, Gandhi was convinced that force and violence are the inalienable aspects of the nature of the state. The state cannot come out of its inherent nature as much as a leopard cannot change its spots under any circumstances. Gandhi subscribed to the view that even if an

---

41. *The Moral and Political Thought of Mahatma Gandhi*, p. 255.
42. Jaya Prakash Narayan, *Panchayat Raj as the Basis of Indian Polity*, p.13.
43. M.K. Gandhi, *The Modern Review*, p. 412.
44 Hobbes, *Leviathan*, Introduction, p. xxiv.

individual is morally deprived, he is not beyond redemption. His acquisitive and exploitative tendencies can be curbed under the moral treatment.[45]

Gandhi felt that state is not the same as the individual to be beyond redemption. He pointed out:

> The individual has a soul but as the state is a soulless machine, it can never be weaned from violence to which it owes its very existence.[46]

So Gandhi was optimistic and visionary of an ideal state of statelessness which he termed as the state of enlightened anarchy. The existence of state in any form is a hindrance to the moral development of the individual, as morality necessitates the freedom of the will of the individual. The authority of the state depends upon the authority of the laws. To attend to other aspects of politics or to enforce its law, coercive power is essential for state. The laws of the state have to be obeyed as they represent the general will.[47] The general will is held to be of general interest to be persuaded as it is rational and promotes the real good of each individual. Since the state promotes the common good of the individuals, the laws of the state are the concrete expression of general will.[48] Disregard of the general will results in a disaster. Hobbes maintained that the power of the sovereign depends upon the general will and if the sovereign disregards the general will, no legal or constitutional machinery would avert the disaster.[49]

In the true test of democracy, it attempts to replace force and violence by social will. Gandhi wrote:

> In democracy, the individual will was governed and limited by the social will which was the state, which was governed

---

45. Benudhar Pradhan, *The Socialist Thought of Mahatma Gandhi*, Vol. II, p. 523.
46. M.K. Gandhi, *Modern Review*, October, 1955, p. 412.
47. D.D. Raphael, *Problems of Political Philosophy*, p. 98.
48. *Ibid.*, p. 100.
49. Hobbes, *Leviathan*, Introduction, p. xxiv.

by and for democracy.[50]

Democracy and violence cannot go together. So they cannot be reconciled. The positive aspect of non-violence is the largest love and the greatest charity. The follower of non-violence, loves the enemy and follow the path of truth and righteousness. He cannot deceive the loved one. He paves the way for an honourable understanding.[51] This results in the elimination of the distrust and suspicion of the person concerned.

Perfect democracy is possible only when there is perfect non-violence. The modern states became totalitarian and if they want to become democratic they must truly and courageously become non-violent.[52] If a revolutionary movement asserts its power by exercising violence and justifies under the pretext of the establishment of non-violence, it betrays a failure to grasp the interaction between violence and power.[53]

In order to facilitate the full growth and progress of the individual, a democratic society must have its basis in rational understanding, mutual cooperation and concern for the well-being of all. The main principle of human love inspired the votary of non-violence to seek good of himself in the good of all and sacrifice his life to realise the ideal.[54]

The spirit of democracy flourishes with the voluntary efforts of the individual and it has to come from within.

Gandhi says,

> True democracy or the Swaraj of the masses can never come through untruthful and violent means, for the simple reason that the natural corollary to their use would be remove all opposition, through the suppression or extermination of the antagonists. That does not make for

50. *Harijan*, 28.9.1947, p. 350.
51. *Speeches and Writings of Mahatma Gandhi*, 4th edn., p. 346.
52. *Gandhi Marg*, Vol. 17, Sep. 1995, p. 226.
53. Raghavan Iyer, *The Moral and Political Thought of Mahatma Gandhi*, p. 222.
54. M.K. Gandhi, *Sarvodaya*, p. 4.

> individual freedom. Individual freedom can have the fullest play only under a regime of unadulterated ahimsa.[55]

Democracy is the rule by the majority but rule in the absence of non-violence and truth is rather deceptive and fatal. So Gandhi stated that democracy must be based on truth and non-violence.[56]

Gandhi pointed out:

> My notion of democracy is that under it the weakest should have the same opportunity as the strongest. That can be never happen except through non-violence.[57]

Gandhi believed that true democracy is the outcome of non-violence.[58] So no perfect democracy is possible without perfect non-violence behind it.[59] He held that the modern imperialism is frankly based on force in defence of it, and is not consistent with non-violence.[60] Centralised type of democracy cannot be run on non-violent lines. A true democrat defends his freedom and the freedom of the mankind. According to Gandhi,

> Centralisation as a system is inconsistent with non-violent structure of society.[61]

In his view centralisation perpetrates exploitation of the individual materially and intellectually and exploitation is treated by Gandhi as part and parcel of violence.

The victory of truth cannot be achieved through falsehood and democracy through dictatorship.[62] Gandhi stated that "centralisation cannot be sustained or depended without adequate force".[63]

---

55. *Harijan*, 27.5.1939, p. 143.
56. *Gandhi Marg*, Vol. 17, Sep. 1995, p. 224.
57. *Harijan*, 18.5.1940, p. 129.
58. *Gandhiji's Correspondence with the Government*, 1942-4, p. 143.
59. *Harijan*, 2.3.1947, p. 44.
60. *Ibid.*, 5.9.1938, p. 236.
61. *Ibid.*, 18.1.1942, p. 5.
62. Rammanohar Lohia, *Marx, Gandhi and Socialism*, p. 123.
63. *Harijan*, 30.12.1939, p. 391.

Decentralised democracy is consistent with non-violence as it governs the least and no violence or force is needed.

## Decentralisation

In view of the nature of the state which retards the individual initiative, Gandhi advocated the decentralised type of democracy followed by the self-governing and self-sufficient village republics as the nucleus of his political philosophy. It is only when democracy relies on the people and the rule by the people, through the politics of convincing, persuasion without depending on the military or police power; it becomes truly a decentralised democracy.

A democratic government cannot be morally justified as long as it uses police force. It must devolve its real power to the people in the political and economic spheres. The social scientist has to evolve the type of economy and polity that fits in with the pattern of decentralisation. If the power does not remain at the working base, it will only be deceptive but cannot be termed as a real democracy.[64]

Gandhi consistently emphasised upon the individual effort, local reform and village-centred activity. He worked out for societal organisation which has its basis on decentralised villages, industries and self-sufficient rural communities.[65]

Being influenced by Henry Thoreau, the ardent champion of the individual freedom and his classical statement 'the government is best which governs the least',[66] Gandhi believed that the best government is one that governs the least. He held that there are certain things which cannot be done without political power though there are numerous other things which do not depend upon political power.[67] He held that a nation is truly democratic when it runs its

---

64. Ramjee Singh, *The Relevance of Gandhian Thought*, p. 64.
65. Joan V. Bondurant, *Conquest of Violence, The Gandhian Philosophy of Conflict*, p. 180.
66. *Young India*, 2.7.1931, p. 162.
67. Joan V. Bondurant, *Conquest of Violence, The Gandhian Philosophy of Conflict*, p. 183.

affairs smoothly and effectively without much interference of the state.[68]

## Panchayat Raj and its Significance

Panchayat Raj means a political structure with its base at the village level consisting of five members especially of elder statesmen of the community with the functional ability of legislature, executive and judiciary.

Gandhi says,

> The government of the village will be conducted by the Panchayat of five persons annually elected by the adult villagers, male and female, possessing minimum prescribed qualifications. These will have all the authority and jurisdiction required. Since there will be no system of punishments in the accepted sense, this Panchayat will be the legislature, judiciary and executive combined to operate for its year of office.[69]

The village *panchayat* was traditionally organised with a group of members but not an individual as the unit. In many respects, it was nothing but an extension of the Indian family system with a strict patriarchal character.[70]

Gandhi, with his series of experiments with truth and the knowledge and experience he gained thereby about the political institutions of the society, made him to suggest a suitable political organisation that suits to the modern requirements and contributes to the progress of the people from the grass-root village level.

The development has to begin from the bottom, i.e., village level. If the country is to be revived, her roots have to be tended which lies in the village. This programme has to be initiated by the people themselves with proper understanding.[71]

---

68. *Harijan*, 11.1.1936, p. 380.
69. *Ibid.*, 26.7.1942, p. 238.
70. Joan V. Bondurant, *Conquest of Violence, The Gandhian Philosophy of Conflict*, pp. 149-50.
71. S.K. Dey, *Panchayat Raj,* p. 66.

The *panchayat* system as viewed by Gandhi represents a village community to be self-sufficient, especially in the matter of the basic necessities of life. The economic reconstruction would be from the bottom to the upwards and the village unit would constitute the foundation of planning. The *panchayat* will have autonomy as far as the internal village administration is concerned. Unlike the anarchist tradition, some sort of hierarchical pattern could be evolved by linking up the village *panchayat* with the Taluk, District, State and Nation.

Gandhi stood for the freedom of the people that are being ruled. He held that people's independence should begin from the bottom, i.e., from village level. Gandhi pointed out

> Independence must begin at the bottom. Thus, every village will be a republic or Panchayat having full powers. It follows therefore, the every village has to be self-sustained and capable of managing its affairs even to the extent of depending itself against the whole world. It will be trained and prepared to perish in the attempt to defend itself against any onslaught from without. Thus ultimately it is the individual who is the unit. This does not exclude dependence on and willing help from neighbours or from the world. It will be free and voluntary play of mutual forces. Such a society is necessarily highly cultured which every man and woman knows what he or she wants and, what is more, knows that no one should want anything that others cannot have with equal labour.[72]

Gandhi pleaded strongly for decentralized economic and political power through the organisation of village *panchayats*. Gandhi was sure that if the *panchayat* system is worked on scientific lines, it could strengthen in the social and economic spheres and also fortify the national defence against the foreign invasion.[73]

Gandhi held that by serving the villages, *swaraj* (self-rule) could be established. The country's prosperity and progress depends upon the villages. He maintained that if the village perishes, India

72. *Harijan*, 28.7.1946, p. 236.

73. M.K. Gandhi, *Village Swaraj*, Foreword, p. iv.

will perish too. It will be no more India. His own mission in the world will get lost.[74] He stated that

> we have to make a choice between India of the villages that are as ancient as herself and India of the cities which are a creation of foreign domination.[75]

Gandhi admitted that in olden times tyranny and opposition were practised by feudal chiefs. Then odds were even but in the modern times the odds are heavy and it is quite demoralising. In the Gandhian scheme of things, the ancient republican India without tyranny and exploitation serves as a model unit.[76]

Gandhi stated that in the structure composed of innumerable villages there will be ever-widening but never ascending circles.

Gandhi says,

> Life will not be a pyramid with the apex sustained by the bottom. But it will be the oceanic circle whose centre will be the individual always ready to perish for the village the latter ready to perish for the circle of villages till at least the whole becomes one life composed of individuals, never aggressive in their arrogance but even humble, sharing the majesty of the oceanic circle of which they are integral units.[77]

Therefore, the outermost circumference will not wield power to crush the inner circle but give strength to all within and derive its own from the centre. Gandhi was optimistic when he stated that, when the dream of the people of *panchayat raj* comes true, i.e., when true democracy is realised, the humblest and lowest Indian could be equally the ruler of India with the tallest in the country.[78]

If a political system is introduced at the village level, that

---

74. *Harijan*, 29.8.1936, p. 226.
75. *Ibid.*, 20.1.1940, p. 423.
76. Ghan Shyam Shah & H.R. Chaturvedi, *Gandhian Approach to Rural Development*, p. 32.
77. *Harijan*, 28.7.1946, p. 236.
78. *Ibid.*, 18.1.1948, p. 517.

results in the further disruption and disunity of the community. The polity of the *panchayat raj* must necessarily be different from the polity of the mass scale. It is for this reason, Gandhi did not accept the Parliamentary democracy which he called otherwise as the tyranny of the majority.[79] Gandhi was very particular of the inclusion of the topic of village *panchayats* in the constitution for their organisation as they reflect the people's voice.

Gandhi says,

> I must confess that I have not been able to follow the proceedings of the constituent Assembly . . . (the correspondent) says that there is no mention or direction about village Panchayats and decentralisation in the foreshadowed constitution. It is certainly and omission calling for immediate attention if our independence is to reflect the people's voice. The greater the power of the Panchayats, the better for the people.[80]

In recognition of the significance and relevance of the village *panchayats*, Article. 31A has been included in the Indian Constitution.

> That after Article 31, the following new Article be added.
>
> (31A) The states shall take steps to organise village Panchayats and endow them with such powers and authority as may be necessary to enable them to function as units of self-government.[81]

The village *panchayat* is the smallest unit being accessible to the people, and provides scope for direct popular participation. Its role and significance has been recognised. It gives economic and social relief to the undeveloped sections of the community with its main focus on agriculture and small-scale industries for the development of the people.

---

79. Jaya Prakash Narayan, *Panchayat Raj as the Basis of Indian Polity*, p. 12.
80. *Harijan*, 21.12.1947, p. 473.
81. Jaya Prakash Narayan, *Panchayat Raj as the Basis of Indian Polity*, p. 18.

In order to democratise the local institutions, three-tier system of rural and local government has been suggested viz., *panchayat raj*, *panchayat samiti* and *zilla parishad*.[82]

## Three-Tier System of Decentralised Administration

Gandhi insisted that democratic structure should be decentralised to the grass-root level, so that the lowest and the last is empowered in decision-making and for that he felt that the three-tier system of administration is highly suitable.

The village consists of the village elders who are elected by the citizens of the village. The purpose of the village *panchayat* is defeated if it is not checked from time to time. There is need to have a wider institution of the people for which the *panchayat* has to be the cabinet and this institution is recognised to be *grama sabha* consisting of all the adult citizens — men and women, both young and old of the village. It is said to be the counterpart of the National Parliament. Among the members of the *grama sabha*, some have to be elected for *panchayat* as its cabinet to conduct the affairs of the village. The *grama sabha* has to meet periodically and review the work done by *panchayat*. The *grama sabha* has to represent hopes and aspirations, fears and frustrations of the people through village *panchayats*.

At the level of block, the next tier of administration is envisaged. The block *panchayat samiti* consists of the Presidents of the village *panchayats*, alternatively members elected by the electoral college of *panches*.[83]

The block *panchayat samiti* has to coopt representatives of women, scheduled and depressed classes, cooperatives and other special interests which have not been represented in the *samiti*. The object of the *panchayat samiti* is that people of all sections of the community that constitute the population within the block has to be represented.[84]

---

82. Ram Reddy (ed.), *Patterns of Panchayati Raj*, p. 3.
83. S.K. Dey, *Panchayat Raj*, p. 91.
84. *Ibid.*, p. 92.

The third tier of administration is *zilla parishad* consisting of the representatives of the block *panchayat samitis*, the members of the state legislature, members of the Parliament, representatives of the cooperative organisations in the district and any other special organisations.[85] Hierarchical pattern could be evolved by the linkage of village *panchayat* with the block, district, state and nation.

The main aims of the *panchayat raj* were to create institutions at the village, block and district levels to create conditions conducive for self-expression and political representation. At these levels to mobilise the public support and local resources for the development of the programmes and also to decentralise the decision-making which helps to take the local experiences, requirements and aspirations to have their full role in the matter of planning and implementation of the development programme.[86]

The *panchayat* elections are to be conducted without the interference of any political party which helps to restore the traditional values of the village. If any place is given for its vested interests, it gives rise to the projection of some political party. This will not help to combat or cure the ills of the society, viz., casteism, communalism, money, power, etc.

Education has played an important role in the matter of creating awareness among the youth who find place in the *panchayat*. The idea of giving constructive type of leadership out of public interests is gradually emerging at present to usher in a democratic decentralised society and adult suffrage. But the factions among the villagers, their kinships loyalties, and their limited identification with larger groups stand as barriers on the way of development programmes.[87]

Gandhi favoured the village republics. The movements of statutory *panchayats* and the new scheme of democratic decentralisation may be stated to be the amplification of the Gandhian views. As democracy at the grass-roots is practised to a limited extent, the results are not satisfactory.

---

85. *Panchayat Raj*, p. 92.
86. *Gandhi Marg*, Vol. II, Number, 3, p. 264.
87. *Ibid.*, p. 285.

In the modern world, the *panchayat* administration is deviating from the Gandhian ideals. There has been a recognisable growing inequality in the country. Some people who are after money and power, are taking the undue advantage of the new and added sources for the acquisition of wealth. They exploited and acquired wealth and they are becoming the masters of the political power also by capturing it.

Gandhi suggested indirect elections to be conducted through the village *panchayats*. He stated that seven hundred thousand villages of India will be organised in accordance with the will of the citizens through voting. These villages with their voting capacity will elect their district administrations which in turn will elect provincial administrations which again will elect the national chief executive. This results in the decentralisation of power among the seven hundred thousand units. There will be voluntary cooperation among these villages which will produce real freedom.[88]

Gandhi finds a perfect democracy based upon the individual freedom. When the basic material needs of the individual are satisfied, he would be free to pursue higher and spiritual values of life to have greater happiness and peace.

## Duties and Rights

Gandhi could be termed as the greatest champion of the human rights. He fought for the rights of the exploited and the humiliated in the society. He established a correlation between the rights, duties and obligations. He stood against the exclusiveness and special privileges against others.

As a strong believer of the equal rights for all men, he defended the human rights and raised his voice against the illegal, illegitimate and unjust social norms, political conventions and colour prejudices which are in vogue over the ravages of time.[89] For a due recognition of the individual rights, his actions are to be directed towards the moral norms of life. The meaning and purpose of human life is

---

88. Gopinath Dhavan, *The Political Philosophy of Mahatma Gandhi*, p. 298.

89. V.P. Varma, *The Political Philosophy of Mahatma Gandhi*, p. 219.

defeated in the absence of aim or goal and without proper ordering of life. There is need to integrate the rights of the individual with a system of moral ends. The lack of such integration would result in disruption. So the performance of one's own duty is of paramount importance.[90]

Gandhi says,

> Instead of insisting on rights everyone does his duty, there will immediately be the rule of order established among mankind.[91]

The individual's assertion of rights without the corresponding adherence is found to be an anomaly in the modern times. Gandhi wanted to reconcile individual rights with the requirements of social progress. Individual is a participant in the social process and he cannot be allowed to manifest his unrestricted individuality. He has to do his duty. Gandhi pointed out:

> The true source of rights is duty. If we all discharge our duties, rights will not be far to seek. If leaving duties unperformed, we run after rights, they will escape us like a will-o-the-wisp.[92]

The individual has to learn to make the willing submission to the social and moral laws to prevent the lawlessness in the society. True rights might not accrue from the mere legal recognition but from moral advancement and social service.[93]

> The law protects rights and enforces the duties which correspond to rights. This is not to say that the scope of the law takes in the whole domain of moral justice.[94]

---

90. *The Political Philosophy of Mahatma Gandhi*, p. 223.
91. *Harijan*, 6.7.1947, p. 217.
92. *Young India,* 8.1.1925, pp. 15-16.
93. V.P. Varma, *The Political Philosophy of Mahatma Gandhi and Sarvodaya*, p. 223.
94. D.D. Raphael, *Problems of Political Philosophy*, p. 166.

## Significance of Freedom

Freedom implies the absence of restraint. An individual is stated to be free when he is not restrained from doing what he wants to do or chooses to do. The idea of choice itself can be called freedom.[95]

In the Atlantic Charter, President Roosevelt and Mr. Churchill drew up a declaration of 'Four Freedoms' which were: freedom of speech, freedom of worship, freedom from fear and freedom from want.[96] It has been said that freedom is too precious a thing and it is one of the highest values of human life playing a vital and positive role.[97]

Gandhi valued the individual freedom so much. His concept of freedom is not narrow but co-extensive with the freedom of man in all his majesty.[98] He held that no man loses his freedom except through his weakness.[99]

He gave utmost importance to the individual freedom.

He pointed out:

> I value individual freedom but you must not forget that man is essentially a social being. He has risen to his present status by learning to adjust his individualism to the requirements of social progress unrestricted individualism is the law of the beast of the jungle. We have to learn to strike the mean between individual freedom and social restraint. Willing submission to social restraint for the sake of the well-being of the whole society enriches both the individual and the society of which one is a member.[100]

Gandhian conception of freedom can be stated to be a synthesis of the natural right of the individual to achieve political liberty as well

---

95. *Problems of Political Philosophy*, p. 115.
96. *Ibid.*, p. 116.
97. *Ibid.*, p. 117.
98. *Harijan*, 7.6.1942, p. 183.
99. *India's Case for Swaraj* (ed.), by W.P. Kabadi, p. 209, Yeshanand & Co., Bombay, 1932.
100. *Harijan*, 27.5.1939, p. 144.

as moral and spiritual freedom. A person who obtains freedom over his passion will not tolerate the social and economic exploitation.[101] He held that the civil liberties stand as the very basis of democracy. In his speech at the Karachi session of the Indian National Congress, in 1931 he got a resolution on the fundamental rights passed.

He stated that:

> But freedom of speech and corresponding action is the breath of democratic life. Freedom of propagating non-violence as substitute for war in the most relevant when indecent savagery is being perpetrated by the warring nations of Europe.[102]

Political freedom postulates social cohesiveness and disciplined suffering. There is need to combine the quest for the political individuality with the voluntary acceptance of social and political discipline which has the basis of social solidarity and cohesiveness.[103] Gandhi spoke of the possibility of freedom in the modern age under the conditions of the moral regeneration of man.[104] When a new society emerges in the place of the modern civilised society followed by the centralised type of government with its characteristic of exploitation and the depravity of the individual freedom real individual freedom could be thought of.

The individual freedom is at stake as the state poses a great threat to the individual who is above the institution. The state represents violence in an organised way which obviously perpetrates on the people. Freedom does not come from any external agencies but only through the inward change brought about. Real freedom is one's own rule over himself.[105]

---

101. V.P. Varma, *The Political Philosophy of Mahatma Gandhi and Sarvodaya*, p. 226.
102 *Harijan*, 22.9.1940, p. 294.
103. V.P. Varma, *The Political Philosophy of Mahatma Gandhi and Sarvodaya*, p. 231.
104. M.K. Gandhi, *In Search of the Supreme*, Vol. I, p. 267.
105. V.P. Varma, *The Political Philosophy of Mahatma Gandhi and Sarvodaya*, p. 231.

For Gandhi, freedom is the essence of man. In the modern age, it is possible to have freedom if there is moral regeneration of man. If the individual is entitled to have his complete freedom, he must learn to discipline himself. He must not infringe on the freedom of others. He has to be of service for the benefit of his fellow men and community at large.[106]

## Satyagraha as a Political Weapon

*Satyagraha* is the most dynamic and significant legacy that Gandhi left behind for India and the world. It has religious and moral sanction and history made a record of the people who were drawn to this concept to experiment with it. Gandhi used *satyagraha* as a political weapon to fight against injustice and exploitation and for the redressal of grievances. It is otherwise known as non-violent resistance. He held that it is an extension of the rule of domestic life into the political life

The term *satyagraha* implies holding on to Truth or abide by love. It also means truth force and soul force. *Satyagraha* excludes the use of violence in any form as man is not capable of knowing the absolute truth and therefore he is not competent to punish. The word *satyagraha* was coined by Gandhi in South Africa from the contemporary passive resistance of the suffragettes and others.[107] He found in his early stage that the pursuit of truth did not admit of violence to be inflicted on one's opponent but he must be weaned from error by patience and sympathy for what appears to be truth to one person may appear to be error to the other. In his view patience is self-suffering. The doctrine of *satyagraha* is used for the vindication of truth. It is not by inflicting suffering on the opponent but on one's own self.[108] Gandhi translated the idea of *satyagraha* into action in South Africa and it began to evolve into a rational and communicable manner.

Self-suffering differs from violence. Violence inflicts, injury on others whereas self-suffering inflicts suffering on the person

106. Sibnarayana Ray, *Gandhi, India and the World,* p. 228.
107. M.K. Gandhi, *Satyagraha*, p. 3.
108. *Young India*, 14.1.1920, p. 5.

concerned or invites suffering on himself who exercises the technique of *satyagraha*. The important characteristic of *satyagraha* as way of life is never to tolerate or submit either to evil or to injustice or tyranny of any kind. The technique of *satyagraha* suggests the rigorous discipline to make resistance on active force. The elements such as self-sacrifice and self-suffering are stated as the alternatives to violence. Gandhi attaches the great importance to the individual integrity and freedom.

According to Joan V. Bondurant, *satyagraha* provides key to an understanding of Gandhian Political Philosophy.[109] *Satyagraha* is interpreted as non-violent direct action by the techniques such as non-cooperation, civil disobedience, fasting and other forms of non-violent direct action, which do not exhaust the content of *satyagraha*. *Satyagraha* is the relentless pursuit of truthful ends by non-violent means.[110] *Satyagraha* wins by resulting in the conflict resolution and attempts to find higher truth and persuades the opponent not to triumph over him.[111]

In order to turn the moral indignation and resistance of the individual into an active social and political force, Gandhi developed his technique of *satyagraha*. The object of *satyagraha* is to come out victorious in the conflict situation followed by the increasing insight into truth, and persuasion of the opponent.[112]

The Philosophy of *satyagraha* being practical, is concerned itself primarily with the means. However, it does not ignore the end. As the end grows out of the means, the progressive use of the non-violent way is everything to the *satyagraha*.[113] In the contemporary times, the critics have not been willing to understand the implications

109. Joan V. Bondurant, *Conquest of Violence, The Gandhian Philosophy of Conflict*, p. 7.
110. Gopinath Dhavan, *The Political Philosophy of Mahatma Gandhi*, p. 126.
111. Joan V. Bondurant, *Conquest of Violence, The Gandhian Philosophy of Conflict*, p. 33.
112. Gene Sharp, *Gandhi as a Political Strategist*, p. 63.
113. Gopinath Dhavan, *The Political Philosophy of Mahatma Gandhi*, p. 5.

of the Gandhian method of *satyagraha*. There is an honest failure in the recognition of the potentiality of *satyagraha*. The political methods adopted conventionally are based upon violence, causing precisely violence is inclusive of hatred.[114] But the politics of *satyagraha* does not carry with it, the elements of violence in any form.

Gene Sharp says,

> Satyagraha as a concrete expression of the principle of moral approximation of the end and the means, can be regarded as the most unique contribution to the philosophy and technique of revolution in our time. What is attained by love is retained for all time, while what is obtained by violence has within it the seeds of its own destruction.[115]

*Satyagraha* is a method of protest made by the aggrieved party to take recourse to an appropriate non-violent action. *Satyagraha* sets in new moral values, a new moral order in the state as it is founded on truth. Its application in the political arena would result in drastic changes in the political authority.[116]

A *satyagrahi* is not merely concerned with working of his own existence that detaches him from society at large. While discharging his duty, he discovers his duty towards his fellowmen. He is aware that "to die in the service of the community or in the pursuit of some other good aims is in reality not to die but to live".[117]

*Satyagraha* promises a transformed individual with integrity and sets in a new social order which is non-exploitative, non-oppressive, just and non-violent governed by the values of truth, love, cooperation, equality and brotherhood.

Gandhi wrote in 1931:

> In the method we are adopting fraud, lying, deceit, and all ugly brood of violence and untruth have absolutely no

114. Joan V. Bondurant, *Conquest of Violence, The Gandhian Philosophy of Conflict*, p. 185.
115. Gene Sharp, *Gandhi as a Political Strategist*, p. 5.
116. Dr. S.A. Bari, *Gandhi's Doctrine of Resistance*, p. 63.
117. *Indian Opinion*, 22.10.1910.

room. Everything is done openly and above board, for truth hates secrecy. The more open you are, the more truthful you are likely to be.[118]

## Application of Satyagraha

As violence interrupts the process and prolongs the real revolution of the whole social structure, non-violent resistance to fight against the evil has assumed much significance. Gandhi called this *satyagraha* a universal principle of universal application.

Gandhi says,

> It is a force that may be used by individuals as well as by communities. It may be used as well as in political as in domestic affairs. Its universal applicability is a demonstration of its permanence and invincibility. It can be used alike by men, women and children.[119]

*Satyagraha*, in its practice, excludes the use of violence in any shape or form whether in thought, word or deed and it demands the observance of absolute non-violence. The practice of *satyagraha* involves suffering of one who has the readiness and capacity to undergo suffering.

*Satyagraha* is held to be of service as a supplement and stands as a substitute to law in some cases in the modern context based upon the rule of law.

> If the laws are unjust or oppressive and constitutional remedies are not available owing to the attitudes of the rulers or majorities, *satyagraha* is a legitimate weapon of the injured individuals or groups.[120]

In the political context Gandhi holds:

> Its use is based upon the immutable maxim that government

118. *Young India*, 21.12.1931.
119. *Ibid.*, 3.11.1927, p. 369.
120. Raghavan Iyer, *The Moral and Political Thought of Mahatma Gandhi*, p. 317.

> of the people is possible only so long as they consent either consciously or unconsciously to be governed.[121]

It must be accepted that most of the hunger-strikes in the country are undertaken for this trivial issues without previous preparation and adequate thought. If this system continues the efficacy of the higher strike will be reduced to a mere mockery.[122]

## Non-cooperation

One of the off-shoots of *satyagraha* is non-cooperation. It is

> a protest against an unwilling and unwilling participation in evil. . . . Non-cooperation with evil is as much a duty as cooperation with good.[123]

Gandhi held that a *satyagrahi* obeys the laws of society intelligently and of his own free will as he considers it to be his sacred duty to do so and it is only when a person has obeyed the laws of society scrupulously, that he is in a position to judge as to which particular rules are good and just and which are unjust and iniquitous.[124]

Gandhi postulated non-cooperation with a view to redress the wrongs.[125] Law must be moral to be obeyed. An individual cannot obey an immoral law though it is framed constitutionally as he cannot obey ignoring the dictates of his conscience. Disobedience to an immoral law is the same as his obedience to a higher moral law and his adherence to truth and justice.

The theory of general interest or common good is held by the utilitarians who hold the view that all the moral obligations depend upon their utility for the promotion of the general happiness and general interest. The state plays an important role in securing a substantial part of the moral end. So the people are obliged to obey the law as an essential condition of fulfilling the general moral

---

121. *Young India*, 3.11.1927, p. 369.
122. M.K. Gandhi, *Satyagraha*, p. 321.
123. *Young India*, 1.6.1921, p. 172.
124. M.K. Gandhi, *The Story of My Experiments with Truth*, p. 347.
125. *Ibid.*, p. 367.

obligations. The state carries out its functions by laying down the rules and regulations and also by framing the laws. The state creates an awareness of its functions among the people being backed by force to make the individual to refrain from doing crimes and actions that affect the common good and to contribute to such of the services such as defence, public utility and other social services which result in the common good.[126]

Whether an action is good or not is judged by its consequences. If the policies of the government are good, they bring about good results in turn and preserve self-respect, mutual consent and the spirit of reverence among the people. Gandhi held that to judge morality of otherwise of an action, the motive of the doer has to be taken into account. The very same action could be termed as moral or immoral depending upon the motive that prompts it.[127]

Non-cooperation could stand as a way to resolve the conflicts. This technique of non-violent non-cooperation promotes the individual relationships. On the other hand, the strained and unjust relations in the socio-economic scenario could be transformed into the just and harmonious relations through the application of Gandhian non-violent, non-cooperation. The non-violent non-co-operation has been formed into an integral part of application to all kinds of human relationships and it is not limited to the political system alone.[128] Non-violent non-cooperation could secure the cooperation of the opponent consistently with truth and justice. It seeks to liquidate the antagonism and transforms the human relationships.[129] The transformation of the opponent could be possible through the soul force, manifested through self-suffering and persuasion.

Non-cooperation finds the rational and moral basis of justification. By the withdrawal of co-operation from the evil, the non-cooperator arouses moral consciousness and brings about transformation in the human relations on the moral grounds. On

---

126. D.D. Raphael, *Problems of Political Philosophy*, p.106.

127. M.K. Gandhi, *Ethical Religion*, p. 9.

128. *Gandhi Marg*, December 1994, p. 284.

129. *Harijan*, 29.4.1939, p. 101.

the other hand, when the non-cooperation does not accept any kind of assistance or help from the state, individual or society. It boosts him morally and gives him moral strength. Thereby it enlightens and educates both the parties. While the non-cooperator relies on his moral and soul force, the latter imbibes what is right under his influence. The Gandhian technique of non-cooperation brings about a moral revolution thereby. The social evils of the opponent group or the society such as drunkenness or gambling could be eliminated and transformation could be brought about through the application of non-cooperation by arousing their moral consciousness.

Gandhi made non-cooperation a sacred duty of every individual. He wanted to uphold the dignity and the moral values of the individual to enable him to be worthy to fit himself into the moral frame.

Gandhi states:

> I am by instinct a cooperator, my very non-cooperation is intended to purge cooperation of all meanness and falsity, for I hold that such cooperation is not worth the name.[130]

## Civil Disobedience

Gandhi stated that non-cooperation and civil disobedience as different branches of the same tree called *satyagraha*.[131] He defined civil disobediences as civil breach of unmoral statutory enactments without the feat of its sanctions. This expression was coined by Henry Thoreau to signify his own resistance to the laws of a slave state. He left a masterly treatise on the duty of civil disobedience. While Thoreau limited his breach of statutory laws to that of the revenue law in regard to the payment of taxes, probably the term civil disobedience as was practised by Gandhi during 1919 covered a breach of any statutory and unmoral law signifying the resister's outlawry a civil in a non-violent manner. He invoked the sanctions of the law and cheerfully suffered imprisonment.[132] It is stated to be of a fierce type.

130. *Young India*, 26.12.1924, p. 429.
131. M.K. Gandhi, *Satyagraha*, pp. 3-4.
132. *Ibid.*, pp. 3-4.

When the laws of the state or the measures taken by the state are immoral and unjust, disobedience can be directed against such state. The purpose of civil disobedience is to compel the government to withdraw an unjust law or to paralyse the government if it has become corrupt in the resister's view to have a moral and non-violent state in its place.

The nature of *satyagraha* is marked by the politics of mass participation and mass involvement. It is democratic and voluntaristic without the use of compulsion to gain support and cooperation. The relevance of *satyagraha* depends upon its context necessity and immediacy. It is not a politics of disorder and violence. The politics of *satyagraha* could be conceptualised as the purified version of liberal democracy. The connection between the ideals of liberal democracy and institutional realities, is considered closely for a principled democrat to give his allegiance. The *satyagrahi* questions the legitimacy of the laws and acts of the authority.[133]

Gandhi demonstrated the power of *satyagraha*. It is proved to be successful as it is basically non-violent, moral and religious, finds its expression in Hindu, Muslim and Christian religions. The method of *satyagraha* is intended to fight against the evils that beset the society such as exploitation, oppression, injustice, inequality, corruption, etc. The efficacy of *satyagraha* depends upon its observance with integrity and self-sacrifice for a good cause. In the modern world of violence and terrorism which assume great proportions, *satyagraha* stands as a great political weapon of non-violent resistance to redress all grievances, wrongs and to combat evil as it has its basis in love and truth. Therefore it bears greater relevance than before. When people observe *satyagraha* and follow its constructive programme with a firm conviction and strong determination to resist evil, they would live freely without any fear.

---

133. *The Indian Journal of Political Science*, Vol. XXXVIII, March 1977, p. 29.

# 6

# Global Issues and Gandhian Solutions

THE modern world is confronted with the unprecedented crisis caused by violence, terrorism, ecological imbalance, mounting tensions and wars which are interconnected. Gandhi demonstrated the practical applicability of non-violence in all the spheres of the human endeavour and its usefulness to the whole world. The concept of non-violence as interpreted by Gandhi assumes ecological significance for its sustainability and enables people to live in harmony with nature without exploitation and stands as a solution and an alternative to violence and terrorism. The technique of non-violence is a way of life to the humanity at large and helps to achieve permanent and enduring global peace.

## Environment — Its Sustainability and Challenges

The humanity is advancing towards the twenty-first century with an unprecedented growth of industrialisation and technological progress in all spheres. Balancing the technological progress with that of environmental protection to make it sustainable should be given the top priority. The dynamics of heavy industrialisation and technological development have far-reaching effects on the modern society. Without proper protection of the environment, the growth envisaged may result in an ultimate disaster. The industrial development and the protection of the environment are inextricably bound up with each other.

Gandhi has not made much reference in his writings and speechs about the environmental sustainability and its protection for the reason that the problem of environment was not much during his time and he might not have anticipated the terrifying dimensions of the environmental degradation as it is in the modern times. As a man of action with great insight about the environmental conservation and its sustainability, he formulated certain concepts and stood against the introduction of large-scale industrialisation.

Gandhi stated that industrial society is no longer ecologically sustainable and it has come true. He held that the industrial civilisation is all evil and a disease. It is in no way indispensable for the permanent welfare of the human race.

Gandhi says,

> Machinery is like a snake hole which may contain from one to a hundred snakes. Where there is machinery there are large cities. . . . Honest physicians will tell you that where means of artificial locomotion have increased the health of the people has suffered.[1]

In the good olden days people used to work in the open air which they liked much but in the modern times people work in the heavy industries at the risk of their lives in their most dangerous occupations to their great disadvantage.[2]

The attitude of man changes depending upon the stage of progress in the socio-economic spheres. In the times immemorial, the primitive man treated nature as wilderness and he recognised it as a source of his sustenance whereas the modern industrial man treats it as something to be tamed and subordinated.

> The technological revolution has gone several steps further in moulding the attitude of man. The Baconian creed that scientific and technological knowledge means control and power over nature, arose from the writings of Francis Bacon in the seventeenth century, but it has found its fullest expression in the last one hundred years. The development of electrical energy and the internal combustion engine, and in one word modernisation,

---

1. M.K. Gandhi, *Hind Swaraj*, p. 96.
2. *Ibid*., pp. 36-7.

> urbanisation and industrialisation gave man unprecedented power for transportation, production and environmental modification. These new tools, as products of scientific technology, strengthened the belief that science held sovereignty over nature.[3]

Gandhi raised his voice strongly against the cultural degradation and moral decadence in his book *Hind Swaraj* published in 1908. The book was a reaction against the modern civilisation and the baneful effects following heavy industrialisation. What Gandhi wanted was not mass production but production by the masses. Heavy industrialisation leads to the exploitation of the masses and nature. The existing situation of environmental pollution-prevails because of the attack of modern man on nature and his attempt to conquer nature. Man can tame or destroy the nature and environment.

The recent scientific discoveries have not added even an inch to the moral height of mankind,[4] when measured in the moral context. On the other hand, science manifested its superiority over the nature through the rapid industrialisation, urbanisation and the material progress without heeding to the devastating consequences that the present type of modernisation is leading to. It is the onerous responsibility of the people to initiate pollution control and the conservation of natural resources to dispel the false dilemma of environment and development. In order to avoid the environmental hazards, people have to have better planning and regulation in the industrial sectors by encouraging small-scale industries whereby pollution and other evils associated with the large-scale industries could be minimised, job opportunities could be increased and pollution problem could be solved.

Gandhi held that modern civilisation does not take note of morality or religion. People are afflicted by this type of civilisation. Those who are under its influence defend it. Modern man is attracted towards the civilisation as it increases the bodily comforts.

---

3. Charles H. Southwick, *Ecology and the Equality of Our Environment*, p. 79.
4. *Young India*, 8.12.1927, p. 414.

Gandhi states that a time is coming when those, who are in the mad rush today for multiplying their wants, vainly think that they add to the real substance and real knowledge of the world. They will retrace their steps and say, "what have we done?"[5] with an enormous increase in the size of the population and the multiplication of wants, so much stress has been laid on the environment because of the massive consumption of non-renewable natural resources, resulting in pollution on a large-scale and affecting thereby the environmental sustainability and ecological balance.

Schumacher held that the modern economy does not distinguish between renewable and non-renewable materials. Its method is to equalise and quantify everything by means of the fixation of a money price. When the various alternative fuels like coal, oil, wood or waterpowers are taken into consideration, the modern economy thinks in terms of the relative cost of each equivalent unit. It would be uneconomic if the cheapest is not preferred. That man has not recognised the essential difference existing between the non-renewable fuels like coal and oil on the one hand and the renewable fuels like wood and water-power on the other, cannot be simply overlooked. Non-renewable oils must be judiciously and carefully used if they are indispensable with utmost care and the most meticulous concern for conservation. Their heedless use with extravagance is an act of violence. The world's resources of non-renewable fuels such as coal, oil and natural gas are exceedingly unevenly distributed all over the globe and they are limited in the quantity at the same time. Exploitation of these natural resources in an ever-increasing rate is held to be an act of violence of man against nature.[6]

So, industrialised nations have to understand the problems created by them and evolve a new lifestyle with new methods of production and new patterns of consumption. It is a non-violent life-style designed for permanence and sustainability.[7]

The modern world is threatened today with the prospect of

5. *Young India.*
6. E.F. Schumacher, *Small is Beautiful*, p. 55.
7. *Ibid.*, p. 17.

shrinking food supplies with a steady increase in the population of the world. Soil erosion and constant impairment of the fertility of the soil have become growing problems of the world. Experts warn that the desire to exploit nature for quick profits results in setting of the deserts on the march. In order to avoid decline, people have to return from the economy of exploitation to the economy of conservation. This enables the largest concentration of population to rely on soil for its maintenance, health and reasonable comfort without impairing the soil fertility.

The outstanding features of this system are stated as:

1. Intensive, small-scale, diversified farming as opposed to mechanised, large-scale collective farming, the total yield, as against yield per agricultural worker, being the highest under this system;
2. Development of cottage crafts as ancillary to agriculture.
3. Cattle-based economy, with strict enforcement of the 'Law of Return', viz., to return to the soil in organic form what is taken out of the soil, without which the health and fertility of the soil cannot be fully maintained;
4. Proper balance and relationship between animal, human and plant life—social health and stability being essentially the product of a symbiosis of the three; and
5. Voluntary protection of both human and animal power against the competition of machinery as the price of social insurance.[8]

Man is an integral part of the nature and he cannot be free to maintain a separate existence. Man interacts with the biophysical environment through his culture, values, organisations, scientific knowledge and social arrangements. Man uses and exploits resources available in the biosphere for his immediate gain.[9] It is very much essential for man to have an understanding of the exploitation of the resources and the evil effects following from it before he uses the natural resources.

---

8. Pyaralal, *Gandhian Techniques in the Modern World*, pp. 39-40.
9. Desh Bandhu, *Environmental Education for Conservation and Development*, p. 61.

Land is constantly being eroded and polluted due to pesticides and fertilizers. These are the great disturbing features of the environment. It is learnt that around 424 nuclear reactors are being operated worldwide and some in addition have been planned for future. These are proved to be very dangerous and pose a great threat to environment and the human health.[10] There is need to have cattle-based economy to enforce the 'law of return' to the soil on organic form taken out from the solid to restore the fertility of the soil and promote human health. Proper balance has to be maintained between the animal and plant life.[11]

Man exploits and controls the environment. So he is on the losing side. He has to realise that if the unbreakable relationship with nature is broken, the quality of human life will be badly affected in socio-moral, socio-economic and cultural spheres and he is confronted with the predicament due to his ruthless assault on nature.

Petra K. Kelly says,

> The Ozone depletion acid rain and global warning are all related to human-generated emissions into the atmosphere changes in conditions on our planet manifest themselves in cancer rates, leukaemia, destruction of lakes and forests, melting of the polar ice caps and weather inequalities and subsequent flooding and loss of coastal land.[12]

Proper ecological understanding could be promoted when people think globally and act locally. There is need to be provid the impetus for non-violent and radical, social and economic transformation throughout the world to put an end to the destruction of the environment.[13]

> The modern man must re-establish the broken link with nature and with life. He must again learn to invoke the

---

10. Anil Dutta Mishra, *Gandhian Approach to Contemporary Problems*, pp. 194-5.
11. K.P. Misra (ed.), *Gandhi and the Contemporary World*, p. 44.
12. *Gandhi Marg*, Vol. II, Number 2, September 1989, p. 192.
13. *Ibid.*, p. 195.

> energy of the growing things and to recognise as did the ancients in India, centuries ago, that one can take from the earth and atmosphere only so much as one puts back into them.[14]

It is appropriate time for every individual to think of achieving a state of harmony with nature. Ecology is to live in harmony with the living organisms. It is a positive balance of multi-dimensional matrix or web of interdependent life and growth.[15] Man has to make the proper use of the land for land is the greatest material resource. The modern man does not make proper use of the land, for getting the reality that he is the child of nature, and he acts as the master of the nature.

> Civilised man was nearly always able to become master of his environment temporarily. His chief troubles came from his delusions that his temporary mastership was permanent. He thought of himself as 'the master of the world' while failing to understand.
>
> Man whether civilised or savage, is a child of nature. He must confirm his actions to certain natural laws if he is to maintain his dominance over his environment. When he tries to circumvent the laws of nature, he usually destroys the natural environment that sustains him. And when his environment deteriorates rapidly his civilisation declines.[16]

While giving a brief outline of history of the earth and the role of a civilised man, a writer stated that a "civilised man has marched across the face of the earth and left a desert in his foot-prints".[17] This statement has the basis of truth.

People in the past have not recognised the significance of environment and its sustainability and despoiled their environment. They depleted or destroyed their natural resources. They cut down

14. Desh Bandhu, *Environmental Education for Conservation and Development*, p. 2.
15. O.P. Dwivedi, *World Religions and Environment*, p. 37.
16. E.F. Schumacher, *Small is Beautiful,* p. 93.
17. *Ibid.*

or burned most of the timber in use from forested hill sides and valleys. Most of the wildlife was killed. Man allowed the erosion of his topsoil for the production of his farm. He allowed the erosion of soil to clog the streams and fill his reservoirs and irrigation canals. In most of the cases he used and wasted most of the easily mined metals or other needed minerals. Then the human civilisation witnessed a decline amidst the spoils of their own land.[18]

The conciliation of man with the natural world is not merely desirable but it has become a necessity. Man has to search for policies needed to reconstruct rural culture instead of drifting from agriculture. He has to make the land open for the gainful occupation to large number of people. There is need to orientate all over actions on the land towards the threefold ideal of health, beauty and goodness.

Schumacher says,

> The social structure of agriculture which has been produced by and is generally, held to obtain its justification from large-scale mechanisation and heavy chemicalisation, makes it impossible to keep man in real touch with living nature, infact it supports all the most dangerous tendencies of violence, alienation, and environmental destruction.[19]

The proposition of the replacement of thousands of millions of tons of fossil fuels, every year, by nuclear energy means to 'solve' the fuel problem is creating an environmental and ecological problem of such a monstrous magnitude. It is nothing but to solve one problem by shifting it to another sphere to create an infinitely bigger problem.[20]

The most notable and relevant concept of 'non-violence' as interpreted by Gandhi assumes great ecological significance. He stated that the human salvation lies in non-violence. He holds that "non-violence is the law of the human race".[21] Non-violence has to

---

18. *Small is Beautiful*, p. 94.
19. *Ibid.*, p. 105.
20. *Ibid.*, p. 16.
21. *Harijan*, 5.9.1936, p. 236.

be applied in all spheres of the human life as it is the law of life. "It must pervade the whole being but not to the isolated acts",[22] he said. His concept of non-violence is not merely limited to the human alone but to the nature and the whole universe also.

Gandhi pointed out:

> Non-violence is the greatest weapon at the disposal of mankind. It is mightier than the mightiest weapon of destruction, devised by the ingenuity of man. Destruction is not the law of the humans.[23]

As violence and exploitation are involved in the large-scale industries followed by its evils of pollution and heavy consumption of non-renewable natural resources. Gandhi believed in adopting a simple and ennobled life of evolving a non-violent technology by developing small-scale and cottage industries as a solution to the growing human problems and as a part of human duty towards the groaning world. He says,

> High thinking is inconsistent with complicated material life based on high speed. . . . All graces of life are possible when we learn the art of living nobly.[24]

What the people in the modern times need is a different lifestyle — a lifestyle to live nobly a simple life in harmony with nature with the spirit of conservation of natural resources by developing a non-violent technology in the place of heavy industries which finds employment to the poor and needy and reduces the problem of pollution to a greater extent. This helps to preserve the sanctity of the environment and saves the humanity from the environmental crisis and enables them to meet the environmental challenges non-violently and makes the ecology sustainable.

## Terrorism and the Modern World

In the modern industrial world the misguided youths without any

---

22. *Harijan*.
23. *Ibid.*, 20.7.1935, pp. 180-1.
24. *Ibid.*, 1.9.1946, p. 285.

respect for human values are on the increase. They are discontented and frustrated. As they are desperate, they resort to all evils. In the affluent societies, these young people resort to vandalism with bitter feeling as an escape from boredom. Due to lack of income, they resort to crimes for their sustenance. The growth of heavy industrialisation appeared to Gandhi as a great source of menace for the realisation of basic moral values in the human society. Several evils have beset the modern industrial world as it is vulnerable to them.

Riots may arise due to social, industrial and political causes. In the modern times, some resort to stealing, kidnapping, maiming and killing for their material gain.[25] Unlike the time of Gandhi which has registered sporadic incidents of violence and terrorism, the modern times witness terrorism on a much larger scale at an increased rate in an organised manner primarily because it is remunerative and the political blackmail gets immediate results. In this connection the terrorists who are convicted of crime, are released and huge ransoms are paid in the short-term. The terrorist ideas travel much faster than the terrorist themselves because of the latest modern communication network. Though their underlying politics is not initially violent, they carry the seeds of violence.

There is need to understand the problems of the terrorists, and their weak points and study their operations and techniques to suggest alternative methods and solve their problems amicably and non-violently. The terrorists export money or promise or engage in political blackmail for the release of their fellow terrorists who have been taken as prisoners and also they demand for the changes in the laws already in force to suit their convenience. The urban guerrillas aim to provoke repression specifically to make the government to govern without it to harass the people by searches, curfews, arrests and detentions by creating a feeling of fear and insecurity.[26]

The total numbers of terrorists constitute a very small group. Most of them are deeply indoctrinated with ideological beliefs and

---

25. Richard Clutterbuck, *The Future of Political Violence* p. 5.
26. Richard Clutterbuck, *Living with Terrorism*, p. 22.

they are convinced that their acts are in the best interests of the common people, though the common people reject them. They collaborate internationally and it is not possible to counter them locally. So it is necessary to mobilise international collaboration against them.[27]

The two reasons for the prevalence of terrorism in the modern times are due to the leaders and agencies of force in the state who acquired the preponderance of coercive power in total disregard of the underlying values and norms of the law in force with impunity within their domain. On the other hand, the tyrannical dictators or totalitarian governments subvert and manipulate the legal structure in their attempt to consolidate their position and power and oppress their internal opponents.[28]

The contemporary political process is marked by the established vital connection of force and violence. Political violence represents a disturbance to the political equilibrium of a state.[29] Political protest is generated more by people who have educational opportunities to participate in the most affluent modern society but prefer to reject its values for ideological and environmental reasons. The rejection is manifested in the form of disruption, sabotage or malicious damage, bombing, personal attack or other forms of terrorism.[30] Political terrorists may broadly be subdivided depending upon their motivation into nationalist, religious or ideological spheres.[31]

Terrorism is distinguishable from violence. It is a special kind of organised violence. Terrorism in its essence "is the use or threat of violence against small numbers to put large in fear".[32]

Terrorism may be defined as

---

27. *Living with Terrorism*, p. 28.
28. Linus Pauling (ed.), *World Encyclopaedia of Peace*, Vol. 3, p. 452.
29. Carl Leuden and Karl K. Schmith, *The Politics of Violence Revolution in the Modern World*, p. 3.
30. Richard Clutterbuck, *The Future of Political Violence*, p. 11.
31. *Ibid.*, p. 21.
32. *Ibid.*, p. 20.

> the systematic use or threat of murder, injury, and destruction to create a climate of terror to publicise a cause, and to coerce a wider target into submitting to the terrorist's aims.[33]

Terror is a symbolic act designed to influence a political behaviour by extra normal means, entailing the use or threat of violence.[34] The development from peaceful protest to terrorism is a gradual one. Only a small number of protesters in fact do become terrorists among whom most of them dropout being unable to adjust with the exercise of violence on the way.[35] The exercise of violence is designed to overthrow the government in the separatist context, aimed to pressurise the foreign governments to accede to their demands for independence.[36]

> The purpose of terrorism is to terrorise. When a child is caught in their cross-fire or a worker killed by a bomb their deaths represent not mistakes but an integral part of the business of terror.[37]

The object of the terrorist is to shake off the faith of a man in the street in the government and in its local representatives, especially the police, so that in the end a desperate people would seek his security from the terrorists and his political allies but not from the authorities concerned.[38] Terrorism is designed to terrorise the innocent people by the exercise of organised violence as a psychological and political weapon in accord with other tactics to overthrow the democratic system and control the population.[39] The success or failure of terrorism depends upon the nature of the

---

33. Linus Pauling (ed.), *World Encyclopaedia of Peace*, Vol. II, p. 451.
34. Thomas Peny Thornton, *Terror as a Weapon of Political Agitation*, p. 73.
35. Richard Clutterbuck, *The Future of Political Violence*, p. 22.
36. Anthony M. Burton, *Urban Terrorism*, Preface, p. ix.
37. *Ibid.*, p. 5.
38. *Ibid.*
39. Richard Clutterbuck, *The Future of Political Violence*, p. 177.

society and its socio-economic and political conditions and the manner of dealing with it.

Terrorism thrives under certain conditions. Sir Robert Mark says,

> Where there is an unbridgeable gulf between government and the governed — between rich and poor. Where the police are generally detested and the courts regarded as a tool of government, where franchise is not universal and the government self-perpetuating, there you are likely to find terrorism. And there, also, it is likely to flourish.[40]

The terrorists have been indoctrinated with a type of ideology supporting violence and terrorism. The national and international incidents of terrorism are on rapid increase. International terrorism takes the form of terrorist movements being operated in other countries like hijacking, kidnapping or killing those people who travel within or outside their own countries. The terrorists who operate their activities outside their own countries may aim to coerce a foreign government, or to intimidate their nationals or refugees working abroad. On the other hand, the terrorists acting on their own country against foreign visitors or residents may aim to coerce governments.[41]

In order to avert violence, terrorism and bloodshed, Gandhi aimed at a non-violent society and a non-violent state. He advocated the doctrine of trusteeship to realise the ideal of economic equality for the emergence of an egalitarian society basing on non-stealing and non-possession to avoid exploitation. This includes the abolition of eternal conflict between the capital and labour by means of levelling down of the rich in whose hands the bulk of nation's wealth is concentrated on the one hand, and levelling up of the semi-starved naked millions on the other. He held that a non-violent system of government is an impossibility as long as the wide gulf between the rich and the poor exists. He added that a violent and a bloody revolution would be one day a certainty unless people voluntarily abdicate their riches and the power that follows from

---

40. *The Future of Political Violence*, p. 161.
41. *Ibid.*, p. 25.

those riches and share them for the good of the common people.[42] Gandhi could foresee the outburst of violence in an organised manner and in such a state bloodshed is inevitable and terrorism flourishes. This could be averted when the gulf between the rich and the poor is bridged.

Gandhi, on the other hand, stood for the emergence of a non-violent decentralised democracy which promotes the full growth of all the individuals by promoting fellow feeling, mutual trust and cooperation. He held that the best type of government is such that it governs the least which gives the weakest the same opportunity as the strongest. When the government is non-violent and all the people are involved in the affairs of the state, it results in a healthy and dignified interdependence, protecting the freedom and independence of all the individuals. When the rule of the government is based on the consent of the people, there would be no problem. Everybody is a ruler in such a state, without being a hindrance to his neighbour. In such a type of government terrorism would not flourish unlike in the authoritarian and ruthless governments which are based on force and violence. In a liberal decentralised democracy which is based on universal franchise with its multi-party system followed by freedom of expression, terrorism would not flourish and, even if any incidents of it occur, could easily be suppressed or controlled.

Gandhi spoke of the futility of violence, love in the place of hatred and non-violent social structure in the place of existing social structure which supports violence in an organised manner. He stood against terrorism as a means, and held that the means adopted should necessarily be as pure as the end and did not agree with the view that end justifies the means. For Gandhi, means and ends are convertible terms. He pointed out that the opposite theory that end justifies the means leads to arrive at the conclusion that violent means that are dangerous and ethically unsound could be applied which give recourse to violence and terrorism. He states "I object to violence because, when it appears to do good, the good is only temporary, the evil it does is permanent".[43] He stated further

42. M.K. Gandhi, *Constructive Programme*, pp. 20-1.

43. *Young India*, 21.5.1925, p. 178.

that "the method of violence cannot do good in the long run".[44]

The act of terrorism and revolutionary activity is suicidal to the progress of the nation. By the heinous act of violence, the terrorists drag down themselves and the dignity of mankind and thereby they violate the human rights and stand as a great threat to the human security in the modern times.

Even if the terrorists justify their act as the expediency or for a good cause, Gandhi never accepted such acts. He stated,

> I do not regard killing or assassination or terrorism as good in any circumstances whatsoever.[45]

There is a Gandhian solution as an alternative method to terrorism if the cause is reasonable and just for the common good inclusive of non-cooperation and civil disobedience based upon the well organised and well defined non-violent principle which prove more potential morally and extremely effective for the removal of unjust and unscrupulous elements and all other evils that have beset the modern society, without relying on terrorism and the exercise of violence. Gandhi did not repose his faith on terrorism.

Gandhi says,

> My experience teaches me that truth can never be propagated by doing violence. Those who believe in the justice of their cause have need to possess boundless patience.[46]

## Non-Violence and World Peace

The issue of peace assumes greater significance than before in the modern times. Peace is held to be not merely a state of the absence of war, stress, strain, conflict and disturbance, but it is a positive state of contentment, blissfulness and love. The concept of peace has been discussed endlessly at the national and international

---

44. *Young India*, 9.6.1920, p. 3.
45. *Ibid.*, 9.4.1925, p. 126.
46. *Ibid.*, 28.4.1920, p. 8.

levels by the statesmen, thinkers and social reformers. They have struggled relentlessly to find the possible solutions to end the internal and external wars between the nations and within the nations. It is more relevant and proper to give a serious thought for the establishment of an enduring and lasting peace in this world.

> Stable international peace — peace that brings security and happiness to the citizens of all countries, must mean much more than the simple obscene of war. It must eliminate violence and the abuse of wealth and power.[47]

The human life becomes meaningful and purposive and gains significance and relevance when the long cherished dream of world peace is realised. Peace cannot be achieved by mere craving or desire. Peace prevails only under certain circumstances. Peace demands sacrifice and the total human effort.

Gandhi thoroughly studied the concept of non-violence and found it to be the basic tenet of human existence. He conducted a series of experiments with non-violence and made it applicable to resolve the national and international problems. He demonstrated to the whole world that non-violence is the only indisputable way to attain peace and tranquillity is more palpable. The concept of non-violence as interpreted by Gandhi is not merely an anti-thesis of violence but it is multi-dimensional. It is a way of life and a conduct to sustain order. It sets in a new world order in the modern civilisation and transforms the existing social order based on violence through its application.

The successful application of non-violence ushers in a new peaceful world order, involving a great deal of moral strength, and readiness to undergo self-suffering on the part of the person who applies it. The success of the application of non-violence depends upon the conviction of the person which has to be gradual, with the attitude that one step is enough for me. The beginning will be small and the rest will follow, says Gandhi.[48]

Non-violence plays a vital role to this tension-ridden, weary

---

47. *The Encyclopaedia of America*, Vol. 29, p. 439.

48. *Harijan*, 28.1.1939, p. 442.

and disturbed world carrying with it the message of the change of heart, to result in the ultimate transformation of the modern society for its betterment. The world has been dominated by the politics of power, balance of power, diplomatic relations and other constraints. So non-violence and love have to be brought about in the place of violence and hatred for the establishment of a new peaceful world.

Gandhi held that non-violence is the law of human race, infinitely greater than violence. It could be exercised by all.

> Non-violence is the greatest force at the disposal of mankind. It is mightier than the mightiest weapon of destruction devised by the ingenuity of man.[49]

The observance of non-violence is of absolute necessity in the modern world. Gandhi stated that "unless now the world adopts non-violence, it will spell certain suicide for mankind".[50] Peace is the absence of physical and mental violence between nations, regions, religions, creeds, races, classes, sexes and between man and man and man and nature. It is only by love and unadulterated non-violence, that peace could be established.[51] The belief in the ability of man to live peacefully is contradiction in terms to the belief of the present world with its unending violence and constant conflict due to the result of biological and psychological drives inherent in mind.[52] So there is no option for man except to rely on non-violence and practise it to realise truth and experience peace in this modern world.

The modern world is beset with nuclear arms race, civil wars, ethnic and religious conflicts. All these have greatly contributed to the internal insecurity, international armament, mutual disbelief, etc. The following remedial measures offered by Gandhi help to resolve the conflicts and solve the problems.

I. Both the national and international leaders must believe

---

49. *Harijan.*, 20.7.1935, p. 180.
50. *Ibid.*, 29.9.1946, p. 335.
51. *Gandhi Marg*, Vol. 17, Number 1, April-June, 1995, p. 7.
52. David Brook (ed.), *Search For Peace*, p. viii.

in peace and cooperation and sincerely work in that direction.

II. Powerful nations must give up their imperialist designs to dominate and exploit other nations.

III. Imperialism of any kind can be abolished if nations restrict their desires to increase their material possessions and learn to lead simple life and

IV. Leaders and peoples of all nations should believe in the oneness of God and oneness of mankind.[53]

Non-violence may not be attainable if a person attempts to obtain it at one rush but people could reach it if they are prepared to work towards it by stage.[54] Gandhi presented non-violence which is the purest, the most elevating and the most inspiring ideal to enable the people to live in peace and progress. Gandhi had firm faith in man. He was hopeful that the future world would be a world of peace, free from wars and bloodshed on the basis of non-violence. He held that the world of tomorrow will be and must be a society based on non-violence. It may seem to be a distant goal and an impractical utopia. It is not unattainable and it could be worked out from now.

> An individual can adopt the way of life of the future — the non-violent way without having to wait for others to do so. And if an individual can do it, cannot whole groups of individuals? Whole nations? Men often hesitate to make a beginning because they feel that the objectives cannot be achieved in its entirety. This attitude of mind is precisely our greatest obstacle to progress — an obstacle that each man; if he only wills it, can clear away.[55]

The practical use of non-violence could be realised when tested.

The virtue of mercy, non-violence, love and truth in any

---

53. *Gandhi Marg*, Vol. 15, Number 4, January-March, 1994, pp. 422-3.
54. S. Radhakrishnan, *Religion and Society*, p. 225.
55. *Ibid.*, p. 230.

> man can be truly tested on when they are pitted against ruthlessness violence, hate and untruth.[56]

Gandhi showed the significance and the applicability of non-violence in a most unique manner as a panacea to the modern world ridden with several evils and problems. He held that violence results in counter-violence and there is no end for violence. Violence could be put to an end only through love or non-violence. It is because that 'love does not burn others, it burns itself.'[57] He objected to violence for the reason when it appears to do good, the good is only temporary but the evil it does is permanent.[58] "The method of violence cannot do good in the long-run",[59] Gandhi said.

The application of non-violence is extendible from the smallest group to the global society. The person who uses non-violence as well as on whom it is used will be blessed because of the tremendous moral force it releases. It creates a climate to promote understanding, good-will, mutual trust and cooperation and puts an end to the prejudices, suspicions, fear, hatred and overall sense of insecurity which are the general causes of violence.[60]

Permanent peace cannot be attained through violence and even if it could be achieved, it is temporary. On the other hand, mutual violence inevitably breeds hatred, revenge and bitterness which stands as a poor foundation for a perfect peace.[61]

> Peace imposed by violence is not psychological peace but a suppressed conflict. It is unstable, for it contains the seeds of its own destruction. The outer condition is not a true reflection of the inner condition. But in peace secured by any inner conflict a new channel is found, in which both the formerly conflicting energies are at work in the same

---

56. M.K. Gandhi, *Non-violence in Peace and War*, Vol. II, p. 85.
57. M.K. Gandhi, *Satyagraha*, p. 78.
58. *Young India*, 21.5.1925, p. 178.
59. *Ibid.*, 9.6.1920, p. 3.
60. S.C. Biswas (ed.), *Gandhi, Theory and Practice. Social Impact and Contemporary Relevance*, p. 507.
61. Richard B. Gregg, *The Power of Non-violence*, p. 112.

> direction and in harmony. Here the outer condition truly reflects the inner condition.[62]

For the last several centuries, war and violence have been tried as a means to achieve peace and prosperity. In the modern times, they threaten the very existence of the human race and there has been the growing conviction among the sane people that non-violence is the only means to avert the catastrophe.[63]

Gandhi had a global perspective — a world-view which has dimensions — sacrifice and coherence. His world-view has become an experienced feeling of non-violence and truth which universalises his ethics and he ethicises world-view. "To Gandhi, world-view is at once an intellectual framework, an emotional attitude and a social reality."[64]

The principle of non-violence is based on love, not limited merely to the personal relations, but extendible to the national and international level. For a person following non-violence, the whole world is one family.[65] Gandhi firmly believed in the doctrine of the absolute universal love.

He stated thus:

> It is my firm belief that if love that sustains the earth. There only is life where there is love. Life without love is death. Love is the reverse of the coin of which the obverse is truth. It is my firm faith and it is my experience that we can conquer the world by truth and love. Love conquers hate.[66]

In the modern world, the fact that human life is surrounded by strife and bloodshed is undeniable. It is only through the practice

---

62. *The Power of Non-violence*, p. 63.
63. Gopinath Dhawan, *The Political Philosophy of Mahatma Gandhi*, p. 4.
64. Y.G. Krishna Murty, *Neo Gandhism*, p. 53.
65. *Harijan*, 21.7.1940, p. 214.
66. *The Collected Works of Mahatma Gandhi*, Vol. XXV August, 1924-January 1925, p. 259.

of non-violence that man could fulfil his destiny and his duty towards his fellow men.[67] The non-violent resistance has its basis on the idea of unity. It is because

> non-violent resistance demoralises the opponent only to re-establish in him a new morale that is finer because it is based on sounder values. Non-violent resistance does not break the opponent's will but alters it, does not destroy his confidence, enthusiasm and hope but transforms them to a finer purpose".[68]

Non-violent resistance influences other people intellectually and morally.[69]

Non-violence implies the elimination of petty jealousies of the local group, caste and communal discriminations. It signifies the recognition of the national community based on suffering, tolerance and self-abnegation.[70] As the national problems could be solved by non-violence, the torchlight of non-violence has to be kept burning with greater brightness ever in the midst of the encircling gloom.

V.P. Varma sums up the firm merits of non-violence as a technique for political action

> First, it strengthens the foundations of democratic behaviour. Secondly, it prevents the emergence of counter-revolution. Thirdly, it serves as a morally oriented conceptual pattern for judging political action. Fourthly, it pleads for the negation of Machtpolitik.[71] (Politics of Power)

Gandhi had the vision of the unity of all mankind and he firmly believed in this ideal. Though he was intensely attached to the concept of Indian nationalism, he was an internationalist and emphasised his role as a citizen of the world.

---

67. M.K. Gandhi, *For Pacifists*, p. 4.
68. Richard B. Gregg, *The Power of Non-violence*, p. 76.
69. *Ibid.*, p. 164.
70. V.P. Varma, *Political Philosophy of Mahatma Gandhi and Sarvodaya*, p. 161.
71. *Ibid.*, p. 176.

Gandhi says,

> It is impossible for one to be internationalist without being a nationalist. Internationalism is possible only when nationalism becomes a fact, i.e., when people belonging to different countries have organised themselves and are able to act as one man. It is not nationalism that is evil, it is the narrowness, selfishness, exclusiveness which is the bane of modern nations which is evil.[72]

Gandhi held that all people are the members of the vast human family. So love of the human mind is an aspect of non-violence. The universal love of humanity finds its concrete expression in the internationalism. India has to be free before she could cooperate herself on equal terms with other nations. Similar is the opinion of Kant who held that practical idea of federation of states has to be extended gradually over all the states with a compact between them for the establishment of perpetual peace.

Immanuel Kant postulated the law of world citizenship as a precondition for the establishment of perpetual peace. In his famous book *Perpetual Peace*, a philosophical essay, he stated thus:

> Without a compact between the nations, however, this state of peace cannot be established or assured. Hence there must be an alliance of a particular kind which we may call a covenant of peace, which would differ from a treaty of peace in this respect that the latter merely puts an end to one war, while the former would seek to put an end to war forever. This alliance does not aim at the gain of any power whosoever of the state but merely at preservation and security of the freedom of the states at the same time. The latter do not however, require for this reason to submit themselves like individuals in the state of nature to public laws and coercion. The practically or objective reality of this idea of federation which is to extend gradually over all states and led to perpetual peace can be shown.[73]

72. *Young India*, 18.6.1925, p. 211.
73. Immanuel Kant, *Perpetual Peace—A Philosophical Essay*, p. 17.

Kant further stated:

1. The civil constitution of every state should be republican.
2. The Law of Nations shall be founded on a Federation of free states.
3. The Law of world citizenship shall be limited to the conditions of universal hospitality.[74]

Bertrand Russell, the world renowned philosopher, also aimed at a world government for the establishment of world peace. He maintained that the world government should be federal with a constitution, embodying the principle which should control the entire federation, and the federal government should concern itself with the external acts of constituent states or at any rate with such of these states which affect interests of other states directly.[75] He advocated the ideal that "mankind is one family with common interests".[76]So cooperation is much more important than competition. To love one's own neighbour is not only a moral duty but it is the wisest policy to promote the human happiness.[77]

Gandhi visualised a plan of human unity to be realised by federal organisation of friendly interdependent states. He had a great devotion to realise the noble goal of international peaceful cooperation and universal harmony. What is needed is not dependence but the interdependence of the states.

Gandhi says,

> The better mind of the world desires today not absolutely independent states warring one against another, but a federation of friendly interdependent states. The consummation of that event may be far off. I want to make no grand claim for our country. But I see nothing grand or impossible about our expressing our readiness for universal interdependence rather than independence.[78]

---

74. *Perpetual Peace — A Philosophical Essay*, pp. 98-102.
75. Bertrand Russell, *Fact and Fiction*, p. 121.
76. Arthur Barker (ed.), *Bertrand Russell Speaks his Mind*, p. 42.
77. *Ibid.*, p. 43.
78. *Young India*, 26.12.1924, p. 425.

Gandhi stood for a world federation of free and independent states to realise the kingdom of God within themselves. He could foresee that possibility of the world to be united under the central governing body composed of representatives of the component parts as the only condition on which the world could safely exist.[79]

He stated that

> The structure of a world federation can be raised only on foundation of non-violence, and violence will have to be totally given up in World affairs.[80]

Though Gandhi stood for the village republics, for the individual initiative and his involvement, he aimed at the necessity of mutual dependence. When the individual is developed fully in the moral and social spheres, he would develop passion for humanity breaking the national and geographical limitations. He stated that no culture could be claimed to be exclusive or superior over the other. He stood for acculturation and cultural synthesis for the cultural advancement of the humanity at large. He drew the inspiration from the Indian nationalism which has its source of belief from the national integrity despite its seeming diversity. This forms the logical basis for nationalism to make its way into internationalism.

Gandhi says,

> Through realisation of freedom of India, I hope to realise and carry on the mission of brotherhood of man. My patriotism is not an exclusive thing. It is all-embracing and I should reject that patriotism which sought to mount upon the distress or the exploitation of other nationalities. The conception of my patriotism is nothing if it is not always in every case without exception consistent with the broadest good of humanity at large.[81]

So, love and concern for the humanity that Gandhi had, broadened his outlook to be a nationalist as well as an internationalist.

---

79. M.K. Gandhi, *Sarvodaya*, p. 80.
80. *Gandhis's Correspondence with the Government*, 1942-4, p. 143.
81. *Young India*, 4.4.1929, p. 107.

Gandhi point out:

> Just as the cult of patriotism teaches us today that the individual has to die for the family, the family has to die for the village, the village for the district, the district for the province and the province for the country, even so a country has to be free in order that it may die, if necessary for the benefit of the world. My love, therefore, of nationalism or my idea of nationalism is that my country may become free, that if need be the whole of the country may die, so that the human race may live. There is no room for race hatred there. Let that be our nationalism.[82]

The establishment of international peace requires the development of a world community. This creates a mood of mutual tolerance, respect and goodwill needed for the establishment and operation of such a community in social practice by the use of non-violent resistance for the rectification of the defects and correcting the wrongs.[83]

Leo Tolstoy says,

> The miseries of men are due to their discord. And their discord results from their not following the truth which is one, but falsehood which is legion. The only means by which men can be united is by union in the truth. And therefore the more sincerely men seek the truth the nearer will they approach to union.[84]

Gandhi stated that non-violence is the means and truth is the end. He says that "ahimsa is not the goal. Truth is the goal. But we have no means of realising truth in human relationship except through the practice of ahimsa."[85] Gandhi was confident of the permanent peace. He says that "if the world is to have peace, non-violence is the means to that end and no other".[86]

---

82. Mahadev Desai (ed.), *Gandhiji in Indian Villages*, p. 170.
83. Richard B. Gregg, *The Power of Non-violence*, p. 120.
84. Leo Tolstoy, *The Kingdom of God is Within You*, p. 410.
85. *Harijan*, 23.6.1946, p. 199.
86. M.K. Gandhi, *Communal Unity*, p. 670.

A single Airforce plane 'Enola Gay' dropped an atom-bomb over the city of Hiroshima. A mushroom-shaped cloud of boiling dust which is of churning debris rose over 20,000 feet into the air within a few minutes. Later on it was learnt that 60 per cent of the built up area of the city was completely destroyed. This is how the atomic age of terrifying dimensions entered into the life of mankind. The world could not adjust with this potential means of vast destruction or to have international violence as an integral element in interstate relationships. In the modern times the search for peace is of great significance than everbefore.[87]

After the Second World War, human security is at stake and there has been a growing feeling of the global crisis as the values on which the humanity has been laid, started warning with the emergence of modern civilisation. Gandhi held that the modern civilisation is a disease and self-destructive. It is because the brilliant inventions and discoveries have not added an inch to the moral height of mankind.

The modern world is beset with several evils. The nature of the modern world is marked by the defects and evils.

> The tumult of violence, the excitement of anger, the rivalry for power and maintenance and preservation of world bodies in spite of their defects are the birth pangs of the new world.[88]

Although man strives for peace, in this modern age he discovered the most dreadful atomic weapons to establish his military superiority. The modern nuclear weaponry is most powerful enough to completely annihilate the very existence of human civilisation. The super powers acquired more than needed capacity to destroy each other's nations with the latest technologically developed nuclear weapons of stock piles. This could be triggered off by a nuclear exchange resulting in the total annihilation of the human race. The leader of the super powers are under the moral obligation to give a serious thought to this questionable dreaded nuclear weaponry and to destroy the stockpiles at any cost.

---

87. David Brook (ed.), *Search for Peace*, Preface, p. vii.
88. Ramjee Singh, *The Relevance of Gandhian Thought*, p. 72.

The human progress to a greater extent is crippled because of the militarisation of the scientific endeavour.

Gandhi says,

> I am convinced that unless India develops her non-violent strength, she has gained nothing either for herself for the world Militarisation of India will mean her own destruction as well as of the whole world.[89]

There is need for India to develop her non-violent strength to be a good example to the whole world and to usher in a peaceful world order. Man could get out of violence only through non-violence and hatred can be overcome only by love.[90] War knows no moral law except that of might is right.

Permanent peace cannot be established through superior violence for it inevitably leads to atom-bomb and the mass destruction it causes. It is the negation of non-violence in its fullness and of democracy which is not possible without the former.[91] Thus violence could never be ended by counter violence. The only effective alternative being the way of non-violence.[92]

Those who take to the sword, they perish by it and those who seek peace and who act in a friendly manner in offensively, forgetting and forgiving offences, for the most part enjoy peace.[93] The military illusions are that some nuclear weapons could be used to gain some military advantage in a war. But there cannot be direct military utility. The military might expect that the war could be small and limited. It is a total illusion. Those that use the nuclear weaponry confidently think that they are on the winning side but a nuclear war means mutual suicide.[94]

---

89. *Harijan*, 14.12.1947, p. 471.
90. M.K. Gandhi, *Non-violence in Peace and War*, Vol. II, p. 97.
91. *Ibid.*, p. 234.
92. *Harijan*, 30.3.1947, p. 88.
93. Leo Tolstoy, *The Kingdom of God is Within You*, p. 20.
94. Devavrat N. Pathak, "Peace Education", article submitted to the Workshop on Peace and Disarmament Studies held during 16-20 Feb. 1987, at the Department of Defence Studies, Voorthhes College, Vellore, p. 6.

The final document of the 10th special session of the General Assembly stands for the disarmament as the programme of action on top priority.

> Nuclear weapons pose the greatest danger to mankind and to the survival of civilisation. It is essential to halt and reverse the nuclear arms race in all its aspects in order to avert the danger of war involving nuclear weapons. The ultimate goal in this context is the complete elimination of nuclear weapons.[95]

When the nuclear tests are conducted, the radio activity emanates from those tests. It represents a greater degree of danger to all parts of the world. The bad effects following it could be felt not alone in the first generation but also by the succeeding generations. Future generations would witness the birth of the increasing number of children with mental defects and physical deformities. The land on which the people inhabit become uninhabitable after the end of the atomic war. It is for this reason that the scientists demand for an international understanding and agreement for the end of the nuclear tests.[96]

Bertrand Russell aptly puts about the modern weapons in the following words:

> Since modern weapons leave us with no choice except all to live together or all die together, the preservation of the human species demands a greater degree of natural tolerance than has ever before been necessary.[97]

In a nuclear war, the states possessing nuclear arsenals themselves may suffer the heaviest casualities and the most extensive damage. The nations in the world would experience grave physical consequences. Radio-active fallout is held to be a serious problem especially in countries adjacent to the belligerent states and during the decades after a major nuclear war, fallout would take a toll of

---

95. *Report of the Secretary General on the Nuclear Weapons*, p. 3.
96. Albert Sweitzer, *Peace or Atomic War*, pp. 12-13.
97. Bertrand Russell, *Fact and Fiction,* George Allen & Unwin Ltd., London, 1961, p. 275.

millions worldwide in present and future generations. Besides this, the world economy and the vital functions of the international community would suffer the evil global consequences.[98]

Gandhi held that peace through the armed peace will be broken at any moment.[99] The values of life such as truth, goodness, righteousness and social justice cannot be resulted from the use of atomic war. So science has to adopt the values of life to contribute for creativity, cooperation and human progress.

The cataclysmic changes that have been brought about in the modern world because of the nuclear weaponry and stockpiles did not change the attitude of Gandhi. He adhered to his faith in non-violence and truth. He held that they constitute the greatest and mightiest force at the human disposal and atom-bomb has no effect before it. He emphasised the need for the humanity to recognise the significance of non-violence and escape from self-destruction.

Gandhi pointed out:

> The moral to be legitimately drawn from the supreme tragedy of the bomb is that it will not be destroyed by counter-bombs even as violence cannot be by counter-violence. Mankind has to get out of violence only through non-violence. Hatred can be overcome only by love. Counter-hatred only increases the surface as well as the depth of hatred.[100]

At the time of conventional warfare, the military doctrines of various kinds have been used to describe the intended conduct of future wars; to control or guide the use of force and to determine the conditions. Due to the existence of nuclear weapons and the rapid technological development during the last few decades, numerous military doctrines in regard to the use or threat of nuclear weapons came into force and they are under the constant revision.[101] The significance and relevance of the military doctrines depends upon the military and political

---

98. *Report of the Secretary General* on *Nuclear Weapons*, p. 182.
99. *Harijan*, 10.1939, p. 296.
100. *Ibid.*, 7.7.1946, p. 212.
101. *Report of the Secretary General on Nuclear Weapons*, p. 108.

purposes they serve. A particular doctrine may have the form of operational concepts for the conduct of war but its objective is to serve as a political declaration for the promotion of peace. The credibility of a certain doctrine depends upon the means for its implementation.[102]

Notable doctrine concerning the nuclear weapons is the doctrine of nuclear deterrence which has its basis on a threat of mutual suicide.[103] This theory gives threat of the use of force to prevent someone from carrying out his intentions. Unlike the deterrence with conventional weapons, the nuclear deterrence under the present conditions is immediate, total and global. In this nuclear age, it is possible to carry out an attack within a few hours and even minutes. In the past it was never possible to carry out such destruction on a mass scale on any part of the globe.[104]

It has been stated that

> enduring international peace and security cannot be built on the accumulation of weaponry by military alliances nor be sustained by a precarious balance of deterrence or doctrines of strategic superiority.[105]

The statement of Immanuel Kant about the evil effects of war and the mass destruction of both the parties bears relevance to the modern nuclear age.

> It follows that a war of extermination in which the destruction of both parties and of all justice can result, would permit perpetual peace only in the vast burial ground of the human race. Therefore, such a war and the use of all means leading in it must be absolutely forbidden.[106]

Gandhi gave the message of peace and concord to the modern world. His ideal was concord in the place of discord, peace in the place of strife, progress in the place of retrogression and life in the place of

102. *Report of the Secretary General on Nuclear Weapons*, p. 109.
103. K. Subrahmanyam (ed.), *Nuclear Myths and Realities*, p. 53.
104. *Report of the Secretary General on Nuclear Weapons*, p. 110.
105. *Ibid.*, pp. 183-4.
106. Immanuel Kant, *Perpetual Peace—A Philosophical Essay*, p. 90.

death.[107] It is the human responsibility to keep the desire for peace alive and make the mankind to relentlessly strive for it for "peace makes people to dwell in safety".[108] It is only when the people depart from evil that they could do good. "Depart from evil and do good; seek peace and pursue it."[109] Gandhi maintained that not to believe in the possibility of permanent peace is to disbelieve in the Godliness of human nature.[110] Permanent peace is a human possibility as well as the human responsibility to usher in a peaceful world order.

Gandhi held that if the leaders of the world who have control over the nuclear weaponry renounce their use wholly, being fully aware of its implications, permanent peace could be established.[111] As he aptly puts, "peace will never come until the Great Powers courageously decide to disarm themselves".[112] The non-violence has to be made as the governing principle of all the individuals of all the nations as their social conduct for the establishment of world peace.[113] Thus, the practice of non-violence contributes to progress and peace to the humanity at large.

---

107. *Harijan*, 30.11.1947, p. 436.
108. *Holy Bible*, Psalms 4:8.
109. *Ibid.*, Psalms 33:14.
110. M.K. Gandhi, *For Pacifists*, p. 81.
111. *Harijan*, 16.5.1936, p. 109.
112. *Ibid.*, 24.12.1938, p. 395.
113. *Gandhi Marg*, April 1982, p. 22.

7

# Summary and Conclusion

UNLESS the teachings and the aspects covered in the moral, religious, socio-economic and political spheres have applicability bearing significance and relevance on the modern life, they cannot make any lasting impact on the society. Mahatma Gandhi thoroughly studied, and applied the teachings and moral ideas of the great teachers of the world and demonstrated their practical applicability because of their relevance and significance. The philosophic ideals and ideas will have significance, meaning and purpose if they are related to the human life, described as mundane. Gandhi did not draw any line of separation between mundane and transcendental, worldly and other-worldly. He did not view the socio-economic, moral-religious and political aspects of the human life as watertight compartments. He held that all the aspects are related and connected to the human life acting and reacting on one another, cannot be kept separate.

Gandhi was open-minded and accommodative at the same time. Apart from the influence his parents exerted on him which is a common and normal feature with all the persons, his honest confession lies in his admittance of the influence that his nurse, Rambha had made to that of the thinker and writers of eminence like Leo Tolstoy, John Ruskin, etc.

The influence of his parents especially his mother left on him a lasting memory of saintliness, religiosity and practice of truth. He was laid firmly on the foundations of saintliness, religiosity and truthfulness and never deviated from these values since his childhood. The experience he had with his father helped him to know of the ways and means to solve the most intricate problems.

This experience helped him to solve the national problems and find solutions in his later life to the global issues also. The impression of Shravana was lasting and prompted him to render service to the humanity and the play Harischandra captured his heart and made him to learn that there is no higher value than truth and the absolute truth is knowable through the relative truth commonly experienced in the human relations. His preparedness to sacrifice anything including non-violence for truth speaks of his reverence and commitment for truth.

The influence of Jainism and Buddhism which lays more stress on non-violence in reverence for life was noticeable. While the follower of Jainism observes non-violence to keep himself pure from this world, Gandhi interpreted non-violence in a new perspective and made it more relevant and applicable in the religio-moral, socio-economic and political spheres of this world. He made it a mission of his life to see that non-violence gets a proper place and observed it in all human relations as the human life is an undivided whole. In the modern context, non-violence has become more relevant. Both Jainism and Buddhism lay more stress on celibacy, non-violence, non-stealing and non-possession which are relevant in the modern times.

Renunciation of objects without renunciation of desires is short-lived. So Gandhi held that one has to act without hankering after fruit. The central teaching of *Gita* is bounded by truth and non-violence. The words such as *aparigraha* (non-possession) and *sambhava* (equability) gripped him. Non-possession implies that one should not possess things not more than one needs for the day. He should not preserve anything for the future. While the rich have a superfluous store of things which they do not need, the poor are neglected and starved to death for want of sustenance.[1] Equability implies that one should possess the things in accordance with his needs and requirements. The concept of non-possession leads to the theory of trusteeship. The rich should voluntarily abdicate their surplus riches and become trustees to establish an equitable economic society so that an egalitarian state may prevail.

---

1. M.K. Gandhi, *From Yervada Mandir*, pp. 19-20.

The influence of Raichand helped him to imbibe the religious consciousness. Mahabharata is a war between the Pandavas and Kauravas in which many millions were engaged in the colossal conflict resulting in a bloodshed. This establishes the futility of war and violence and salvation lies only in non-violence and truth.

Gopalakrishna Gokhale influenced Gandhi to recognise the significance of the spiritualisation of the politics. This paved the way to Gandhi to purify politics by refusing any dichotomy between religion and politics. His another concept of the purity of means and ends is significant. This made Gandhi to state that end does not justify the means. For Gandhi means and ends are convertible terms.[2]

Vivekananda exerted profound influence on Gandhi. His conception that 'service to the poor is service to God' impressed Gandhi. In Vivekananda the combination of two ideals — the individual salvation and the universal well-being could be found. Vivekananda brought social context to religion to make it meaningful and purposive. Gandhi humanised religion by making the individual supreme. He could not find God apart from rest of the human activity. He made religion, the religion of service and he held that God could be realised only through service.[3] The experience of Swami Dayananda at Murvi made Gandhi to assess his religious faith rationally for one has to give sufficient reason for the faith he has.

The influence of Dadabhai Naoroji from whom Gandhi learnt the first lesson of non-violence, to fight against the evil not by violence but by love made Gandhi in his later life to fight non-violently against any heaviest odd. Gandhi found non-violence as a panacea to rid the evils that have beset the modern society. Lokamanya Tilak taught Gandhi to adopt the truthful and non-violent means. It is only when the cause is just and truthful, that one could adopt non-violent and truthful means to achieve the goal. The setting of non-cooperation by Tilak made Gandhi to fight against the evil by non-cooperating with evil at the later stage of his political career.

---

2. M.K. Gandhi, *Hindu Dharma*, p. 5.
3. M.K. Gandhi, *The Story of My Experiments with Truth*, p. 118.

It was under the Western influence that Gandhi learnt about non-violence and truth. He had great admiration for Socrates who was deeply committed to truth. Socrates resisted the superstitious beliefs non-violently and did not refrain from preaching what he believed to be truthful and bravely suffered the punishment of death. This helped Gandhi to stand for truth at any cost and fight for a just cause non-violently.

The teachings of Jesus especially the *Sermon on the Mount* appealed to him greatly. He found the spirit of renunciation present in the *Sermon on the Mount*. Through Theosophy he learnt to give the equal treatment to all religions which promoted religious tolerance, interreligious dialogue, ridding from tensions arising out of religious difference. This attitude ultimately helped to arrive at the conclusion that "Religions are different roads converging upon the same point",[4] "that all religions are true".[5] He felt that no religion denies the ethic of non-violence and truth. He held that all religions are meant to bind and unite the people but not to separate them.

The influence of the Russian sage Leo Tolstoy was profound on Gandhi. It was under his influence that Gandhi could become a firm believer of non-violence. Under the influence of the writings of Tolstoy Gandhi could explore and "realise more and more the infinite possibilities of universal love".[6] The writings of Tolstoy helped Gandhi at his later stage to leave his scepticism and become a firm believer of non-violence. Tolstoy preached what he practised. Gandhi took him as a model and made his life a series of experiments with truth and practised what he preached.

It was from the Russian writer T.M. Bondureff that Gandhi learnt work ethic and the concept of bread labour who stated that "If a man work not, neither shall he eat".[7] This made Gandhi to find expression also present in *Gita* that he who eats without offering sacrifice, eats stolen food and the Biblical expression. "In the sweat of thy brow shalt thou eat thy bread". "This further led Gandhi to

---

4. *Harijan*, 30.1.1937, p. 407.
5. *Young India*, 12.5.1920, p. 2.
6. M.K. Gandhi, *The Story of My Experiments with Truth*, p. 119.
7. Pyarelal, *Mahatma Gandhi, Early Phase*, Vol. I, p. 667.

identify himself with the poor and made him to state

> I cannot imagine anything nobler or more national than that for, one hour in the day, we should all do the labour that the poor must do and thus identify ourselves with them and through them with all mankind.[8]

The writings of the modern writer, John Ruskin influenced Gandhi and brought about an instantaneous change in him. The writings of Ruskin were intended for the human welfare and to uphold the dignity of labour and social equality. It is only when the individual develops the social affection that he could develop an attitude of social equality irrespective of the position that one holds. Ruskin made it clear that society can make its real progress only under certain moral conditions, and Gandhi made these principles to apply in his life.

The influence of Henry David Thoreau, his lifestyle and his famous concept of Civil Disobedience helped Gandhi to resist the unmoral laws of the state and to set a moral order by disobeying the unjust laws framed by the state non-violently. The classical statement of Henry Thoreau "the government is best which governs the least"[9] finds expression in making the individual supreme and involve him actively in the affairs of the state. The government that governs the least could be found in the decentralised democracy which results in the individual initiative and his involvement in the political affairs.

Gandhi has been described as the seeker of truth and his search is marked by the scientific temper as his life is a series of experiments with truth. He studied the ethico-religious principles found in different religions of the world and made them applicable in a more effective manner. He studied all religions and found that they bear common thread of love and compassion.

His religious philosophy was characterised by upholding truth, non-violence and religious tolerance. He rationally assessed different religions to find common factors if any to find the possibilities for better improvement and progress for their peaceful co-existence.

---

8. *Young India*, 20.10.1921, p. 329.
9. *Ibid.*, 2.7.1931, p. 162.

He upheld the moral and spiritual values of all religions to have peace, happiness and progress. He wanted to eliminate such of the elements which stand as barriers, to have the experience of reality.

The moral virtues viz., non-violence, truthfulness, non-stealing, non-possession and celibacy have their significance and perennial relevance for the world is governed by the moral law. Every action has its own effect whether good or bad. The good action results in good results. The purity of life can be maintained when the human life is pure in word, thought and deed. The importance of non-violence and its applicability cannot be ignored. In the modern times, it gained more significance and relevance. Non-violence contributes highest good to mankind. It is the basis and law of life, progress and peace. Non-violence at the same time is a matchless weapon unparalleled in the modern times. Truth is the highest value and for Gandhi it is a sovereign principle. Truth knows no geographical limitations. In his relentless non-violent fight against the evil, he realised truth. The ethical maxims like non-stealing and non-possession forbid the mankind from possessing anything or holding anything more than they need. Non-possession leads to the voluntary reduction of wants and real happiness and mankind will develop an attitude of contentment and with a tendency of increasing capacity to render selfless service to the society. This attitude of life results in peaceful co-existence and ushers in an egalitarian society. One needs to have control over his passions. When he cannot conquer himself or his passions, he cannot lead others on the right path. People have to be brave and fearless. He who is fearless could sacrifice himself for the good of the mankind.

The concepts that influenced Gandhi, viz., non-violence, truth, service, renunciation are commonly found in all religions. They are of greater significance and bear perennial relevance. His comparative study of religions and inter-religious dialogue reveal his comprehensive view of religion. He held that the ethical points are common to all religions. Gandhi brought down religion from the cloistered seclusion of *yogic* contemplation to man's socio-economic and political plane[10].

The equal treatment of all religions as they are based on the

---

10. M.K. Deva Raja, Philosophy, *Religion and Culture*, p. 206.

same truth and morality made Gandhi to think of universal religion. For him all religions are equal and one in essence. This tendency promotes the essential human unity and rids the barriers. As he stated that "religion binds man to God and man to man"[11]. So it promotes human unity.

Gandhi gave utmost importance to the purity of means and ends in recognition of the significance of the moral law binding on man. Gandhi studied and evaluated the human situation to take non-violent action in the event of necessity, without losing sight of purity of means and ends. While the traditional political thought assumed a different position by separating ends and means which has proceeded to eclipse over the primacy of ends and established an unseparable nexus between these two. He stood against the theory that end justifies the means. His dictum "means and ends are convertible terms",[12] was his philosophy of life. This avoids the problem of employing the immoral means which give recourse to violence, untruth and other evils. The adoption of purity of means has great significance bearing on human life and relevance to the modern world. To realise truth, non-violence is the means. This protects the purity of means and ends.

Generally religion and politics are held to be two separate realms between which a line has been drawn. Politicians do not rely on religion and they have different set of methods to be successful in their endeavour. "Can politics be conducted without killing, hurting, conquering, becoming sad and making others sad in any society as it is?" Gandhi revolutionised politics.

Gandhi curbed the dichotomy existing between religion and politics by bringing politics and religion together for the purification of politics as politics cannot be purified without religion. His political ideas were different from those of the political thinkers like Kautilya and Machiaville for whom end is significant and end justifies the means. For Gandhi politics and religion are inseparable. The politics unguarded by moral values has to be shunned as it is a disvalue. When religion is brought closer to politics, politics

---

11. *Harijan*, 4.5.1940, p. 117.

12. *Young India*, 26.12.1924, p. 424.

becomes valuable and moral. Gandhi held that religion must pervade the entire texture of the human life. Gandhi refused any division of human life into social, religious, moral, economic and political watertight compartments for all act and react on one another. When an individual enters into politics with religious consciousness, he could check the evils that entered into politics and remove them.

> Enunciating the maxim that right ends should be won by right means and that means are as important as ends, he tried to introduce into politics a code of conduct which only strictly religions men usually practised.[13]

When politics is divorced from religion, it has absolutely lost its true meaning and purpose. In the modern times, what people need is the religion that which contributes to the national integration for the progress and mutual cooperation, and that which keeps politics at the service of mankind but not the religion which separates people or religion that supports fundamentalism resulting in bloodshed.[14]

Social philosophy is broader in scope. The social issues are very significant, having great bearing on human life. Gandhi conceptualised the social issues. He made them relevant and dynamically operative to the modern world. No social idea could be claimed to be final, as it undergoes changes from time to time and it is subject to the acid test of human experience on rational and moral grounds. Thereby the social issues become significant and relevant to the modern times and the future generations to come.

Gandhi stood against the evil manifestation of caste and untouchability. In the West, this tendency is manifested in the form of colour prejudices, racial apartheid and class struggle. Gandhi personally experienced humiliation arising out of racial discrimination as a victim of colour prejudices. He was not allowed to travel in a first class compartment though he was entitled to it while travelling from Durban in South Africa.[15] The recent remembrance of Gandhi and righting of a century-old wrong — the

13. K. Satchidananda Murty, *The Indian Spirit*, p. 230.
14. Ramjee Singh (ed.), *Aspects of Gandhian Thought*, p. 91.
15. M.K. Gandhi, *The Story of My Experiments with Truth*, pp. 80-1.

most notorious symbol of discrimination by the proclamation of the message of the restoration of human dignity as uttered by the South African President Nelson Mandela to atone for the shame, speaks of the relevance, significance and the victory of non-violent resistance against the racial apartheid. At times, a century may have to elapse for a noble thought to capture action or a succeeding generation has to rectify the mistake by taking an appropriate action.

At the outset, Gandhi attempted to purify the existing *varna* system and stated that outcasteness has altogether to be destroyed. He worked for the removal of untouchability though he adhered to the *varna* system to promote mutual love, cooperation and realise an egalitarian society. He envisaged a classless and casteless society. Gandhi held that

> though Varna is determined by birth could be retained only by observing the obligations. Even if one is born of Brahmana parents, if his life fails to reveal the attributes of Brahmana cannot be called Brahmana. On the other hand even if one who is not a Brahmana but reveals the attributes of a Brahmana through his conduct will be regarded as Brahmana".[16]

This reveals the established fact that caste is determined not by one's own birth but by character.

While the thought of Gandhi was evolutionary depending on the socio-economic and political situation in which he did not lose sight of moral values, the changes he brought about are revolutionary to suit the modern society. Because of his profound influence of

---

16. *Harijan*, 28.9.1934, p. 261.

    C.F. Caste in Buddhism has been determined not by one's own birth but by character.

    "Him I call indeed a Brahmana who finds no fault with other beings whether feeble or strong and does not kill nor cause slaughter. Him I call Brahmana, who is tolerant with the intolerant mild with fault finders and free from passion among the passionate."

    Max-Müller, *The Sacred Books of the East*, Vol. X, p. 92.

Hindu philosophy, he gave an impression of a conservative and he was in defence of caste system. He considered the four divisions of the *varnashrama-dharma* to be fundamental, natural and essential. But he opposed the casteism when it degenerated with its evil manifestation of untouchability. So he did not subscribe to the fanatical view that a brahmana born of brahmana ever remains brahmana by virtue of his birth. This upholds the fact that caste is determined not by one's own birth but by the character he possess.

Gandhi was opposed to the restrictions imposed on inter-dining and inter-caste marriages and stated that it is misrepresentation of the Hindu *dharma*. Though he felt in 1933 that inter-dining and inter-caste marriage was in no way essential for the promotion of the brotherhood or for the removal of untouchability, he stated in 1935 that there should be no restriction on inter-caste marriage or inter-dining in *varnashrama-dharma*.

In 1946 Gandhi wrote that

> classless society is the ideal, not merely to be aimed at but to be worked for in society, there is no room for classes or communities.[17]

He broke the orthodox Hindu tradition, characteristically he continued further and declared in 1946 that the boys and girls who want to marry cannot be married at Sevagram unless one of the parties belongs to the Harijan community. He refused to attend the wedding unless it was an inter-caste marriage. This makes it very clear that Gandhi wanted to bring about the reformation in the society gradually and aimed to establish a classless and casteless society to promote brotherhood, communal unity and harmony which are very essential for any society to progress and co-exist peacefully. He transformed the traditional concepts for the betterment of all sections of the community and improve their social conditions.

As Joan V. Bondurant aptly puts:

> that the significant contribution of Gandhi lay not in any revival of traditional forms or methods, but in a

17. *Harijan*, 17.2.1946, p. 9.

> transformation of traditional concepts in such a way that only the symbol remained familiar for the symbols were made by Gandhi to stand for a quite different set of values.[18]

In due recognition of the significance of the inter-caste marriages, the government encourages them and extends all possible support and help to such of the couples by giving them incentives and provides them with better job opportunities so that they may lead a dignified and independent life on par with others. This greatly contributes for the establishment of an egalitarian classless and casteless society and to shed the differences and discriminations that commonly exist in the society.

The position of women and their status is marked by the characteristics of exploitation, discrimination and humiliation in the society since the ancient times. Gandhi worked out for their social uplift by upholding the values such as equality and social justice, hitherto unheeded. The idea that woman is no less significant than man, has acquired a new dimension and women have got to play a vital role in the modern society. The age-old social custom — *purdah* which keeps the woman away from playing her role in the society was not acceptable to Gandhi. The women are not merely meant for the household work but they are intended to stand for the better and higher cause of society. He pleaded for their proper education to make them more sensitive to the glaring social inequalities. No women should suffer legal disability. The Fourth World Conference on Women held in Beijing in 1995 viewed that gender equality in laws could be pursued as a desired objective.

The Indian Parliament proposed to introduce a bill on women's reservation for their social uplift and active participation on all affairs. The Prime Minister Shri I.K. Gujral emphasised the need to have a nation wide debate on the women's reservation relating to the extension of Reservation Bill to the women to be introduced in Parliament which would result in drastic changes in the social fabric. It is obvious that progressive legislation has always been opposed by socially conservative and fundamentalist forces.[19]

---

18. Joan V. Bondurant, *The Conquest of Violence*, p. 5.
19. *Indian Express*, 17.5.1997.

Gandhi had great concern for the plight of the millions of women who became widows. He held that a social reform should be brought about in case of those who suffer from the enforced widowhood by getting them married. He called the system of dowry as a degrading social practice and pleaded for its abolition. He wanted that a strong public opinion should be created in condemnation of the degrading practice of dowry. The dowry deaths have become common these days. Some brides are subjected to harassment and humiliation and are set on fire for the sake of dowry. Many ignoble incidents of the nature have been recorded. These heinous acts mock at the basic human values and norms of the human dignity.

The Fourth World Conference held in Beijing stated that if any woman is harassed with the demand of dowry or caused considerable agony, anguish and trauma, her husband accused of this cruelty would be sentenced to imprisonment under the Section 498-A. Several anti-dowry movements have been organised by the progressive organisations. Gandhi stood for the freedom of women, their rights and social justice. He pleaded for the equal status. He stated that women could fight non-violently against any abuse of power or social evils.

Gandhi stated that alcohol ruins people physically, morally and intellectually.[20] Moral regeneration is need of the day and man needs to have control over his passions. Mere prohibition or legislation would not bring about the desired change. Many instances have been recorded of innocent people who died for consuming the poisonous liquor. The preparation of alcohol was to be stopped at any cost. Awareness has to be created among the people about the evil effects of alcohol and rid of them of this evil practice.

Education plays a significant role in the human life. Education draws allround out of the best in child and man, body, mind and spirit.[21] By restructuring education, it could be made meaningful, purposive and relevant to the needs of the modern man. When education lacks moral values for inculcation, the purpose and

20. M.K. Gandhi, *Key to Health*, p. 36.

21. N.K. Bose, *Selection from Gandhi*, p. 251.

meaning of education is lost. Education is a powerful media for social change in the emerging new world order. So education has to be value oriented and related to human life and its problems and be able to find possible solutions.

In the modern times, the students' unrest is a major problem as unemployment is on increase. So Gandhi advocated basic education which does not only help to acquire knowledge but it is also inclusive of imparting some sort of training useful to do work and to develop an attitude of dignity of labour and become independent and self-sufficient. He wanted that every child has to be taught of some useful handicraft. This type of education brings about a revolutionary changes with far-reaching consequences. It is not sufficient if elementary education is made compulsory, but it ought to be made self-supporting also. It has neither to be politicalised nor commercialised.

Adult education is a modern trend in education which is of great significance and relevance. The tradition of adult education in India is as old as the civilisation itself. With the emergence of a new pattern of education in the British regime, adult education slowly geared to economic activity and state policy.[22] The project of adult education was imbued with the philosophy of Gandhi in search of truth by self-purification, self-reliance and leading an exemplary life. Sarvodaya which aims at the welfare of all and uplift of all, was designed to bring about a revolutionary changes in the socio-economic spheres. Its aim is to educate the people and make them to learn the habit of sacrificing and serving others without any exploitation.

The educational system that Gandhi devised was aimed at the development of:

> an all round vigorous personality, physically and mentally alert, keenly aware of his environment and fired with the desire to improve it and endowed with the scientific spirit, power of decision, strong will and the power to take initiative.[23]

---

22. Anil Bordia (ed.), *Adult Education in India*, p. 11.
23. Nayar, D.P., *Building for Peace*, p. 11.

Gandhi met the challenge of adult education very early in his public career. When he launched his non-violent struggle in South Africa, his only instrument was the people in whom he was to generate the spiritual strength so that they could offer themselves in the struggle against the tyrannical rule. The technique of adult education which he developed earlier, was perfected later on through the *ashrams*. His aim was to educate them to gain certain basic competence and imbibe certain moral values before they could be used before the public.

Gandhi with a great insight and forethought, made innovations in the field of education to make it relevant to the needs of the people. His concept of education also gave a moral boost to the society. The educational idea of Gandhi is realised into action in view of its significance. The modern government gives more preference to the job oriented courses to make the students who pursue such courses self-sufficient and to have better professional opportunities to them.

Gandhi was a true economist who stood for the well-being of the masses. His crusade against exploitation, poverty, the recognition of the economic order upholding of the moral value system and the introduction of trusteeship to establish economic equality which stands as a poverty alleviation programme are the ample proofs to bring about revolutionary changes in the economic sphere.

Gandhi realised the need of the rich and the poor to be morally conscious and they have to be aware of their duties, defects and the weaknesses for the removal of the inequalities existing in the society. He found that without the economic equality, non-violent independence cannot be achieved. Economic equality involves the abolition of the eternal conflict between the capital and the labour.

> It means the levelling down of the few rich in whose hands is concentrated the bulk of the nations wealth on the one hand, and the levelling up of the semi-starved naked millions on the other.[24]

Gandhi appealed to the rich and the poor for the establishment of an egalitarian society. He appealed to their reason to be morally

24. M.K. Gandhi, *Constructive Programme*, p. 20.

conscious. This is a progress from rationality to morality and from morality to spirituality which makes people to lead an austere life to identity with all sections of the people by sharing their problems in a spirit of renunciation by broadening their outlook and rising above their self.

Gandhi appealed to the rich of their duty towards the starving poor as, "the rich not only refuse food to the poor, they refuse wisdom, they refuse virtue, they refuse salvation".[25] Gandhi wanted to bring about a total transformation in the economic sphere through his non-violent method of trusteeship for the establishment of economic equality. The existing capital order of society has to be transformed into an egalitarian society. By economic equality Gandhi meant that "everyone must have a balanced diet, a descent house to live in, facilities for the education of one's children and adequate medical relief".[26]

John Ruskin says,

> Inequalities of wealth unjustly established have assuredly injured the nation in which they exist during their establishment, and, unjustly directed, injure it yet more during their existence. But inequalities of wealth, justly established, benefit the nation in the course of their establishment; and nobly used, and it yet more by their existence.[27]

So Gandhi advocated the theory of trusteeship. The capitalists have to be the trustees by voluntarily giving away their surplus riches for the common good and realisation of the economic equality. Gandhi on the other hand was very practical when he admitted that if the capitalists do not act up to this theory, it is not due to the defect of the theory of trusteeship or its falsity but due to the weakness of the wealthy.[28]

Today we do not find the rich voluntarily abdicating their

---

25. John Ruskin, *Unto This Last*, p. 89.
26. *Harijan*, 31.3.1946, p. 63.
27. John Ruskin, *Unto This Last*, pp. 34-5.
28. *Harijan*, 16.11.1939, p. 376.

surplus riches or voluntarily disclose their accumulated capital to lead an austere life due to their weakness. Since the theory of trusteeship could not be operative, the government has no other option except to take the alternative measures to bring out the accumulated wealth and ill-gotten gains disproportionate to the earnings of the rich by drawing their attention to the fact that the rich could voluntarily disclose their accumulated wealth on payment of 30 percent tax of their unaccountable money to the Income Tax Department. This is for the common good and it is a good measure to reduce the disparities existing between the rich and the poor at an optimum level.

Like Ruskin and Tolstoy, Gandhi felt industrialisation to be a great menace to realise the basic moral ideals of the human society. Gandhi considered the village as the basic and primary unit for political set-up. He challenged the basis of modern civilisation which was solely responsible for impoverishing the Indian villages.[29] The evils in the industrial world have been manifested in the form of exploitation, colonial expansion, imperialism, commercial monopoly, diplomatic mechanisms for keeping down the economic and political growth of the rivals followed by the myths of cultural, racial and religious superiorities of the exploiters. All these follow in a ceaseless train demoralising the whole world.[30] The technological advancement erodes the moral fibre of the society and has bad effect on the value system. Many people drift to the cities to improve their living conditions but they experience break in their family ties and neighbourly relations.

For Gandhi, man is the supreme consideration[31] and he has got to play a vital role in the society. But in the industrial civilisation, the significance of man is reduced to nothing and he got no important role to play. He is reduced to a mere cog in the machine. Human life is reduced to a mere mechanical drudgery. He seeks gross sensual pleasures like drinking, gambling and other evils for his relief and recreation. This type of mechanical life leads to dehumanisation.

---

29. Ramjee Singh, *Gandhi and the Modern World*, p. 153.
30. D.M. Datta, *The Philosophy of Mahatma Gandhi*, p. 112.
31. *Young India*, 13.11.1921, p. 378.

The capitalists are after the material advancement thinking vainly that material progress and the real human happiness go together. So they lay more stress on industrialisation, large-scale production, growing mechanisation, automation and the multiplicity of wants.[32] But they do not take moral values into consideration. So Gandhi vehemently opposed the modern civilisation. He measured the progress in terms of moral values. The real happiness and progress do not lie in the material progress. Russell defined civilisation as "the pursuit of objects not biologically necessary for survival".[33] Modern civilisation does not take moral values into consideration. People go on multiplying their wants and they value quantity but not quality. The industrial civilisation is self-defeating. It results in the environmental pollution and the health of the modern man suffered to a greater extent on account of this.

Gandhi did not stand against the machinery but what he objected to was the craze for machinery which tends to save labour and deprives the labour of their employment opportunities making them to die of starvation.[34] Gandhi was fully aware of the socio-economic conditions and the growing unemployment problem of the country.

The present use of machinery tends to concentrate its wealth more in the hands of a few, in total disregard of the millions who are deprived of their basic requirements. Gandhi vehemently opposed this tendency as "abundance of money particularly in the hands of a few is a highly dangerous phenomenon".[35] Gandhi pointed out that "I want the concentration of wealth not in the hands of a few, but in the hands of all". As E.F. Schumacher observed, industry is a pace-setter of the modern life. He presented his views on the lines of Gandhian economics and stated that people could show interest in the evolution of small-scale industries which tends to be a non-violent technology, and a technology with a human face. This gives a meaning and purpose to the lives of the working class. Gandhi

---

32. Ramjee Singh, *Gandhi and the Modern World*, p. 156.
33. Bertrand Russell, *The Prospects of Industrial Civilization*, p. 39.
34. *Young India*, 13.11.1924, p. 378.
35. *Kurukshetra*, October 1994, p. 10.

measured the progress of the society or nation in terms of moral values and human welfare.

The reduction or elimination of poverty, inequality and unemployment is considered to be an important sign of economic development. Rural development should be looked upon as a joint venture of public, corporate, cooperative and private sectors. A systematic approach should be followed to bring about allround and balanced development of the economy. The government should help the rural poor in an organised manner within the framework of the institution that is capable enough to give access to the nation's economic and political systems.[36]

Some highly urbanised nations believe that urbanisation as the sign of progress, was not acceptable to Gandhi. He was convinced of the fact that the villages can become the nurseries for rearing a new humanity on self-reliant, non-exploitative truthful and healthy living lines. He did not see anywhere the need to discard the foundation of village life to build up an urban euphoria. He was very much inclined to retain the village as the base.[37] He declared that "if the villages perish, India will perish too".[38]

In order to be compatible with the decentralisation, village-based economy, industry has to be on small-scale and traditional, employing a non-violent, non-alienating technology which would add a maximum of human dignity and moral substance to the labourers.[39] Gandhi wanted the villages to be free from the influence of industrialisation. He held that by developing cottage industries, India could lead on ennobled and peaceful life in the world. The introduction of small-scale industries is technologically possible, operationally feasible, economically viable and socially desirable.

The revival of rural industries is possible and could be successfully operated without exploitation. Industrialisation thrives on exploitation and competition to market their finished goods. So

---

36. Katar Singh, *Rural Development*, p. 315.
37. S.C. Jain, *Rural Development, Institutions and Strategies*, p. 127.
38. *Harijan*, 29.8.1936, p. 226.
39. Mark A. Lutz & Kenneth, Lux, *Humanistic Economics - The New Challenge*, p. 305.

village has to be made self-contained to manufacture its finished goods for the use of their people. Gandhi stood for everything 'that promotes the well-being of the villagers".[40] Rural industries create new opportunities for gainful employment, particularly to the underemployed during the lean periods in the absence of agricultural operation.[41] As the establishment of village industries solves the problem of growing unemployment and a mad rush to settle in the cities to a greater extent, it is relevant to the modern times especially to country like India.

Gandhi stated that the real planning of the nation consists in the best utilisation of the whole manpower and the distribution of the raw production of the country in her numerous villages instead of rebuying the finished goods outside at fabulous prices.[42] In the recent times some countries like India have exported the iron ore and other raw products to Japan and other countries at a cheaper rate and bought finished goods at higher prices. It is quite uneconomical and undesirable.

Gandhi introduced hand spinning which is not costly but economic and within the reach of the common man to make the people self-sufficient and self-reliant. He encouraged the village population to rely on *khadi* as it teaches them to be self-reliant, and self-dependent and improve themselves by their own efforts. *Khadi* revives the economy and makes the people self-sufficient and restricts them primarily to the needs of the village.

Gandhi thoroughly studied the socio-economic conditions of the country. He was convinced that the revival of hand-spinning and hand-weaving would make great contribution to the economic and moral regeneration of the country. The spinning-wheel serves the needs of the poor and restores the villagers to their rightful place. It abolishes the distinction persisting between the high and the low. The art of spinning is held to stand as a symbol of "commercial peace but not of commercial war". It is "the livery of

40. *Harijan*, 27.1.1940, p. 428.
41. R.P. Mishra, *Rural Industrialization in the Third World Countries*, p. 143.
42. *Harijan*, 23.3.1947, p. 79.

Indian freedom"[43] in the poetic expression of Jawaharlal Nehru. The promotion of *khadi* and village industries contributes to the true economic independence to the millions of the countrymen and helps to build a joint national family based on peace, harmony and love.

The message of spinning-wheel presupposes man to lead a simple life and his preparedness to render service to the mankind at large. The spinning-wheel being a small-scale machinery tends to keep mankind at the proper place, from the state of exclusiveness and exploitation without reducing him to a small, subordinate and insignificant part in the machine, unlike in the case of heavy industrialisation.

Gandhi believed that agriculture provides the only unfailing and perennial support to the people of this country. There is need to refashion the village communities into an ideal type and make them adapt to the modern methods of cooperative operation.[44] The modern world moves towards the ideal of collectives or cooperative effort which stands as a welfare measure. There is no place for evils such as selfishness and inhumanity in the cooperative effort.

The urbo-rural disparities are on increase and there is need to reduce such disparities and maintain a balance between the city and rural life in the modern times. The villages have to be further improved and several programmes have to be taken up for the poverty alleviation by creating job opportunities to the unemployed youth and rural development for the avoidance of evils arising out of mass unemployment and mass migration into the cities. This requires the adoption of agro-industrial and urbo-rural culture. The cities are under the moral obligation to realise their duty towards the villages in the matter of making an adequate return for their strength and sustenance.

> It is only when the cities realise the duty of making an adequate return to the villages for the strength and sustenance which they derive from them instead of selfishly

43. M.K. Gandhi, *Constructive Programme*, p. 12.
44. B.N. Ganguli, *Gandhi's Social Philosophy, Perspective and Relevance*, p. 147.

> exploiting them that a healthy and moral relationship between the two will spring up.[45]

Gandhi thoroughly studied the drawbacks, various forces and evils of the industrial society in the modern times. He examined whether the individual could morally progress and such society would enable the individual to have freedom, welfare and progress. He measured the progress of the nation in terms of moral values and human welfare. He stated that he could find the real happiness and human welfare in the villages. Gandhi was frank in admitting that "you cannot build non-violence on a factory civilisation, but it can be built on self-contained villages".[46]

Although Gandhi did not proceed from any specific political ideology, his contribution to political theory and the inclusion of values into politics is noteworthy to meet the modern challenges. There has been a noticeable distinction between the social and the political but social philosophy is a wider term than that of the political as it deals with everything relating to the activities of man in relation to the society.[47] Similarly, Gandhi did not make any wall of separation between the social, economic, religious and political. He gave a concrete expression of the human life as an integral whole.

Gandhi felt the need to maintain a harmonious balance among the moral and social, economic and political spheres to avoid the possible domination of one sphere over the other which may destroy the identity of one with the other.[48] The main object of politics is the pursuit of power or the capture of power. The political theory formulated by Gandhi challenges the substantial presupposition of the mainstream of political theory.The method that Gandhi introduced in the domain of politics is not power-based but based on spiritual values. This has gained great relevance and significance in this modern age, as its institutions relies on the politics of power.

---

45. *Harijan*, 9.10.1937, p. 293.
46. *Ibid.*, 4.11.1939, p. 331.
47. D.D. Raphael, *Problems of Political Philosophy*, p. 1.
48. *Gandhi Marg*, Vol. 18, No. 2, Sept. 1996, p. 214.

Russell held that the present institutions rest upon two important things namely property and power, but the problem is that they are unjustly distributed.[49]Gandhi believed in the ideal of decentralisation of power and economy. Gandhi stood against the centralisation of power and concentration of wealth in the hands of a few. He wanted that power and wealth have to be shared equally by all. He gave utmost significance to the individual. He stated that the individuals have to work for and be placed in a social order where "the poorest and the most helpless man" would have "control over his own destiny".[50] This he felt could be provided by a decentralised democratic state based on truth and non-violence.

Gandhi held that the individual-will is governed and limited by the social-will in the democracy. The individual cannot take law into his own hands. If it is so happens there would be no state and the state becomes anarchy without any social law, leading to the destruction of liberty.[51]

Gandhi differed from the political thinkers, like Austin and Weber who justified the exercise of physical force to make the state strong enough to effectively implement its rules which they considered as legitimate. Unless the state is efficiently tyrannous, the citizens may have every good reason to disobey the state if they are proved to be morally repugnant. Thereby they remove the essential characteristic of the state.

Jawaharlal Nehru pointed out that Gandhi applied moral values into political action. Gandhi believed in the convertibility of means and ends and they can never be separated, for means ultimately govern the end. If the means are evil the end itself becomes distorted and becomes evil. Any unjust society must necessarily have the seeds of conflict and decay within it as long as it does not get rid of that evil.[52]

Gandhi stood against the modern political theory of the state. He stood against the increase of the power of the state. He states that:

---

49. Bertrand Russell, *Political Ideas*, p. 14.
50. *Gandhi in a letter to a Bengali friend.*
51. *Harijan*, 29.9.1947, p. 350.
52. Jawaharlal Nehru, *India's Foreign Policy*, p. 182.

> I look upon an increase in the power of the state with the greatest fear because although while apparently doing good by minimum exploitation, it does the greatest harm to mankind by destroying individuality which lies at the root of progress.[53]

In a democracy the will of the people must rule, says Gandhi. Even if democracy is a rule by the majority and follow the opinion of majority for all practical purposes, the majority rule should necessarily promote the interests of all. This helps to avoid the possible tyranny of the majority. It is for the reason that majority does not represent the will of the people. So Gandhi held that in the matter of conscience, the law of majority has no place. He believed on the other hand that "the minority has a perfect right to act differently from the majority".[54] Minority at the same has not to be coerced but convinced, persuaded and respected.

Gandhi advocated the idea of the limitation of the state power. He laid more stress on the controlling rather than the increase of the authority of the state. When the state seizes power, the role of the individual is reduced to nothing.

Since the state is born of violence and force, Gandhi was convinced of the fact that both of them are the inalienable aspects of the nature of the authority of the state. While the individual could be curbed of his acquisitive and exploitative tendencies under moral treatment, the state cannot come out of its inherent nature.

Gandhi says,

> The individual has a soul but as the state is a soulless machine, it can never be weaned from violence to which it owes its very existence.[55]

So Gandhi aimed at an ideal state of statelessness. Gandhi stated that democracy must be based on non-violence and truth. When the democracy is based on non-violence and truth, the weakest will

---

53. *Modern Review*, October 1935, p. 412.
54. *Young India*, 2.3.1922, p. 129.
55. *Modern Review*, October 1935, p. 412.

have the same opportunity as the strongest as non-violence is based on love. But the modern imperialism is based on force in defence of it and it is not consistent with non-violence. Centralisation as a system is inconsistent with non-violent structure of society.[56] Centralisation cannot be sustained with adequate force. On the other hand, decentralised democracy is consistent with non-violence as it governs the least and no violence or force is needed for the implementation of its policies.

In order to achieve the growth of community development, and to bridge the gulf between government at the centre with the people in the country at large, decentralisation at each level is found to be necessary at every level for policy-making and execution of its functions to offer services and to give counsel and advice.[57]

Gandhian concept of decentralised democracy is based on the recognition of the individuality, freedom, and the dignity of the individual. His decentralised type of democracy followed by the self-governing and self-sufficient village republics, forms the nucleus of his political philosophy. He aimed at the individual's initiative and involvement in the affairs of the state. If the power does not remain with people such type of government could be termed as deceptive. He held that the decentralised democracy runs its affairs smoothly and effectively without the interference of the state.

*Panchayat raj* as a political structure at the base of the village level, consists of five members with the functional ability of legislature, executive and judiciary. This system suits to the modern requirements and contributes to the progress of the people from the grass-root village level. If the country has to be revived and make progress, the development has to begin from the bottom. This system represents self-sufficiency of the village, especially in the matter of promoting the basic needs of the people. The *panchayat* will have autonomy as far as the internal village administration is concerned. Unlike the anarchist tradition, some sort of hierarchical pattern could be evolved by linking up the village *panchayat* with the taluk, district, state and nation.

---

56. *Harijan*, 18.1.1942, p. 5.

57. Henry Maddich, *Democracy, Decentralization and Development*, p. 26.

While the traditionally organised village *panchayat* considered a group of members as the unit but not the individual, the village *panchayat* as visualised by Gandhi having full powers has ultimately considered individual as the unit. Gandhi pleaded strongly for the decentralised economic and political power through the organisation of village *panchayats*. He felt that if the *panchayat* system is worked on scientific lines, it could strengthen the social and economic base as the economic and political power would be decentralised under such system. The progress and prosperity of the nation depends upon the villages. He held that if the village perishes, India too will perish.

In recognition of the contemporary relevance and significance of the village *panchayats*, Article. 31A has been included in the Indian Constitution according to which "the states shall take steps to organise village panchayats and endow them with such powers and authority as may be necessary to enable them to function as units of self-government.[58] The village *panchayat* is the smallest unit within the reach of the people, which provides great scope for direct popular participation. It gives the economic and social uplift to the underdeveloped sections of the community with its main focus on agriculture and small-scale industries for the progress and development of the people.

The three-tier system of rural and local government, viz., *panchayat raj*, *panchayat samiti* and *zilla parishad* has been introduced in order to democratise the local institutions. Hierarchical pattern could be evolved by the linkage of village *panchayat* with the block, district, state and nation to create conditions conducive for the individual initiative, self-expression and political representation. If the *panchayat* elections could be conducted without the interference of any political party, there will be no scope for the vested interests. This rids the evils of the society such as casteism, communalism, power, money, etc.

The moments of statutory *panchayats* and the new scheme of democratic decentralisation could be termed as the amplification of

---

58. Jaya Prakash Narayan, *Panchayat Raj as the Basis of Indian Policy*, p. 18.

the Gandhian views. But in the modern times, the *panchayat* administration is deviating from Gandhian ideals as there has been a growing inequality which is recognisable in the country. Some persons who are after money are following unscrupulous methods for the acquisition of their wealth. They have exploited the people and acquired wealth.

Gandhi could be termed as the greatest champion of the human rights. He fought for the human rights and for the proper place of those who were exploited and humiliated in the society. On the other hand, he established co-relation between the rights, duties and obligations. He never encouraged exclusiveness and special privileges in the case of anybody. He raised his voice against the illegal, illegitimate and unjust social norms, political conventions and colour prejudices and abuse of power. In order to set in a moral order in the society, he integrated the rights of the individual with the duties. This avoids disorder and disruption in the society. "Instead of insisting on rights, everyone does his duty there will immediately be the rule of order established among mankind."[59] says Gandhi. For him the true source of right is duty. So true rights do not accrue merely from the legal recognition but from the moral advancement and social service.

Gandhi gave utmost importance to the individual freedom. It prevails only under certain moral conditions depending on the moral regeneration of man. If an individual is immoral or does not adhere to the moral values, his freedom comes in conflict with the freedom of other individual resulting in chaos and disorder in the society. The freedom of an individual must not infringe on the freedom of others.

Gandhi used *Satyagraha*, a non-violent resistance, to fight against injustice, exploitation and for the redressal of grievances. It is the most significant and dynamic legacy that Gandhi left for India as well as for the whole world. It excludes the use of violence in any form. The object of *satyagraha* is that the opponent must be weaned from error by patience and sympathy which involves self-suffering. Joan V. Bondurant held that *satyagraha* as a political weapon provides key to an understanding of the political philosophy

---

59. *Harijan*, 6.7.1947, p. 217.

of Gandhi.[60] It is the relentless search for truthful ends by the aggrieved party to seek recourse to an appropriate non-violent action.

In the contemporary times the critics have not been willing to understand the implications of Gandhian method of *satyagraha*. There has been an honest failure in the recognition of the potentiality of *satyagraha*. The conventional political methods adopted are based upon violence which result in hatred and antagonism.

*Satyagraha* results in a moral order as it is founded on non-violence and truth. Its application results in drastic changes in the political authority. *Satyagraha* transforms the individual and society and ushers in a new socio-economic and political order which is non-exploitative, non-oppressive and just, governed by non-violence, truth, love, cooperation, equality and brotherhood. *Satyagraha* assumes greater significance and relevance than before to fight against the evils that have beset the modern society. As it is a moral principle founded on truth and non-violence with religious sanction behind, it has the universal applicability.

> If the laws are unjust or oppressive and constitutional remedies are not available owing to the attitudes of the rulers or majorities, *satyagraha* is a legitimate weapon of the injured individuals or groups.[61]

The concepts of non-cooperation and civil disobedience are the offshoots of *satyagraha* designed to fight against the evil as a part of human duty for the establishment of a just society. Gandhi postulated non-cooperation to redress the wrongs. Disobedience to an immoral law is same as obedience to a higher moral law, and adherence to truth and justice. By withdrawing the support, the non-cooperation arises moral consciousness and brings about moral transformation in the individual or the society or the state and also in the human relations for the common good. Gandhi suggested non-cooperation as a potent weapon to fight against the evil as a sacred duty of every individual.

---

60. Joan V. Bondurant, *Conquest of Violence*, p. 7.
61. Raghavan Iyer, *The Moral and Political Thought of Mahatma Gandhi*, p. 317.

When the laws framed by the state are immoral or the measures taken up are corrupt and unjust, disobedience could be declared against such state. The purpose of civil disobedience is to compel the government to withdraw the unjust law or to paralyse the government if it has become corrupt and unjust in the resisters view to have a moral and non-violent state in its place.

The relevance of *satyagraha* depends upon its context, necessity and immediacy. It is not a politics of violence or disorder. Gandhi demonstrated the efficacy of *satyagraha* and it is proved to be successful if it is non-violent and moral. *Satyagraha* finds its expression especially in Hindu, Muslim, and Christian religions. The success of *satyagraha* depends upon its observance with integrity and self-sacrifice for a good cause.

In the past, politics was a matter of sacrifice and service. Leaving their possessions, and by sacrificing their riches, some people came forward to render their selfless service to the people. In the modern times, politics has become a means of change from one party to the other for their political gains and politics is reduced as a matter of business, corruption and exploitation which result in hatred and antagonism and violence. *Satyagraha* as a political weapon resists non-violently against the evil and redresses the grievances and wrongs. The solutions *satyagraha* finds are, permanent and lasting, as it has its basis in love and truth. The success of *satyagraha* depends upon its cause. If the cause is good and the people are firm in their resolve and non-violently resist the evil and exploitation, success is a certainty.

If the cause is intended to promote the interest of a section of the society and the people are misguided and drawn to fight for such cause, people would come to know of the cause whether it is just or not sooner or later. Public opinion is a potent weapon to fight against the evil and Gandhi gave utmost importance to it.

Tolstoy stated that:

> The power of the government rest upon public opinion and possessing power they can always support the sort of public opinion they require by whole organisation, officials, law courts, schools, the church and even the press. Public opinion produces the power. Power produces public opinion

and it seems as if there were no escape from this position.[62]

If the cause is unjust, *satyagraha* is bound to fail. When the people are exploitative and unjust they tend to resort to the evil methods to achieve their unjust cause. Gandhi vehemently opposed such movements. Unfortunately such movements have become very common in the modern times. Gandhi brought out the full implications of non-violent principle and a truly non-violent person will refuse to be a party to any kind of exploitation.[63]

The modern world is confronted with the unprecedented crisis due to violence, terrorism, ecological unsustainability, mounting tensions and wars which are interrelated and have great impact on the world. The humanity is advancing towards the twenty-first century which is witnessing the unprecedented growth of industrialisation and technological progress in all spheres. Although Gandhi did not make much reference to the environmental degradation its sustainability and protection in his writings and speeches, as the problem was not much during his time, or he might not have anticipated the terrifying dimensions of the environmental degradation as it is in the modern times, the concepts he formulated and the ideals he translated into action speak of his great insight about the conservation of natural resources and environmental sustainability.

Gandhi stood against the introduction of heavy industrialisation and the baneful affects following it. The heavy industrialisation results in the massive consumption of the natural resources which are limited, non-renewable and unevenly distributed in the world. The existing environmental pollution prevails because of man's attack on nature and his multiplicity of desires resulting in the heedless consumption of the natural resources. "One should live so as to have the best for oneself and one's family and not to try to be wiser than life and nature."[64] Gandhi raised his voice time and again against the heavy industrialisation and the ceaseless evils following it.

---

62. Leo Tolstoy, *Christianity and Patriotism*, p. 526.

63. K. Satchidananda Murty, *The Quest for Peace*, p. 58.

64. B.R. Nanda, *Mahatma Gandhi — A Biography*, p. 73.

Science establishes its superiority over nature through the rapid industrialisation, urbanisation and the material progress without taking moral values and the role of the individual into consideration. It is the onerous responsibility of the people to initiate pollution control and the conservation of natural resources. In order to avoid the environmental hazards, people should have better planning and regulation in the industrial sectors. There is need to have environmental clearance and pollution check at the time of setting up of the industries. If the industries are set-up without observing these norms, they would be a great hazard to the nation. The Central Pollution Control Board has to thoroughly study all the aspects keeping in view of the larger interests of the people.

The establishment of small-scale and cottage industries not only solve the unemployment problem but they also control the evils arising out of large-scale industries such as environmental hazards and pollution problems to a greater extent. The small-scale and cottage industries stand for the greatest good of all.

Real happiness does not consist in the multiplication of wants resulting in a luxurious and complicated material life. Gandhi believed in leading a simple and ennobled life. Gandhi says that

> high thinking is inconsistent with the complicated material life based on high speed. . . . All graces of life are possible when we learn the art of living nobly.[65]

So the industrial nations have to understand the problems created by them and evolve a new lifestyle — a non-violent lifestyle designed for permanence and sustainability with new methods of production and new patterns of consumption.[66] Man has to live in harmony with nature and evolve a non-violent culture. It is not merely desirable but it has become a necessity. This attitude helps to conserve the natural resources and preserves the environmental balance.

Terrorism is a special kind of organised violence or a threat of violence by the small number to put large in fear and it is on

---

65. *Harijan*, 1.9.1946, p. 285.

66. E.F. Schumacher, *Small is Beautiful,* p. 17.

increase in the modern times. The object of terrorism is to shake off the human faith. In the modern society, the wealth is concentrated in the hands of a few and they become richer under certain economic conditions conducive to them by their acquisitive and exploitative tendencies and the poor become poorer and they are dissipated. Under these circumstances, the outburst of violence or bloodshed is a certainty which cannot be averted. So in an atmosphere of growing economic inequalities, terrorism flourishes. Gandhi stood for economic equality for non-violent system of government presupposes egalitarian society.

Gandhi stood for the emergence of a non-violent decentralised democracy which promotes the full growth and development of all individuals by promoting fellow feeling, mutual trust and cooperation. He held that the best type of government is that which governs the least and which gives the weakest the same opportunity as the strongest. In such type of government terrorism would not flourish, unlike in the authoritarian and ruthless governments which are based on force and violence.

Gandhi believed in the purity of means and ends. He stood against the opposite theory that end justifies the means as it leads to arrive at the conclusion that violent and immoral means that are dangerous and ethically unsound could be applied which give recourse to violence and terrorism. He stated that "I object to violence because, when it appears to do good, the good is temporary, the evil it does is permanent."[67] Gandhi held that the adoption of violence as a method cannot do good in the long-run.[68] So people have to follow the non-violent method to achieve their goals and promote their interests. In this context the offshoots of *satyagraha* — non-cooperation and civil disobedience which are based on non-violence in their application bear great relevance and significance, as alternative methods which are just and moral and extremely effective for the redressal of grievances and removal of evils that have beset the modern society, without resorting to violence and terrorism.

The issue of peace has become more significant and of greater relevance than before. The real human happiness lies in the

67. *Young India*, 21.5.1925, p. 178.
68. *Ibid.*, 9.6.1920, p. 3.

experience of real peace. Gandhi advocated the principle of non-violence as the only way of life. Its application results in a moral reordering of the world order to usher in a new peaceful world order.

The outstanding contribution of Gandhi lies in his presentation of truth and non-violence to the human civilisation to be observed in every walk of the human life. Gandhi held that truth and non-violence are not the matters merely intended for the individual practice but they are extendible for practice by groups, communities and nations also.

Non-violence plays a vital role in the tension ridden, weary and disturbed modern world. It carries with it, the message of love and the change of heart to result in the ultimate transformation of the modern society for its betterment. The modern world is dominated by the politics of power, balance of power, diplomatic relations and other constraints. As John Ruskin pointed out money power is imperfect and doubtful. The real human happiness lies in the experience of virtues.[69] So non-violence and love have to be brought together in the place of violence and hatred, for the establishment of a new peaceful world order.

There is no alternative to non-violence for the establishment of peace in this modern world as "it is the greatest force at the disposal of mankind. It is mightier than the mightiest weapon of destruction devised by the ingenuity of man"[70] says Gandhi. He held that unless the world adopts non-violence, it will spell certain suicide for mankind.[71] Peace could be established only through non-violence.

Richard B. Gregg says,

> Through non-violent resistance we can reach an active, reasoned belief in the conditions capable of continuous practice in all grades of life and all sorts of conflict so as to educate everyone into a conviction that they give better results, more efficiently, than violence.[72]

---

69. John Ruskin, *Unto This Last*, p. 42.
70. *Harijan*, 20.7.1935, p. 180.
71. *Ibid.*, 29.9.1946, p. 335.
72. Richard B. Gregg, *The Power of Non-violence*, p. 120.

The establishment of international peace requires the development of a world community which creates a sense of mutual tolerance, respect and goodwill needed for the establishment and operation of such community in social practice by the use of non-violence to rectify the defects and correcting the wrongs.[73] Nehru aimed at the World Government. He stated that it must and will come as there is no other remedy for the world's sickness.[74]

Though Gandhi was intensely attached to the concept of Indian nationalism, he was an internationalist and he emphasised his role as a citizen of the world. He says that

> it is impossible one to be internationalist without being a nationalist. Internationalism is possible only when nationalism becomes a fact.[75]

The principle of non-violence is based on love and it is extendible from personal relations to that of the national and international relations. For a person following the universal principle of non-violence, the whole world is a family for him. Gandhi had global perspective.

The modern world by its nature is marked by several defects and evils.

> The tumult of violence, the excitement of anger, the rivalry for power, and maintenance and preservation of world bodies in spite of their defects are the birth pangs of the new world.[76]

There is need to have international understanding and cooperation without any difference on the grounds of geographical, political, lingual, economic or cultural matters. The spirit of love and brotherhood animating from non-violence has to be carried to the international level. The international problems have to be sorted out, discussed and solved in good faith by adopting the method of

---

73. *The Power of Non-violence.*
74. Jawaharlal Nehru, *India's Foreign Policy*, p 183.
75. *Young India*, 18.6.1925, p. 211.
76. Ramjee Singh, *The Relevance of Gandhian Thought*, p. 72.

persuation, negotiation, adjustment and compromise without resorting to violence, by being rational and moral. By being united, the fear of unseen peril arising out of division could completely be avoided.

Like charity, peace must begin at home and it has to be global to the extent. Immanuel Kant could see no prospect of world, state or republic overriding the local or personal relationships of men in their nation states. It is moral obligation of the people to see that besides their duties within their immediate society, they have a duty to see humanity beyond to secure peace among the free autonomous nations. To seek peace is a human duty.

Although man strives for peace, the most dreadful atomic weapons have been discovered in the modern age to establish the military superiority of the different nations and also as a measure of their security and defence. The modern nuclear weaponry is powerful enough to completely annihilate the very existence of human civilisation. On the other hand, the human progress to a greater extent has been crippled because of the militarisation of the scientific endeavour and most part of the national income is diverted for the military expenditure. Permanent peace cannot be established through the superior violence for it leads to the use of nuclear weapons which cause mass destruction. Violence could be ended by the non-violence — the only alternative which is the greatest moral force at the disposal of mankind. The civilisation rests on non-violence and truth and it could be saved to the extent to which they respond to these principles. It is the human responsibility to work out for it.

In the modern world some nations engage in the proliferation of nuclear weaponry and other nations justify the doctrines such as the doctrine of deterrence as a measure of security. But the doctrine of deterrence result in mutual suicide as it operates only under certain conditions. This doctrine in no way does contribute to the world peace but results in the mutual terror at the same time.

> Enduring international peace and security cannot be built on accumulation of weaponry by military alliances nor be sustained by a precarious balance of deterrence or doctrine of strategic superiority.[77]

77. *Report of the Secretary General on Nuclear Weapons*, pp. 183-4.

Gandhi held that peace cannot be established through arms and it will be broken at any time. The values of life such as truth, goodness, righteousness and social justice cannot be resulted from the use of the atomic weaponry. "Instead of thinking in terms of peace and acting in violence, the nations must think in terms of peace alone."[78] The atomic and nuclear energy harnessed by the scientists for the purpose of destruction could be utilised for the constructive purpose, is a human possibility. Science has to adopt the values of life and contribute for creativity cooperation and human progress. There is need to adhere to the principle of non-violence and recognise its significance and relevance to escape from self-destruction.

The leaders of all the countries have to courageously disarm themselves.

> Even if the road to nuclear disarmament is a long and difficult one, there is no alternative. Peace requires the prevention of the danger of a nuclear war. If nuclear disarmament is to become a reality, the commitment to mutual deterrence through a balance of terror must be discarded. The concept of the maintenance of world peace, stability and balance through the process of deterrence is perhaps the most dangerous collective fallacy that exists.[79]

Gandhi gave the message of peace and concordia to the modern world. It is the human responsibility to keep the desire for peace alive and make the mankind relentlessly to strive for it, for "peace makes people to dwell in safety".[80] Permanent peace is a human possibility and human responsibility. In recognition of the lasting impact that the practice of non-violence has made, and its growing significance, it has to be made as the governing principle of all the individuals and nations as the social conduct for the establishment of lasting and enduring world peace.

---

78. V.P. Gaur, *Mahatma Gandhi — A Study of His Message of Non-violence*, p. 121.
79. *Report of the Secretary General on Nuclear Weapons*, p. 191.
80. *Holy Bible*, Psalms, 4:8.

There is need to examine how Gandhian ideals have been followed in India as well as in other parts of the world and how they take a new shape in their social action against the existing order based on violence and exploitation. There have been several challenges faced by the Gandhian thought theoretically and practically.

The follower of Gandhi, Vinoba Bhave, proposed the Sarvodaya Samaj. He emphasised the need to have purity of means to usher in an ideal society based on truth and non-violence. He stood against the caste ridden society, acquisitiveness and exploitation. He wanted that there should be full scope for the development and welfare all the individuals. Sarvodaya is a concept of social engineering and an instrument of social transformation. He extended the meaning of Sarvodaya to make it relevant with practical implications. The *bhoodan* (donation of land by landowners to the landless poor), *gramadan* (donation of village for its development), *shramadan* (rendering free service for the community development) aroused most interest in some of the countries of the world.

Mathew Zachariah holds that Sarvodaya movement which Vinoba Bhave guided since many years after the assassination of Gandhi, stands as an expression of a revolutionary Gandhian with three major aims.

> To change the hearts and minds of the people so that they may pursue truth, to enable people to practice a lifestyle which will encourage them to pursue truth and to change current social structures enough so that new centralised structures that facilitated personal pursuit of truth with a nurturing community are possible.[81]

When the Bhoodan movement was widened, it became *gramadan* with greater relevance. The idea of Vinoba Bhave was to establish a new world order by change of human heart. He felt that co-operative, non-violent structure of economy based on *gramadan* would act as a real defence of the nation rather than the National Five Year Plans which become ineffective in the event of world war.

81. Matthew Zechariah, *Revolution Through Reform*, p. 20.

Though Jaya Prakash Narayan was drawn by communism in early part of his life, he was drawn to the Gandhian ideals subsequently. His thought has undergone an evolutionary change. He made a voyage from communism to socialism and from socialism to *sarvodaya*. After the completion of his studies, Jaya Prakash Narayan associated himself with the independence movement. Being aware of the implications and the principles laid down in socialism, Jaya Prakash Narayan remarked that socialism must eventually merge with *sarvodaya*.[82]

Socialism with *sarvodaya* could be merged only when socialism gives up its inborn tendencies, viz., the exercise of violence and the concentration of power. It is only when the purity of means is adopted as advocated by Gandhi and non-violent principle is adopted, the non-violent power could be emerged. It is only when there is diffusion of power, there could be decentralised democracy established.

As Ramjee Singh observes:

> It seems that nearly after three and half decades after his death, Gandhi has become more relevant. True, Gandhi and Gandhian thought has suffered a callous neglect in the land of his birth but a distant — Martin Luther King, a Walesa in prison inspiring lakhs of Polish people to rise against the Martial Law regime in a non-violent manner, a Sukhorov fasting for the reunion of his daughter with her husband, a Mother Teresa serving the wounded and afflicted in the war-torn Lebanon have taken up the Gandhian path. Thus Gandhi has become a world phenomenon.[83]

Martin Luther King was greatly influenced by the teachings of Gandhi. He later adopted his non-violent doctrine as the most powerful weapon against the colour prejudices in USA. In the Montgomery bus boycott launched by Martin Luther King against

---

82. Jaya Prakash Narayan, *Socialism, Sarvodaya, Democracy*, p. 138.
83. Ramjee Singh, *The Relevance of Gandhian Thought*, Preface, p. vii.

the racial segregation, he instructed his followers about the necessity of love to be shown to all (agape). It virtually brought to him into a position of national and international prominence and made his emergence as a symbol of racial justice. After the boycott, the King's devotion towards Gandhian non-violent method increased.

It was under the leadership of Nelson Mandela who stated "The struggle is my life", the African National congress (ANC) resisted non-violently against the South African government for democracy, freedom, justice and equality. The ANC along with other allies organised the defiance campaign against the specific unjust laws of racial apartheid. He fought for the equal political rights of the people.

He stated:

> I have cherished the ideal of democratic and free society in which all persons live together in harmony and with equal opportunities. It is an ideal which I hope to live for and to achieve. But if need be it is an ideal for which I am prepared to die.[84]

Nelson Mandela was successful in his non-violent resistance against the colour prejudices and in achieving freedom and democracy. He became the President of South Africa. Gandhi was remembered recently of an incident that took place 100 years ago in which he become a victim of the racial apartheid. He was not allowed to travel in a first class compartment though he was entitled for it at Pietermaritzburg and he was thrown out of the train on racial grounds. Mandela stated that the South African government righted a century-old wrong. The grandson of Gandhi Mr. Gopala Krishna Gandhi, the Indian High Commissioner of South Africa received the Freedom of Pietermaritzburg award on behalf of Gandhi on 26 April 1997. This speaks of Mandela's commitment and reverence for the teachings and ideals of Gandhi.[85]

Thus, as was in the past, the ideals of Gandhi have been cherished and practised in India and other parts of the World in the

---

84. Nelson Mandela, *Struggle is My Life*, p. 2.
85. *The Hindu*, 27.4.1997.

modern times because of the durable results that have been achieved. This is because of the fact that his philosophy bears greater relevance and significance to the modern times than before as his ideals are laid down on the firm foundation of the immutable moral maxims — truth and non-violence.

# Select Bibliography

Alfred Tennyson, *The Princes*, Mac Millan and Co. Ltd., London, 1907-8.

Alvin Tofflar, *Future Shock*, Bantham Books, New York, 1981.

Anand T. Himgorani (ed.), *Science of Satyagraha*, Bharatiya Vidya Bhavan, Bombay, 1962.

———, (ed. & Published), *To the Women*, Karachi, 1946.

Anil Bordia (ed.), *Adult Education in India*, Nachiketa Publications Limited, Bombay, 1973.

Anil Dutta Mishra, *Gandhian Approach to Contemporary Problems*, Mittal Publications, New Delhi, 1996.

Anthony M. Burton, *Urban Terrorism*, Leo Cooper, London, 1975.

Arthur Barker (ed.), *Bertrand Russell Speaks His Mind*, London, 1960.

Augustine St., *Confessions*, tr. by William Watts, The Loob Classical Library, London, 1931.

Bakshi, S.R., *Gandhi and Status of Women*, Criterion Publications, New Delhi, 1987.

———, *Gandhi and Status of Harijans*, Deep & Deep Publications, New Delhi, 1987.

Bari, S.A., Dr., *Gandhi's Doctrine of Resistance*, Kalamkar Prakashan Pvt. Ltd., New Delhi, 1971.

Basant Kumar Lal, *Contemporary Indian Philosophy*, Motilal Banarsidass, Delhi, 1973.

Benoy Gopal Ray, *Gandhian Ethics*, Navajivan Publishing House, Ahmedabad, 1950.

Benudhar Pradhan, *The Socialist Thought of Mahatma Gandhi*, GDK Publications, Delhi, 1980.

Bertrand Russell, *The Prospects of Industrial Civilization*, George Allen & Unwin Ltd., London, 1925.

———, *Fact and Fiction*, George Allen & Unwin Ltd., London, 1961.

———, *Political Ideas*, Unwin Paperbacks, George Allen & Unwin Publishers, London, 1977.

Bhararatan, Kumarappa (ed.), *Collected Works of Mahatma Gandhi*, Government of India Publication Navajivan Trust, Vol. 1-90, Ahmedabad, 1958-84.

Bhattacharya, Buddhadeva, *Evolution of the Political Philosophy of Gandhi*, Calcutta Book House, Calcutta, 1969.

Biswas, S.C. (ed.), *Gandhi, Theory and Practice Social Impact and Contemporary Relevance*, Indian Institute of Advanced Study, Simla, 1969.

Bondurant, Joan V., *Conquest of Violence, The Gandhian Philosophy of Conflict*, Princeton University Press, New Jersey (USA), 1958.

Carl Leiden And Karl M. Schmitt (ed.), *The Politics of Violence Revolution in the Modern World*, Prentice Hall, Inc., USA, 1968.

Charles, W. Hendel (ed.), *The Philosophy of Kant and our Modern World*, The Liberal Arts Press., Inc., New York, 1957.

David Brook (ed.), *Search For Peace*, Dodd, Mead & Company, New York, 1974.

Davies, Ross, *Women and Work*, Hutchinson & Co. Ltd., London, 1975.

De Bary, W.M., Theodore, *Sources of Indian Tradition,* Motilal Banarasidass, New Delhi, 1972.

Desai. V.G. (tr.), *Ashram Observances in Action*, Navajivan Publishing House, Ahmedabad, 1959.

Desh Bandhu & G. Berberet (ed.), *Environmental Education for Conservation and Development*, Nataraj Publishers, Dehradun, 1987.

Devaraju, N.K., *Philosophy, Religion and Culture*, Motilal Banarsidass, Delhi, 1974.

Dewey John, *Democracy and Education*, Light & Like Publishers, New Delhi, 1916.

———, *Experience and Education*, The McMillan Company, New York, 1957.

Dey, S.K., *Panchayat Raj*, Asia Publishing House, Bombay, 1961.

Dhavan, Gopinath, *The Political Philosophy of Mahatma Gandhi*, Navijivan Publishing House, Ahmedabad, 1946.

Dutta, D.M., *The Philosophy of Mahatma Gandhi*, The University of Wisconsion Press, Canada, 1953.

Dutta, D.K., *Social, Moral and Religion Philosophy of Mahatma Gandhi*, Intellectual Book Corner, New Delhi, 1980.

Dwivedi, (ed.), *World Religions and Environment*, Gitanajili Publishing House, New Delhi, 1989.

Erikson, Erik H., *Gandhi's Truth*, Faber & Faber, London, 1970.

Gandhi, M.K., *Women and Social Injustice*, Navajivan Publishing House, Ahmedabad, 1942.

———, *For Facifists*, Navajivan Publishing House, Ahmedabad, 1949.

———, *Non-Violence in Peace and War*, Navajivan Publishing House, Ahmedabad, 1949.

———, *Communal Unity*, Navajivan Publishing House, Ahmedabad, 1949.

———, *Hindu Dharma*, Navajivan Publishing House, Ahmedabad, 1950.

———, *Satyagraha,* Navajivan Publishing House, Ahmedabad, 1951.

———, *Drink, Drugs and Gambling*, Navajivan Publishing House, Ahmedabad, 1952.

———, *Sarvodaya,* Navajivan Publishing House, Ahmedabad, 1954.

———, *From Yervada Mandir*, Navajivan Publishing House, Ahmedabad, 1957.

———, *My Experiments with Truth,* Navajivan Publishing House, Ahmedabad, 1959.

———, *Key to Health*, Navajivan Publishing House, Ahmedabad, 1960.

———, *In Search of the Supreme*, Compiled and ed. by V.B. Kher, Navajivan Publishing House, Ahmedabad, 1961.

———, *Hind Swaraj*, Navajivan Publishing House, Ahmedabad, 1962.

———, *Village Swaraj,* Navajivan Publishing House, Ahmedabad, 1962.

———, *True Education,* Navajivan Publishing House, Ahmedabad, 1962.

———, *Ethical Religion,* Navajivan Publishing House, Ahmedabad, 1968.

———, *The Voice of Truth*, Navajivan Publishing House, Ahmedabad, 1969.

———, *Constructive Programme — Its Meaning and Place*, Navajivan Publishing House, Ahmedabad, 1981.

———, *Khadi, Why and How?* Navajivan Publishing House, Ahmedabad, 1995.

———, *The Bhagavad Gita*, Orient Paperbacks, New Delhi.

Ganguli, B.N., *Gandhi's Social Philosophy Perspective and Relevance*, Vikas Publishing House Pvt. Ltd., Delhi, 1973.

Gene, Sharp, *Gandhi Wield's The Weapon of Moral Power*, Navajivan Publishing House, Ahmedabad, 1960.

———, *Gandhi as a Political Stratagist*, Porter Sargent Publishers Inc., Beacon St. Boston, 1979.

George. H. Sabain, *A History of Political Theory*, G. Harrop, London, 1975.

George Kotturan, *Ahimsa : Gautam to Gandhi*, Sterling Publishers, New Delhi, 1973.

George L. Abernethy & Thomas, A. Langford, *Philosophy of Religion*, McMillan Company, New York, 1968.

Ghan Shyam Shah & Chaturvedi, H.R., *Gandhian Approach to Rural Development*, Ajanta Publications, Delhi, 198[illegible].

Gora, *An Atheist With Gandhi*, Navajivan Publishing House, Ahmedabad, 1951.

Hardayal, L., *Thoughts on Education*, Viveka Swadhyaya Mandal, New Delhi, 1969.

Hemalata Swarup Sarojini Bisaria (ed.), *Women Politics and Religion*, A.C. Brothers, Etawah (UP), 1991.

Herman Levy, *Drink*, Routledge & Kegan Paul Ltd., London, 1951.

Himgorani A.T. (Ed. & Published), *To the Women*, Karachi, 1946.

Hobbes, *Leviathan*, J.M. Dent & Sons Ltd., London, 1962.

Immanuel Kant, *Perpetual Peace, A Philosophical Essay*, The Liberal Arts Press, New Work, 1948.

Ishwara Jopa, *Ethos of Non-violence*, Navajivan Publishing House, Ahmedabad, 1964.

Iyer, Raghavan, *The Moral and Political Philosophy of Mahatma Gandhi*, Oxford University Press, London, 1973.

Jain, S.C., *Rural Development, Institutions and Strategies*. Rawat Publications, Jaipur, 1985.

Joe Park (ed.), *Selected Readings to the Philosophy of Education*, The McMillan Company, London, 1968.

John Ruskin, *Unto This Last*, Appleton-Century-Crofts, Division of Meredich Publishing Company, USA, 1967.

Kabadi, W.P. (ed.), *India's Case for Swaraj*, Yeshanand & Co., Bombay, 1932.

Katar Singh, *Rural Development, Principles, Policies and Management*, Saga Publications, New Delhi, 1986.

Krishna Murty, Y.G., *Gandhism will Survive*, Acharya Ramlochan Saran, Patna , 1949.

Krishna Murty, Y.G., *Neo Gandhism*, Nalanda Publications, Bombay, 1954.

Krupalani, J.B., *The Gandhian Way*, Publications Division, New Delhi, 1953.

Kshira Sagar, R.K., *Untouchability in India Implementation of the Law and Abolition*, Deep & Deep Publications, New Delhi, 1986.

Leo Tolstoy, *Essays and Letters*, tr. by A. Maude, Oxford University, London, 1925.

———, *The Christianity and Patriotism*, Oxford University Press, London, 1960.

———, *The Kingdom of God and Peace Essays*, Oxford University Press, London, 1960.

Lewis Mumford, *Techniques and Civilization*, Routledge & Kegan Paul, London, 1955.

Linus Pauling (ed.), *World Encyclopaedia of Peace*, Pergon Press, England, 1986.

Louis Fischer, *The Life of Mahatma Gandhi*, Jonathan Cape, London, 1957.

Mackenzie, J.S., *A Manual of Ethics*, University Tutorial Press Ltd., London, 1929.

Mahadev Desai (ed.), *Gandhiji in Indian Villages*, S. Ganeshan, Madras, 1927.

Mahadev Desai, *The Gita According to Gandhi*, Navajivan Publishing House, Ahmedabad, 1956.

Matthew Zechariah, *Revolution through Reform*, Vistaar Publication, New Delhi, 1988.

Mathur, J.S. & Mathur, A.S. (ed.), *Economic Thought of Mahatma Gandhi*, Caitanya Publishing House, Allahabad, 1962.

Mathur & P.C. Sharma (ed.), *Facets of Gandhian Thought*, Navajivan Publishing House, Ahmedabad, 1975.

Max-Müller, *The Sacred Books of the East*, Oxford University Press, London, 1975.

Misra, K.P., *Gandhi and the Contemporary World — (Studies in Peace and War)*, Chanakya Publications, Delhi, 1981.

Misra, R.P., *Rural Industrialization in the Third World Countries*, Sterling Publishers, Baroda, 1985.

Moore, G.E., *Principa Ethica*, Cambridge University Press, London, 1968.

Nanda, B.R., *Mahatma Gandhi — A Biography*, Unwin Books, 1965.

Narayan, Jaya Prakash, *Panchayat Raj as the basis of Indian Polity*, Indo Prints, New Delhi, 1962.

Natesan, G.A. (ed.), *Speeches and Writings of Mahatma Gandhi*, Ganesan & Co., Madras, 1934.

Nayar, D.P., *Building for Peace*, Navajivan Publishing House, Ahmedabad, 1952.

Nehru, Jawaharlal, *The Discovery of India*, The Signet Press, Calcutta, 1946.

Nehru, Jawaharlal, *Indian's Foreign Policy*, The Publications Division,

Ministry of Information and Broadcasting, Govt. of India, New Delhi, 1983.

Nihal Singh. St., *Dry America an Object Lesson to India,* Ganesh & Co., Madras, 1921.

Niharanjan Ray (ed.), *Gandhi, Theory and Practice Impact and Contemporary Relevance*, Indian Institute of Advanced Study, Simla, 1969.

Nirmal Kumar Bose, *Studies in Gandhism*, Navajivan Publishing House, Ahmedabad, 1972.

———, (ed.), *Selections from Gandhi*, Navajivan Publishing House, Ahmedabad, 1948.

Panikkar, K.M., *Hinduism and the Modern World*, The Allahabad Law Journal Press, Allahabad, 1938.

Prabhu, R.K. & U.R. Rao, *The Mind of Mahatma Gandhi*, Navajivan Publishing House, Ahmedabad, 1969.

Pyarelal, *Epic Fast*, Mohanlal Maganlal Bhatt, Ahmedabad, 1932.

———, *Gandhian Techniques in the Modern World*, Navajivan Publishing House, Ahmedabad, 1953.

———, *Mahatma Gandhi*, Vol.I *Early Phase,* Navajivan Publishing House, Ahmedabad, 1965.

Quinton, Anthony (ed.), *Political Philosophy,* Oxford University Press, Great Britain, 1967.

Radhakrishnan, S., *Indian Philosophy* Vol. I, George Allen & Unwin, London, 1941.

———, *Religion and Society*, George Allen & Unwin Ltd., London, 1956.

———, *Religion in a Changing World*, George Allen and Unwin Ltd., London, 1967.

———, Foreword, Compiled and edited by P.K. Prabhu and U.R. Rao, *The Mind of Mahatma Gandhi*, Navajivan Publishing House, Ahmedabad, 1969.

———, (ed.), *Mahatma Gandhi — Essays and Reflections on His Life and Work*, Jaico Press Private Ltd., Bombay, 1977.

———, *Dhammapada*, Oxford University Press, London, 1980.

———, *Search for Truth*, Hind Pocket Books, Delhi, 1989.

Radhakrishnan, S. (ed.), & P.T. Raju, *The Concept of Man — A Study in Comparative Philosophy*, George Allen & Unwin Ltd., London, 1966.

Rafia Zakaria (ed.), *A Study of Nehru*, A Times of India Publication, Bombay, 1960.

Ramachandran, G., Mahadevan, J.K. (ed.), *Quest for Gandhi*, Gandhi Peace Foundation, New Delhi, 1970.

Ramjee Singh, *The Relevance of Gandhian Thought*, Classical Publishing Company, New Delhi, 1983.

———, *Gandhi and the Modern World*, Classical Publishing Company, New Delhi, 1988.

———, *Aspects of Gandhian Thought*, Indian Society Gandhian Studies, Rajasthan, 1994.

Rammanohar Lohia, *Marx, Gandhi and Socialism*, Nava Hind Publication, Hyderabad, 1963.

Ram Reddy (ed.), *Patterns of Panchayat Raj*, The McMillan Company of India Ltd., Madras, 1977.

Raphael, D.D., *Problems of Political Philosophy*, McMillan and Co. Ltd., London, 1970.

Richard, B. Gregg, *The Power of Non-Violence*, Navajivan Publishing House, Ahmedabad, 1960.

Richard Clutterbuck, *Living with Terrorism*, Faber & Faber, London, 1975.

———, *The Future of Political Violence*, McMillan, London, 1986.

Rolland, Romain, *Mahatma Gandhi*, Publications Division, Government of India, New Delhi, 1969.

Rus Walton, *Biblical Solutions to Contemporary Problems*, Wolgemuth & Hyatt Publishers, Inc., Brentwood, Tennessee, 1989.

Satchidananda Murty, K., *The Indian Spirit*, Andhra University Press, Waltair, 1965.

———, *Indian Philosophy Since 1498*, Aruna Power Press, Visakhapatnam, 1982.

———, *Quest For Peace*, Ajanta Publications (India) Delhi, 1986.

Savita, *Gandhi and Social Policy in India*, The Institute of Constitutional and Parliamentary Studies, New Delhi, 1970.

Schumacher, E.F., *Small is Beautiful*, Blond & Briggs Ltd., London, 1973.

Sen, N.B. (ed.), *Wit and Wisdom of Mahatma Gandhi*, New Book Society of India, New Delhi, 1960.

Sethi, J.D., *Gandhi Today*, Vikas Publication, New Delhi, 1979.

Shakespeare William, Peter Alexander, (ed.), *Hamlet*, Rupa & Co., Allahabad, 1989.

Sibnarayan Ray, *Gandhi, India and the World*, Nechiketa Publication Ltd., Bombay, 1970.

Subrahmanyam, K. (ed.), *Nuclear Myths and Realities*, ABC Publishing House, New Delhi, 1981.

Surendra Varma, *The Metaphysical Foundation of Mahatma Gandhi's Thought*, Orient Longmans, New Delhi, 1970.

Tahtinen Unto, *The Core of Gandhi's Philosophy*, Abhinav Publications, New Delhi, 1979.

Tannebaum, *The Philosophy of Labour*, Albod, New York, 1952.

Tendulkar, D.G., *Mahatma*, Karnatak Publishing House, Bombay, 1944.

Thimmaiah, Y. (ed.), *Studies in Rural Development*, Chugh Publication, Allahabad, 1979.

Unnithan, T.K.N., Dr., *Gandhi and Free India*, J.B. Wotters, Holland, 1956.

Usha Rao, N.J., *Women in a Developing Society*, Ashish Publishing House, New Delhi, 1983.

Varma, K.M.P. (ed.), *Philosophy of Religion*, Clarical Publishing Co., New Delhi, 1982.

Varma, V.P., *The Political Philosophy of Mahatma Gandhi and Sarvodaya*, Lakshmi Narain Agarwal, Agra, 1972.

Vithaldas Kothari, *Why Khadi and Village Industries?*, Navajivan Publishing House, Ahmedabad, 1957.

## Journals

*Fourth World Conference on Women*, Department of Women and Child Development, Government of India, New Delhi, 1995.

*Gandhi Marg*, Gandhi Peace Foundation, New Delhi.

*Harijan*, Navajivan Publishing House, Ahmedabad.

*Humanist*, John's Reprint Corporation, New York.

*The Indian Journal of Political Science*, Vol. XXXVIII, Haridwar Rai, The Indian Political Science Association, University of Bhagalpur, Bhihar, January, March, 77.

*Modern Review*, Calcutta.

Report of the Secretary-General (United Nations), *Nuclear Weapons*, Autumn Press, Massachusetts, 1980.

*Young India*, Navajivan Publishing House, Ahmedabad.

# Index